The Politics of Egalitarianism

Methodology and History in Anthropology

General Editor: David Parkin, Director of the Institute of Social and Cultural Anthropology, University of Oxford

Volume 1
Marcel Mauss: A Centenary Tribute
Edited by Wendy James and N.J. Allen

Volume 2
Franz Baerman Steiner: Selected Writings
Volume I: Taboo, Truth and Religion. Franz B. Steiner
Edited by Jeremy Adler and Richard Fardon

Volume 3
Franz Baerman Steiner. Selected Writings
Volume II: Orientalism, Value, and Civilisation. Franz B. Steiner
Edited by Jeremy Adler and Richard Fardon

Volume 4
The Problem of Context
Edited by Roy Dilley

Volume 5
Religion in English Everyday Life
By Timothy Jenkins

Volume 6
Hunting the Gatherers: Ethnographic Collectors, Agents and Agency in Melanasia, 1870s–1930s
Edited by Michael O'Hanlon and Robert L. Welsh

Volume 7
Anthropologists in a Wider World: Essays on Field Research
Edited by Paul Dresch, Wendy James, and David Parkin

Volume 8
Categories and Classifications: Maussian Reflections on the Social
By N.J. Allen

Volume 9
Louis Dumont and Hierarchical Opposition
By Robert Parkin

Volume 10
Categories of Self: Louis Dumont's Theory of the Individual
By André Celtel

Volume 11
Existential Anthropology: Events, Exigencies and Effects
By Michael Jackson

THE POLITICS OF EGALITARIANISM

Theory and Practice

Edited by
Jacqueline Solway

Berghahn Books
New York • Oxford

First published in 2006 by

Berghahn Books

www.berghahnbooks.com

©2006 Jacqueline Solway

All rights reserved. Except for the quotation of short passages for the purpose of criticism and review, no part of this book may be reproduced in any form or by any means, electronic or mechanical, including photocopying, recording, or any information storage and retrieval system now known or to be invented, without written permission of the publisher.

Library of Congress Cataloging-in-Publication Data

A catalog record for this book
is available from the Library of Congress

British Library Cataloguing in Publication Data

A catalogue record for this book is available from the British Library

Printed in the United States on acid-free paper

ISBN 1-84545-114-7 hardback
ISBN 1-84545-115-5 paperback

CONTENTS

Introduction   1
    Jacqueline Solway

Part I: The Politics and Practices of Egalitarianism

1. All People Are (Not) Good   21
    Bruce G. Trigger

2. Community, State, and Questions of Social Evolution in
Karl Marx's *Ethnological Notebooks*   31
    Christine Ward Gailey

3. Subtle Matters of Theory and Emphasis: Richard Lee
and Controversies about Foraging Peoples   53
    Thomas C. Patterson

4. "The Original Affluent Society": Four Decades On   65
    Jacqueline Solway

5. The Original Affluent Society   79
    Marshall Sahlins

6. On the Politics of Being Jewish in a Multiracial State   99
    Karen Brodkin

Part II: The Kalahari Then and Now

7. The Lion/Bushman Relationship in Nyae Nyae in the
1950s: A Relationship Crafted in the Old Way   119
    Elizabeth Marshall Thomas

8. The Kalahari Peoples Fund: The Activist Legacy of the
Harvard Kalahari Research Group   131
    Megan Biesele

9. Land, Livestock, and Leadership among the
   Ju/'hoansi San of North-Western Botswana   149
      Robert K. Hitchcock

10. Contemporary Bushman Art, Identity Politics, and
    the Primitivism Discourse   159
       Mathias Guenther

11. Class, Culture, and Recognition: San Farm Workers and
    Indigenous Identities   189
       Renée Sylvain

12. The Other Side of Development: HIV/AIDS among Men
    and Women in Ju/'hoansi Villages   205
       Ida Susser

Part III: Richard Borshay Lee: An Appreciation

13. Richard B. Lee and Company: A Kalahari Chronicle,
    1963–2000   223
       Compiled by Jacqueline Solway

14. Richard B. Lee: The Politics, Art, and Science
    of Anthropology   229
       Christine Ward Gailey

Richard Borshay Lee: Selected Bibliography   243
       Compiled by Jacqueline Solway

Notes on Contributors   249

Index   253

ACKNOWLEDGEMENTS

I am very grateful to Christine Gailey who coorganized the initial conference sessions out of which this volume grew and contributed significantly to conceptualizing their transformation into the book. A heartfelt thanks to the participants of the May, 2001 joint meetings of the Canadian Anthropology Society and American Ethnological Association and to those who attended the sessions and whose questions helped refine our analyses. In the transition from conference to text, Robert Hitchcock, Karen Brodkin, and Ida Susser stepped in at key moments with helpful advice and support. Marshall Sahlins graciously allowed me to include his piece and took the time to read and comment upon the version that I abridged and my introduction to it. I wish to thank Sam Grey who used her technical wizardry to transform "The Original Affluent Society" into electronic form and Susan Pheiffer who cast a critical gaze on my introduction to Sahlins's piece. I am especially grateful to Elizabeth Marshall Thomas, who is a professional writer and not a formal academic. Attending the conference and allowing us to publish her paper exemplifies the generous spirit that has shaped this tribute to Richard Lee.

Versions of most of the articles (Solway's introduction, Gailey's article and biography, and the articles by Patterson, Trigger, Brodkin, Thomas, Guenther, Sylvain, Biesele, Susser, and Hitchcock) first appeared in a special issue of *Anthropologica*, the journal of the Canadian Anthropology Society/Société canadienne d'anthropologie in Vol. 45 (1), 2003. These papers benefited from the editorial oversight of several *Anthropologica* editors, including Jean Lapointe, former managing editor, and Sally Cole, former Anglophone editor, and particularly, Winnie Lem, current editor-in-chief, who oversaw the peer review of most of the original articles. I am grateful to Andrew Lyons, current managing editor, who facilitated my obtaining the text files from Wilfred Laurier Press. All have been modified and/or updated for the book. I wish to thank *Anthropologica* and Wilfred Laurier Press, who hold the copyrights, for generously allowing us to reprint the articles. Marshall Sahlins, who holds the copyright for "The Original Affluent Society," granted permission for its reprint.

I am grateful to Richard Lee's family, David Lee, Miriam Rosenberg-Lee, Louise Rosenberg-Lee, and Harriet Rosenberg, who facilitated this project in many ways. Richard provided the photos. It has been a pleasure to work with Marion Berghahn, Vivian Berghahn and Michael Dempsey of Berghahn press. Thanks especially to Debi Howell for her superb copyediting. Michael Lambek, as always, is my main support, critic, and friend. And Nadia and Simon Lambek graciously provided computer expertise and general good humor.

INTRODUCTION
THE POLITICS OF EGALITARIANISM—
ESSAYS IN HONOR OF RICHARD B. LEE

Jacqueline Solway

The essays assembled in this book exemplify the way political anthropologists address a range of problems that deeply affect people throughout the world.[1] The authors draw their inspiration from the work of Canadian anthropologist Richard B. Lee, and, like him, they are concerned with understanding and acting upon issues of "indigenous rights"; the impact of colonialism, postcolonial state formation, and neoliberalism on local communities and cultures; the process of culture change; what the history and politics of egalitarian societies reveal about issues of "human nature" or "social evolution"; and how peoples in southern Africa are affected by and responding to the most recent crisis in their midst, the spread of AIDS.

The authors in this volume discuss the state of a range of contemporary debates in the field that in various ways extend the political, theoretical, and empirical issues that have animated Lee's work. In addition, the book provides readers with important contemporary Kalahari studies, as well as "classic" works on foraging societies.

Three central projects form the basis of this collection. These correspond to the projects that have engaged Lee throughout his career. The first, initiated in the 1960s by Lee and his colleagues, set about to present as complete a picture as possible of the hunting and gathering way of life. As historical (and academic) circumstances changed, Lee's work turned more to an investigation of former foraging societies and their evolving life patterns and political struggles. The latter has increasingly become labeled and encompassed under the rubric of "indigenous rights." The second project entails an examination of the

Notes for this section can be found on page 15.

manner in which historical and evolutionary perspectives and processes can best be combined and complemented to produce a sound understanding of local and global patterns of change. The third project can be broadly characterized as the interrogation and appreciation of egalitarianism as a theoretical possibility, an historical fact, and a political project. All resonate with and derive from a wider concern for social justice and human rights (broadly conceived to include social and economic rights as well as the more narrowly political) and the ways that they can be realized through political praxis. Thus, the topics addressed by these essays include the politics, ethnography, and philosophical basis of egalitarianism and attendant questions regarding varying understandings of human nature and their implications for striving towards a more emancipatory future.

Other chapters examine aspects of "indigenism" (especially in the context of southern Africa), the theoretical importance assigned to evolution and history in understanding processes of change, and the role of anthropology in political critique and activism. Finally, Lee's work draws attention to the role of the four-field approach in North American anthropology and exemplifies the approach at its most productive, in particular the early Harvard-based Kalahari project, and later in his and Ida Susser's work on HIV in southern Africa. In this volume, Christine Ward Gailey pays explicit attention to this topic, while other contributors address it less directly.

Ethnographic Impetus to Theory

Lee's most enduring legacy is the remarkable corpus of ethnographic work and its impetus to theory that stem from his long-term Kalahari research and from the scholars he inspired, encouraged, and mentored. The San[2] and the body of ethnography that has emerged about them join a small group of ethnographic cases (including, for example, the Trobriand Islanders, the Nuer, etc.) that have provided the stimulus for important anthropological theorizing, debate, and analysis. The San have been subject to study and restudy primarily because they are intrinsically interesting, but so are all people. The richness, quality, and reliability of the data collected by Lee and his colleagues have invited further study and enabled restudy to be especially productive. Moreover, the San have generated interest in large part because of the important theoretical questions that Lee has asked of his material and that others have consequently been inspired and provoked to ask of it.

Lee's early work challenged long-held assumptions that hunter-gatherer life was "nasty, brutish and short." Through rigorous empirical research, Lee demonstrated the security inherent in a foraging

Introduction 3

subsistence base.[3] Marshall Sahlins used Lee's material to advance his extremely significant concept of the "original affluent society," which he first presented at the 1966 "Man the Hunter" conference organized by Lee and Irven DeVore and later refined in his 1972 book *Stone Age Economics* (see also Sahlins, Gailey, Susser, and this author's chapter in this volume).

The essay is reproduced here in shortened form. As explored in my introduction to the Sahlins essay, the argument of original affluence continues to stimulate scholarly attention and debates inspired by it show no sign of abating. Using Lee's material, Sahlins was able to pose important questions regarding the ubiquity of the market principle as the mechanism of economic integration in society. Technically, the argument of original affluence takes the market principle as a given, but, in effect, it pierces the very heart of the principle by suggesting that, while human subjects make means-versus-ends calculations, they may not necessarily be doomed to make such decisions under the ubiquitous specter of unlimited ends. Therefore, the possibility of freedom from incessant deprivation exists.

Sahlins's notion of the original affluent society fed into the debate between the formalists and substantivists that loomed large in the field of anthropology at the time he introduced the concept. To simplify, the formalists viewed the economy as composed of (individual) humans attempting to fulfill unlimited wants with limited ends (the market principle), while the substantivists argued that the economy constituted a category of culture that represented the "material life process of society" (Sahlins, 1972: xii). This particular debate no longer commands the attention of anthropologists with the same urgency, but questions (or, in most cases, the blind acceptance) of the universality of the market principle as the basis of the economy remain central not only among academics but also among the governmental and institutional officials and policy makers whose decisions have a profound impact upon the daily lives of people throughout the world. The implicit assumption that the economy consists of "autonomous" individuals making choices (on an even playing field) regarding the most effective means to allocate their scarce resources guides these institutions and their planning. In the current neo-liberal moment, the assumption of market universality is joined by the concomitant normative notion that peoples' well being will be enhanced by granting them even greater autonomy in making such choices. These ideas influence the policies not only of our own governments but also those of the multilateral institutions, such as the World Bank and the International Monetary Fund, that dictate to the governments of poor countries. Such assumptions about the nature of the economy lead ultimately to policies that, for instance, force poor residents of indebted nations to decide between utilizing their scant cash for water (which is being privatized as a result of World Bank policies), school fees, food, or medical care. For this reason, and a host of many others, the lessons of the "original affluent society" and its inherent critique of market universality remain highly salient.

The Theoretical and Ethnographic Basis of Egalitarianism

Many of this volume's essays take their impetus from the same unwavering resolve to understand the nature of human equality and to strive towards its realization that underlies much of Lee's work and political praxis. The optimism inherent in this position does not spring from naïveté but rather from a seasoned realism that endures despite the difficult times and challenging moments that Lee has encountered (see Gailey, this volume). Like many progressive scholars of his generation, Lee has witnessed "heroes and heroic regimes" dissolve into the ordinary, or worse, criminal; he has withstood the cynical prism through which his work has sometimes been viewed; he has experienced a historical period in which activist politics have been increasingly marginalized (if not trivialized) by right-wing governments and by sentiments in the university and beyond; and he has suffered personal tragedy. Yet, despite all, his resolve that the capacity exists for human society to exist under more egalitarian conditions than those characterizing our present predicament remains intact.

Lee's early ethnography provided a critical contribution to the rise of feminist anthropology (see Gailey, Susser, and Thomas Patterson, this volume). By using his own careful measurements and comparative data from other foraging societies, he revealed the importance of collected foods (largely procured by women) in relation to meat in most forager diets. In fact, in acknowledging that a greater proportion of the San diet was supplied by collected vegetable foods, Lee challenged the appropriateness of the term "hunter-gatherer society" and switched to "foraging society" in many of his writings. By demonstrating women's subsistence role in San society, Lee and others were able to question the received wisdom that posited hunting and the division of labor upon which it was predicated, including male predominance, as the evolutionary basis of human social organization. In addition, Lee provided ethnographic evidence of women's political centrality and in doing so contributed to dispelling stereotypes of "primitive patriarchy."[4] His Kalahari colleague, Pat Draper, provided further ethnographic support in an important article that appeared in one of the formative volumes of feminist anthropology (Draper, 1975). In it

Draper offers observation and analysis of greater sexual egalitarianism amongst foraging as opposed to sedentary San.

In the 1980s Lee's theoretical framework shifted explicitly to Marxist political economy, with an emphasis on examining the social and economic basis of egalitarianism. With Eleanor Leacock, he published works that affirmed Karl Marx's construct of "primitive communism" and explored its ethnographic foundations. Lee and Leacock argued that societies exist (or have existed) that have the capacity to reproduce themselves while limiting the accumulation of wealth and power, and they attempted to identify the structures that enabled such societies to do so. Lee's careful elucidation and analysis of the structural mechanisms that inhibit social and economic differentiation amongst the San provided significant inspiration and substance to James Woodburn in developing his important distinction between immediate and delayed return societies in his 1982 article "Egalitarian Societies" and subsequent works (see chapter four, "'The Original Affluent Society': Four Decades On," for further discussion). In this volume, Bruce Trigger, Gailey, and Patterson (and less directly Susser) also address this aspect of Lee's work. Gailey examines Marx's *Ethnological Notebooks*, illustrating how Marx distinguished communal-based social formations, such as those of foraging groups, from those of peasants and how he saw in the former possibilities for an emancipatory future.

The observations of Trigger and Patterson emerge from a similar perspective; they pay special attention to assertions regarding the "nature" of human nature that various writers wish to put forward on the basis of forager ethnography. Because many observers view the societies of contemporary foragers as a prism through which to glimpse human origins, easy license is taken in making assumptions about "primordial" humans as either "noble savages" or "nasty brutes." Renée Sylvain's chapter also draws attention to the impact of Lee's work in the reexamination of the Hobbesian notion of human nature. She then takes the discussion forward by differentiating ideas of human nature from those of identity and interrogating the latter in relation to San studies.

In considering the nature of human inequality, especially gender-based, Patterson identifies liberal views whose theoretical genealogy lies, in particular, with Locke for whom gender inequality is taken as a given and contrasts them with those emerging from a Marxist and Marxist feminist tradition. He notes that Lee's work supports the latter. In addressing the controversies central to the 'Kalahari Debate' (discussed below) he continues the contrast between liberal versus Marxist based perspectives. He includes many of Lee's critics (the "revisionists") in the category of those who grant analytic privilege to the sphere of exchange (in the liberal tradition), in contrast to those who grant theoretical primacy to the sphere of production (following Marx). In so doing, the "revisionists" emphasize San relations with encompassing and extractive political-economic systems in which San interpersonal relationships appear largely as a function of their external subordination. Lee, on the other hand, by keeping the primary (but not exclusive) gaze on production is able to illustrate the means by which the San inhibit both political and economic inequality despite the fact (not because of it, as some critics would have) that they are enmeshed in power relations not of their own making.

In the volume's first chapter, Trigger poses questions about the inherent "goodness" or lack of it in human nature and ponders the degree to which there might be a biological basis for human nature that limits its social construction. Trigger acknowledges the openness of his questions and the difficulties in answering them. But he implores progressive anthropologists to consider the degree to which people in complex capitalist societies might fashion social structures and living arrangements that promote a more equitable sharing of wealth, despite a basic human nature that may be less flexible than we may wish to believe. One of the reasons Trigger finds the San material so compelling is that he shares this political commitment with Lee. Amongst the San, as depicted by Lee, one finds no "noble savage" occupying an original utopia, but rather a group of people who actively resist the rise of inequality. They possess and deploy a set of rules or "instruments" that are, to borrow Pierre Clastres's term, "anti-state"; their existence illustrates, within important limits, the possible.

Praxis

Throughout this volume, several authors highlight the connection between theory and practice by asking what a politically engaged or emancipatory anthropology might look like. Megan Biesele and Susser draw attention to Lee's southern African activism, while Karen Brodkin addresses a more deeply rooted political foundation. With respect to Lee, to herself, and to many other progressive Jewish activists, Brodkin asks, "What kind of Jewishness do Jews create when they pursue social justice in North America today?" She identifies at least two strands of Jewish political activism that are constructed on the basis of different sets of narratives. Some emphasize the Holocaust and solidarity with Israel, while others hark back to memories of immigrants working in sweatshops and to union struggles. Collective memories amongst the latter have been further radicalized through the infusion of feminist politics. Despite the class status they now occupy, contemporary Jews like Brodkin and Lee more strongly identify with the latter

Introduction 7

category, personally and in terms of praxis. As Brodkin illustrates, although most progressive Jews no longer share direct identification with the underprivileged circumstances of oppressed peoples in North America, they can "perform identity work" that enables them to share in their struggles.

Biesele, a member of the original Harvard Kalahari project, chronicles the Kalahari project's remarkable legacy of activism and advocacy. The Kalahari Peoples Fund (KPF), founded in 1973 and funded by publication royalties, donations and grants, has facilitated a wide array of activities designed to promote San empowerment. Efforts have been directed towards the enhancement of livelihood opportunities, leadership development, the struggle for land rights, education and language development, and numerous other projects. Increasingly, the San are defining their own development priorities and assuming managerial responsibilities, while Western-based KPF workers are happily assuming a secondary role. Robert Hitchcock picks up on this theme by highlighting the San land struggles and the range of methods the San, along with their neighbors, deploy in asserting their rights. These efforts have met with mixed results, but some initiatives, such as the various mapping projects, appear to be bearing fruit and give one hope that greater San empowerment will be possible in the future. Hitchcock's essay gives the reader a good sense of the complex mix of characters (multiethnic locals, governmental officials, and expatriates), as well as the various levels (local, regional, state, international, and global) that come into play, intersect, and complement and contradict each other in the world of San activism.

Biesele, Hitchcock, Sylvain, and Mathias Guenther touch on the thorny dilemmas faced by the San with regard to the appellation of the label "indigenous" that is often imposed on and, at times, embraced by the San themselves. One contentious issue in the field is whether the term "indigenous" and the various international declarations and instruments designed to empower indigenous peoples apply outside of the Americas, Australia-New Zealand and perhaps the northernmost zones of Europe (areas that experienced massive influxes of foreign peoples, leaving the previous inhabitants as marginalized minorities). Authors weigh in on both sides of the argument. Kuper (2003, 389) represents the extreme negative opinion. For him, "indigenous" is a gloss for "primitive" and easily transmutes into a racial category. He argues that bearing the indigenous label requires a demonstration of authenticity based on descent that inevitably leads to questions of how much descent qualifies and thus to divisive quarrels about who does or does not belong. Therefore, its adoption introduces the possibility for conflict, pitting groups against each other. Short-term political gains reaped under the indigenous rubric, he argues, may be counteracted by the long-term political consequences of carrying the identity baggage that comes with the indigenous label.

Others recognize the limits of extending the term beyond the Americas and the Antipodes, and acknowledge the risk of romanticizing peoples termed indigenous as Stone Age relics, living in commune with nature and each other, and many of the other hazards identified by Kuper. At the same time, it is evident that many marginalized minorities worldwide became encapsulated within newly emerged nation-states to whose predominant cultures, languages, and social groups they remain subordinated. Furthermore, many of these peoples live in conditions of poverty and despair resembling the more disempowered of the American and Australian indigenous groups. Thus instead of "primitiveness" being the underlying characteristic of indigenism as Kuper asserts, encapsulation, marginalization, disempowerment, cultural and livelihood difference from the dominant society are considered by many activists to be the defining characteristics of the indigenous. The importance of descent as a basis for indigenous identification also varies. In some instances the people themselves emphasize it but in many instances common residence and life circumstances provide a basis for group inclusion. Governments wishing to defuse indigenous claims by stipulating stringent requirements for indigenous entitlement and wishing to foster a divide and rule strategy will often emphasize descent. In addition, a persuasive argument can be made that the political visibility and clout that the indigenous label imparts, especially as the indigenous movement continues to gain more international purchase, may counteract the pitfalls of "strategic essentialism" that is often entailed in its usage (see, for example, Niezen, 2003; Lee, 2000; Hitchcock and Vinding, 2004). In Steven Robbins's words, "essentialist constructions of identity are not necessarily incompatible with an active embrace of the contradictions of modernity and its bittersweet fruits" (2003: 398). This comment resonates with Biesele's observation in this volume that "Today, the indigenous peoples of the Kalahari are remote and untouched only in our dreams (and in bad books and films)."

Further complicating the usefulness and appropriateness of the term "indigenous" are the actions of some of the nongovernmental organizations (NGOs) that operate under the banner of indigenous rights. These are not a uniform lot. For instance, Survival International (a British NGO that in an earlier incarnation called itself the Primitive People's Fund) has launched an aggressive campaign against the Botswana government on behalf of the San. Their tactics have probably done more damage to San relations with their fellow citizens than any other act or organization. Worse, they have undermined the

Introduction 9

efforts of local NGOs and human rights groups in their attempts to work with the San in promoting social justice (see Suzman 2002; Solway, 2005). But Survival International occupies one end of the continuum of NGOs working "on behalf" of marginalized minorities. Its actions contrast greatly both in terms of practice and principles from NGOs such as the Working Group of Indigenous Minorities in Southern Africa (Wimsa), the Kalahari Peoples Fund, and the Kuru Development Trust, which have local San activists as lead members of their boards and governance structures; some groups also include local non-San in their membership (see Guenther, Hitchcock and Biesele this volume). To be sure, the appellation of the term "indigenous" is not without contradictions. It presents serious challenges as well as opportunities for the San; some of the dilemmas of embracing and escaping it are spelled out in the chapters by Hitchcock, Sylvain, and Guenther.

Ethnography

Bronislaw Malinowski may have enjoined us to pitch our tents in the middle of the village, but Kalahari ethnographers have more often pitched their tents at the edge of a waterhole. Lee's own tent was situated near a waterhole called Dobe: so significant has been his pioneering research there that what was a rather obscure place now appears on most Botswana maps. His beautifully vivid and empathetic account of the Kalahari peoples' changing lives has set a high ethnographic standard matched by few.[5] Generations of anthropology undergraduates have come to appreciate a non-Western society by reading his work. Whether describing foraging practices, naming relationships, sexuality, or the politics and poetics of vanity and humility surrounding the presentation of a Christmas ox, Lee's fine attention to detail, lively descriptions, and engaging portrayals of the vitality of San life have given his work a central place in the ethnographic record. Through films and other materials, the general public has also been presented with a sensitive account of an African society. As a result, the San are arguably the most thoroughly documented group in Africa.

Perhaps it is Lee's brilliance as an ethnographer, his ability to keep multiple methodological balls in the air at any given time, and the widespread academic and public recognition of his work, in addition to the role San material has played in theory building, that have made him, his work, and San studies in general such a lightning rod for criticism, discontent, and political and theoretical dispute. In the 1980s,

Lee's early ethnography, as well as the evolutionary analytic framework that informed it, increasingly came under fire. Claiming that he neglected San incorporation into coercive world power structures and arguing that their egalitarianism was a product of their subservience and not a *sui generis* phenomenon, "revisionist" scholars initiated a lively "Kalahari debate" (see Patterson and Gailey this volume). Lee met their challenge by generating detailed historical research (some of it conducted with this book's authors, such as myself and, especially, Guenther) and by refining theoretical models of egalitarianism. As a result of these debates, our knowledge of Kalahari peoples and the models deployed in their analysis have become more sophisticated.

"The Predicament of the Returning Researcher"

Long-term fieldwork presents many opportunities but also many challenges. Lee first went to the Kalahari as a graduate student in 1963 and has returned numerous times since, most recently in 2005. A scholar who returns to the same research location for several decades bears the traces and influences of a succession of academic paradigms, theoretical orientations, and, especially in Lee's case, an ever-changing and growing number of fellow fieldworkers. He or she is faced with the difficult task of disentangling changes in the object from those of the scholar-observer (Haugerud and Solway, 2000). The extent to which longitudinal research produces a greater sense of depth (or paradoxically of superficiality) for the researcher is open to debate. But this is why long-term field research is important; it subverts our "isms," mitigates against the smugness of the present, and reminds us, to borrow Sara Berry's 1993 phrase, that "no condition is permanent."

In the four decades that Lee has visited the Kalahari, the pace of change has been breathtaking, complex, heartening and simultaneously disheartening, and at times, I would think, bewildering. Many of the changes are cited in this volume's contributions by Hitchcock and Biesele; they also form the backdrop to articles by Guenther, Sylvain, and Susser. It has not always been easy or comforting to witness the transformations, but Lee has carefully documented the changes in livelihood strategies; social conditions; local, national, and global political dynamics; the arrival of the AIDS pandemic; and the San's participation in formal institutions and structures. Contrary to the accusations of some critics, Lee has never viewed the San as timeless isolates. Each new version of his ethnography portrays the San as modern subjects and agents of change in the new states of southern Africa. The essays by Hitchcock, Guenther, Susser, Biesele, and Sylvain all illustrate this point.

Introduction 11

Art, Science, and Politics

In his important 1992 article, "Art, Science, or Politics? The Crisis in Hunter-Gatherer Studies" published in *American Anthropologist,* Lee evokes Charles Percy Snow's distinction between the supposedly irreconcilable "humanistic and scientific" academic subcultures. I wish to borrow Lee's title in a slightly altered form in order to suggest that his work as well as that of his collaborators in the Kalahari and elsewhere has sought to bridge the gulf explicit in Snow's dichotomy. Lee's work, in particular, not only embraces and effectively synthesizes both tendencies, but it does so without getting lost in the singular logic of either or indulging in either's excesses. To Snow's classification of art and science, I wish to add, as did Lee, politics. Most of the volume's chapters reflect the ideals and practices that lie at the heart of a politically engaged anthropology whose practitioners are committed to activism inside and outside of the academy.

Snow's distinction speaks intimately to anthropologists, especially those trained in the North American four-field approach, whose discipline has been memorably characterized by Eric Wolf as "the most scientific of the humanities, the most humanist of the sciences" (1964: 88). However, for many in the field, the unity is becoming increasingly difficult to sustain. The epistemological presumptions and methodologies of the more "scientific" subfields of archeology and biological anthropology seem to diverge ever further from those of the more humanistic subfields of social/cultural and linguistic anthropology. While surveys conducted by the American Anthropological Association reveal a wide diversity of opinion on the matter, and many North American departments hold firm to unified multi-subdisciplinary programs, fracture lines have appeared. The fact that Columbia University, the founding four-field department in the United States, now offers students the opportunity to take a full major in cultural anthropology *or* archeology is symbolically potent evidence of a retreat from the early vision of an integrated discipline. Increasingly fewer projects exemplify the bridging of anthropology's subfields; indeed, the field may be diverging at a more rapid pace in the new millennium. However, the interdisciplinary and inter-subdisciplinary Kalahari project that Lee and DeVore initiated in 1963 stands as a hallmark of the best that the four-field approach has to offer. By the 1980s, Lee's work narrowed to a more focused exploration of cultural-historical and political economy questions, but Lee and Susser's recent HIV research strives to reintegrate biomedical and cultural anthropology.

Lee's early research was influenced by cultural ecology and evolutionary studies; his work stands as a paradigm of these approaches and became the exemplar for many who sought to apply similar research methods and analytic tools in the Kalahari and elsewhere. His work, especially the early ecologically oriented writings, employed rigorous scientific methodology. He counted, measured, weighed, and quantified. Lee seemed to have a natural gift for this sort of work; for instance, how many people could eyeball and estimate the weight of an ox within 5 to 10 kilos?[6] He produced models that aided in the understanding of San society, of other hunter-gatherer societies, and of sociocultural evolution. As a result of the team-based nature of the research and Lee's generosity, the integrity of his meticulously collected data and analyses have been scrutinized repeatedly by other team members and have stood the test of time.

The Kalahari project has included experts and students in all four subdisciplines as well as other fields, such as medicine, literature, and history. It has inspired subsequent team research endeavors, such as the Harvard Ituri project. In addition, the 1966 "Man the Hunter" conference that Lee and DeVore organized provided the foundation for ongoing interrogation and theorizing of the very concept and existence of the category "hunter-gatherer." Hunter-gatherer (forager) studies is now well established, with regular international conferences, ongoing research and debate, and productive internal critiques. If some of this work has provided a counterpoint to Lee's, it nonetheless reveals that the significance of his work lies not only in the models and data it has provided but also in its role as stimulus to further reflection, question, debate, controversy, and critical scholarship.

The legacy of Lee's Kalahari work finds expression not only in a voluminous output of books, articles, reviews, and documentary films, as well as newspaper articles and other popular media forms to which he has had direct input, but also, significantly, it finds expression in the work of all of the ethnographers who have followed in his footsteps. They have been animated by his written work; he has tutored them in the language, given access to his field notes, and otherwise encouraged and mentored countless researchers. This volume includes a representative group whose work spans more than half a century of Kalahari research. We begin with Elizabeth Marshall Thomas, whose fieldwork predates Lee's. She first traveled to Namibia (then Southwest Africa) in 1951 with her extraordinary family to conduct fieldwork amongst the San. Renée Sylvain, a student of Lee's, returned from the northern Namibian bush four days prior to the Montreal session, which begot this volume. Susser and this author were in the field as the final touches were being made to this book. I suspect that, in the fifty plus years since Thomas's initial research, there have been few, if any, years during which at least one of us has not been in the Kalahari.

Thomas's essay draws upon her early 1950s fieldwork to highlight the exceptional relationship, or set of "understandings," that existed

Introduction 13

between the San and the local lions. This "Bushman/lion truce" that she describes no longer exists, but that it did is fascinating and crucial to document. Thomas's chapter depicts a past Kalahari and one that she observed only in the "Nyae Nyae" interior. The remaining Kalahari-based chapters are situated in the wider set of relations and present day circumstances, life, and predicaments of contemporary San and their neighbors.

The chapters by Guenther and Sylvain address issues of theoretical and political importance regarding San identity at the turn of twenty-first-century, post-Apartheid, post-Cold War southern Africa, where as elsewhere questions of identity and recognition are becoming increasingly foregrounded and politicized. The contested terrain of San identity, the various stakeholders whose interests are served by fostering a particular label for the San, the possible consequences of applying the different labels, and some of the means by which the San and others attempt to navigate the complexities entailed are examined by Guenther and Sylvain. Guenther highlights the dilemma faced by the San, who, despite their participation in the contemporary everyday world, are continually recast as primitive by a public that wishes to ossify them as living fossils. He exposes a paradox of San artists, who live and work in a very modern world, but cannot escape the hegemonic Western perspective that will only view them and their work through a primitivist lens. The Western-based art consuming audience does this by rejecting artistic pieces that incorporate "modern" images and thus do not conform to outsiders' vision of the San as "primordial" noble savages. More nefarious is the refusal to grant creativity to individual artists and instead to credit the "culture" with "authorship" of the works. Guenther's chapter also follows up nicely on Biesele's, as it illustrates a variety of San organizations and NGOs, some in which expatriate involvement is central and another that is run solely by San.

Sylvain addresses predicaments faced by the Omaheke San of Namibia, who have long been employed as farm laborers. Their political fortunes have been increasingly tied to the politics of recognition. Sylvain explores the identity dilemmas faced by the Omaheke in a number of arenas that tend to mutually reinforce one another. Their fortunes vis-à-vis the state of Namibia, their employment situation, their relationships with NGOs, and their place in the scholarly literature tend to hinge upon a number of contrasting sets of identities. For instance, are the Omaheke "indigenous peoples" or an underclass (and thus invisible to the blossoming NGO world)? Must they be defined by their cultural characteristics or class characteristics? And why must these categories be seen, as they so often are inside and outside the academy, as mutually exclusive? By what standards of "authenticity" are these categories to be measured, and who has the authority to set the standards? As Sylvain points out in her eloquently argued piece, the consequences for the Omaheke are not simply "academic." In addressing these timely questions, Sylvain provides significant insights that add a new analytic layer to the Kalahari debate, to the "identity" literature, and to questions regarding the appropriateness and strategic political wisdom of taking on the indigenous label.

Susser and Lee, in collaboration with southern African scholars and practitioners, are currently engaged in applied research in the struggle against HIV/AIDS. Southern Africa has the world's highest prevalence of documented HIV positive cases. Given that analysts in southern Africa and elsewhere have associated high rates of HIV with poverty and, especially in southern Africa, with women's lack of autonomy, Susser wonders whether the San's legacy of a lack of "relative poverty" (Sahlins's original affluence) might have granted them any small amount of protection against its spread. She also speculates as to whether the San legacy of female political agency depicted so vividly by Lee may have provided the San an added measure of resilience against HIV compared to neighboring groups. While Susser and Lee's results remain preliminary and suggestive at this point, they point to important factors to consider with regards to the spread of—and possible resistance to—AIDS amongst the San.

Conclusion

The chapters explore a number of pressing questions in political anthropology today. Trigger, in particular, poses questions regarding the malleability of human nature and, by implication, casts doubt on the proverbial notion of a "blank slate" upon which culture can shape endless human possibilities. However, acknowledging limits does not necessarily result in a pessimistic scenario in which Hobbes's "war of every man against every man" prevails. Social formations, cultural constructs, and human beings have the capacity to develop structures that can mitigate against such dystopic outcomes. Sahlins's piece provides a theoretical discussion of the possibility that humans can live in a world where some of the mechanisms implicit in Trigger's argument operate to limit both inequality and a perception of deprivation. In turning his gaze on the scholarly interpretation of San material, Patterson shows how an emphasis on exchange relations versus production relations has led analysts to misrecognize the possibilities of egalitarianism present in San society. Similarly, in asking why Marx's later work, the *Ethnological Notebooks*, has been so little studied, Gailey suggests that academics have neglected the communal structures that Marx identified in the more egalitarian of precapitalist structures and

Introduction   15

that may still be evident in some aspects of contemporary communities. These societies hold within them the capacity to enable people to resist oppression, and they provide a basis for a more egalitarian future. Brodkin offers a reflection on the kinds of praxis, in this case identity work, in which we can engage to redress oppression.

Kalahari studies take us from a glimpse into what a world of hunters living amongst hunters (including lions) might have looked like to the San struggling in various ways with the realities of twenty-first century life in an increasingly globalized southern Africa. Hitchcock and Biesele recount the world of San activism with its trials and triumphs. Guenther and Sylvain explore conundrums facing the San in various circumstances and speak to the complexities entailed in the contrasting identities both imposed on and embraced by the San. Susser follows with a discussion of how egalitarian structures may have lessened the San's vulnerability to HIV/AIDS in comparison to their neighbors. The volume closes with Gailey's intellectual biography of Lee written for the original *Festschrift* issue of *Anthropologica*.

Taken together, these works explore both theoretical and practical dimensions of egalitarianism as a political possibility and project. All are a tribute to and a celebration of the inspiring work of Richard B. Lee. His optimism and enthusiasm for new ideas and new people have benefited colleagues, friends, and students.[7] This volume is presented in the spirit of the gift that we so cherish in anthropology—that is, as only one moment in a chain of open-ended exchanges, of generalized reciprocity, that will endure, repeat, expand, and embrace new members over time. Like a trinket in the *hxaro*[8] network or a valuable in the *Kula* ring, we see this as an offering that will be productive of new and more "items" and relations. We can most assuredly count on the fact that Lee will continue his commitment to anthropology, to the peoples of the Kalahari and southern Africa, to his students and colleagues, and to art, science, and politics. And we hope that the critical works that make up this book will serve as a call for further research into the themes and topics explored here.

Notes

1. This book had its genesis at the joint meetings of the Canadian Anthropology Society, American Ethnological Society, and the Society for Cultural Anthropology in Montreal, May 2001, where Christine Gailey and I organized several sessions that explored a set of themes arising from the work of Richard Lee. The sessions

resulted in a special issue of the journal *Anthropologica*. Richard Katz and Patricia Draper also presented papers at the 2001 conference. Susser was a discussant at the conference and has provided a paper for this volume. Brodkin was unable to attend the conference but has contributed a paper. In addition, Gailey conducted an extensive interview with Lee in 2002. From this interview, she produced an intellectual biography that provides a window into Lee's life and better enables us to understand and appreciate the array of factors and circumstances that have shaped the direction of Lee's work (such as family, education, engagement with evolving intellectual developments and perspectives, the radicalized political context of the 1960s, and the antiwar movement). This book includes versions of all of those papers plus an abridged version of Marshall Sahlins's classic piece, "The Original Affluent Society," and a new introduction to the essay.

Since the 2001 conference, two pioneers in the study of the San have passed away—Isaac Schapera and Lorna Marshall. Their pathbreaking work has led the way and formed a sound basis for all subsequent work in the field.

2. "San" is a generic term deriving from the language family of Khoisan. Debate has raged and fashions have changed regarding the correct and/or appropriate appellation to bestow on the former foraging peoples of the Kalahari (and southern Africa). The term "Bushmen," once dismissed as pejorative, is coming back into fashion. Lee worked with people who call themselves Ju/'hoansi and have been called !Kung in much of the anthropological literature (see Gailey, this volume). Because some chapters in this volume, especially those by Guenther and Sylvain, focus on other San groups than the Ju/'hoansi, I employ the generic term "San."

3. The San's diet had been described (see Thomas, 1959), but Lee painstakingly documented how varied and highly nutritious it was.

4. As Gailey notes (in personal communication with the author, March 2003), Lee's depiction of the control women exercised over their own work arrangements and the distribution of products was significant for feminist scholars producing a critique of male bias in anthropology. (See inter alia Slocum, 1975).

5. The number of times key articles such as "Eating Christmas in the Kalahari" and the undergraduate ethnography first published as *The Dobe !Kung* have been reprinted is evidence of this, as is the fact that his first ethnography, *The !Kung San: Men, Women and Work in a Foraging Society*, won the prestigious Herskovits award.

6. This passage derives from Lee's well-known article "Eating Christmas in the Kalahari," first published in *Natural History* magazine. Lee's capacity to make people come alive through his writing, to engage an audience, and to do so through the classic Jewish humorous motif of self-deprecation is exemplified brilliantly in this wonderful narrative.

7. In particular, students have always appreciated his enthusiasm: he not only made us feel welcome, he made us feel interesting.

8. *Hxaro* is a system of generalized gift exchange practiced amongst the Ju/'hoansi (Wiessner, 1982).

References

Berry, S. 1993. *No Condition Is Permanent*. Madison: University of Wisconsin Press.

Draper, P. 1975. "!Kung Women: Contrasts in Sexual Egalitarianism in the Foraging and Sedentary Contexts." *Toward an Anthropology of Women*, ed. Rayna Rapp Reiter. New York: Monthly Review Press, 77–109.

Haugerud, A., and J. Solway. 2000. "Introduction." "The Returning Researcher: Interdisciplinary Perspectives on Long-Term Research, Roundtable." African Studies Association Annual Meeting, Memphis, Tenn.

Hitchcock, Robert, and Diana Vinding, eds. 2004. *Indigenous People's Rights in Southern Africa.* Copenhagen, International Working Group for Indigenous Affairs.

Kuper, Adam. 2003. "The Return of the Native." *Current Anthropology* 44: 389–402.

Niezen, Ronald. 2003. *The Origins of Indigenism.* Berkeley, University of California Press.

Robbins, Steven. 2003. "Comment on Kuper – Return of the Native." *Current Anthropology* 44: 398–99.

Sahlins, M. 1968. "Notes on the Original Affluent Society." In *Man the Hunter,* ed. R. Lee and I. De Vore. Chicago: Aldine.

―――. 1972. *Stone Age Economics.* Chicago: Aldine.

Slocum, Sally. [1971] 1975. "Woman the Gatherer: Male Bias in Anthropology." *Toward an Anthropology of Women,* ed. Rayna Rapp Reiter. New York: Monthly Review Press, 36–50.

Snow, C.P. 1959. *The Two Cultures and the Scientific Revolution.* New York: Cambridge University Press.

Solway, Jacqueline. 2005. "Anthropologist and Accomplice." In *Auto-Ethnographies of Academic Practices,* ed. Anne Meneley and Donna-Jean Young. Peterborough: Broadview Press, 113–25.

Suzman, James. 2002. "Kalahari Conundrums: Relocation, Resistance, and International Support in the Central Kalahari, Botswana." *Before Farming* 1(3). Available at: http://(www.waspjournals.com).

Thomas, Elizabeth Marshall. 1959. *The Harmless People.* New York: Alfred A. Knopf.

Wiessner, P. 1982. "Risk, Reciprocity, and Social Influences in !Kung San Economics." *Politics and History in Band Societies,* ed. E. Leacock and R.B. Lee. Cambridge: Cambridge University Press, 61–84.

Wolf, Eric. 1964. *Anthropology.* New York: Norton

Woodburn, James. 1982. "Egalitarian Societies." *Man* 17: 431–51

For Lee references, see "Selected Bibliography."

PART I

The Politics and Practices of Egalitarianism

Chapter 1

ALL PEOPLE ARE (NOT) GOOD

Bruce G. Trigger

As a result of his early studies of the !Kung San, Richard Lee (1979) reached some very important conclusions about the nature of human behavior in small-scale societies. In this paper, I will consider the implications of these findings for understanding sociocultural evolution and charting the future development of anthropology.

The *San Tzu Ching*, or Three Character Classic, which was composed by the Confucian scholar Wang Yinglin in the late Sung dynasty and served for almost 700 years as a primer for Chinese youngsters learning to read, began as follows:

Jen chih chu	At the beginning of people's lives
hsing pen shan	their human nature is basically good
Hsing hsiang chin	Human natures are close to one another
hsi hsiang yuän	it is their cultural environment that causes them to grow far apart from each other

This summation of Confucian, and Chinese, views about human nature reflects an understanding that is more optimistic and hopeful than the Christian belief that all humans are inherently sinful. The paramount, original sin identified in the Bible was disobedience to God, but, in the patriarchal and hierarchical societies in which the Judeo-Christian tradition emerged and flourished, this form of sinfulness was effortlessly extended to include disobeying kings, officials, fathers, husbands, elders, teachers, and employers. This interpretation survived intact through the European Middle Ages. Following the growth of capitalism, however, many people came to regard greed as the gravest moral vice.

As part of their rejection of religious orthodoxy, eighteenth-century philosophers of the Enlightenment adopted the contrary view that human beings were fundamentally rational and good. This idea may have been encouraged by Jesuit missionaries' accounts of Confucian beliefs, but it was also inherent in the continuing influence of Pelagianism, a minority tradition in Christian theology that stressed God-given reason and free will, rather than divine grace, as a major element in human salvation. In the eighteenth century, these heterodox beliefs took on new life in the context of Deism. In Enlightenment circles, belief in human goodness and rationality powered the conviction that human beings had the ability to build a better future for all humankind. While humanity's innate goodness was thought to become corrupted in rigidly hierarchical and despotic societies, it was assumed that general moral improvement could be brought about by creating progressive societies that were more in line with human nature. It was believed that such societies would liberate the human spirit, progressively eliminate ignorance, curb uncontrolled passions, free human beings from superstition, and unleash human creativity and progressive change (Toulmin and Goodfield, 1966: 115–23).

Karl Marx's ideas about human nature were based on, yet departed from, those of the Enlightenment. He regarded individuals as passionate creatures whose needs and general aspirations were innate and cross-culturally uniform. Yet he rejected the concept of an autonomous human nature. He described human nature as a social construct that altered as social formations were transformed. This view accorded with Marx's burning desire to radically transform Western society. In practice, conservatives generally prefer to regard human nature as biologically grounded and inflexible, while radicals hope that it is situationally determined and therefore capable of swift and radical change. Yet Marx and Friedrich Engels, in conformity with Enlightenment views, also believed that hunter-gatherer societies were characterized by equality and sharing and regarded socialism as the return, at a more advanced level of economic productivity, to a situation that accorded with the original goodness of human beings; a view that Lewis Henry Morgan also held to be true of American republican democracy (Fuller, 1980: 230–64; Geras, 1983).

Lee's ethnographic observations among the !Kung would have pleased Marx. Here was evidence of what Marx had regarded as a "primitive" social formation exhibiting economic and political equality that was not merely the product of an ideologue's or philosopher's imagination. Yet Lee in turn entered new territory when he presented evidence that economic and political equality in small-scale societies did not simply reflect human nature. Self-assertion and greed were kept in line by complex patterns of ridicule and gossip, and by fears of falling victim to witchcraft (Lee, 1979: 458–61; 1990; Trigger, 1990). If the state protects power and privilege in complex societies, ridicule, gossip, and fears of witchcraft protected social and economic equality in hunter-gatherer societies. About the same time Pierre Clastres (1977) argued that people who lived in small-scale societies actively resisted the development of the state. Lee's findings made it clear that groups such as the !Kung were fighting to maintain social and economic equality among themselves. Rather than simply being without a state form of organization and hence lacking something, hunter-gatherer societies possessed their own instruments of political control, of which the state would eventually become the antithesis. The "anti-state," with its use of ridicule, gossip, and witchcraft as equalizing mechanisms, appears to have functioned well as long as societies remained small and all the people who lived in them knew each other personally.

An unanswered question remained: how large could societies be in which anti-state principles remained effective? My Huron ethnohistorical research, conducted in the 1960s and 1970s, had demonstrated that these techniques remained operative in Iroquoian towns with over 1,500 inhabitants and in multicommunity societies that were several times larger still. These remained societies in which, despite elaborate consultative structures and formal political offices, each individual had to personally agree with public policies in order to be bound by them. No individual could tell another what to do, and no localized clan group could be dominated by another. Families and clans that felt pressured by other groups in the community could leave and try to set up on their own or join a more congenial group (Trigger, 1969; 1990). Similar arrangements existed among the Tupinamba in Brazil (Clastres, 1977) and the Kachin in Burma (Leach, 1954). These observations initially caused me to believe that gossip, ridicule, and witchcraft must result in public opinion being an effective curb on individual behavior not only in small-scale, but also in middle-range, societies. Yet many middle-range societies around the world exhibit marked social stratification and economic inequality, as Jérôme Rousseau (2001) has clearly demonstrated. Pastoral societies also display varying degrees of egalitarianism and social hierarchy (Salzman, 1999; 2001). Eventually I became aware that as sedentary and semi-sedentary societies grew larger egalitarianism tended to survive mainly among swidden agriculturalists, especially ones with overall population densities that were low enough that dissidents could easily move away, thereby frustrating the development of chiefdoms and other forms of social stratification.

Some anthropologists who oppose unilinear views of sociocultural evolution have posited that resistance to the development of inequality has been successful at much larger scales, in the form of heterarchical preindustrial civilizations. This would make states an optional, rather than an inevitable, consequence of increasing social complexity and leave open the possibility that states and economic inequality are only accidental features of modern industrial societies. Some archaeologists propose that Teotihuacan, in Mexico, may have been a kingless complex society (Cowgill, 1997) and the Indus Valley civilization a potentially stateless one (Kenoyer, 1997; Maisels, 1999: 186–259; Possehl, 1998). Yet the little that is certain concerning such societies resembles what was known about the Classic Maya prior to the decipherment of their writing system. John Eric Thompson (1954) imagined the Maya to have been a unique society of dispersed farmers, peacefully governed by priests who lived in elaborate but largely empty ceremonial centers. Since the decipherment of their script, Maya society turns out to have been more like that of other early civilizations than Thompson thought possible (Coe, 1993).

Moreover, well-documented, heterarchically structured early civilizations, such as those of Mesopotamia and the Yoruba, were not characterized by the absence of hierarchy and economic inequality, but presented hierarchy and economic inequality in another form (Stone, 1997). My comparative study of early civilizations has produced no evidence of early complex societies in which social stratification did not exist and was not accompanied by massive economic and political inequality (Trigger, 1993). Likewise, there is no evidence of any large-scale societies in which the authority and privileges of the dominant upper classes were not protected by coercive powers. Once a ruling group controls society-wide communication networks, gossip and ridicule can be countered by the administrative interventions of the state. The coercive powers of the state can also be deployed to punish individuals who are suspected of practicing witchcraft against the upper classes (Trigger, 1985).

Where matters of social and political equality are involved, complexity does not produce a wide variety of responses. Early civilizations came in various sizes and differed in their organization. But in all early civilizations, those who managed society as a whole invariably used their coercive powers to accumulate and protect wealth. Even the nuclear family became more hierarchical and authoritarian, as it transformed itself to accord with the image of the state (Trigger, 1985). Such cross-cultural uniformity would be unexpected if the principal human wants and the goals of human life were culturally defined, either wholly or in large part.

All early civilizations, because of their large size and complexity, may have required centralized controls in order to function adequately, and this in turn would have necessitated the concentration of wealth to cover administrative costs and ensure effective government (Trigger, 1976). Yet why, in addition, would ruling elites invariably have opted to accumulate private wealth and indulge in conspicuous consumption on such a massive scale? Why, moreover, would such behavior have been universally respected and have enhanced a ruler's powers, even among subjects who may have resented their monarch's exactions? Something must have encouraged rulers and subjects alike to accept as normal the congruence of political power, social status, and wealth. While I accept that all human behavior is symbolically mediated, cross-cultural uniformity of this sort pushes the understanding of these aspects of human behavior toward a materialist, and possibly even towards a more biologically grounded, view.

Throughout the twentieth century, Marxists and other progressives have treated human behavior as shaped exclusively by social forces and therefore maximally changeable and improvable. Ironically, as Marx and Engels also did, they further hedged their bets by assuming that human beings are basically inclined to be good, thereby following in the tradition of Confucian Chinese and Western Enlightenment philosophers. In operational terms, "good" may be glossed as meaning "socially cooperative" or "altruistic." They have generally ignored evidence that our closest primate relatives, and therefore probably our primate ancestors as well, were not only extremely sociable but also intensely hierarchical (Conroy, 1990). While sociability and competitiveness have been defined and controlled differently in different human societies (Hardin, 1968), their universal importance makes it clear that they are species-specific tendencies that every society has to channel, rather than purely cultural creations. Christian theologians may have evaluated human nature more accurately than did Enlightenment philosophers.

Viewed from this perspective, Lee's findings suggest that social and political equality in hunter-gatherer societies was not a direct expression of human nature. His evidence indicates that hierarchical behavior was actively suppressed in hunter-gatherer societies, where economic and political egalitarianism had great adaptive advantages, as well as in some of the more mobile middle-range societies. Contrariwise, in more complex societies competitive behavior was supported and reinforced by the state. While culturally specific values that channel these tendencies in different ways are built into all societies, support for, or opposition to, these tendencies appears to be controlled primarily by the general sorts of socioregulatory mechanisms that function at different levels of social complexity.

Today we live in a transnational world guided by the ideas of nineteenth-century Liberalism that have been disinterred from the intellectual graveyard. These ideas constituted a doctrine that was discredited as a result of the economic collapse of the 1930s. If they have been altered in any way, it is in the direction of being even less socially responsible than they were in the past, at least partly as a result of the weakened constraints of traditional religious social ethics in modern Western society. Despite the triumphalist platitudes of neoconservatives, practical and theoretical problems abound. Growing worldwide industrialization and the ceaseless search for short-term profits pose major threats to global ecology, unless new, clean, and cheap sources of energy can be developed. Poor societies are being exploited and destabilized as never before, and the poorest members of developed societies are increasingly malnourished and diseased. A pervasive and growing psychological malaise blights the lives of ever larger numbers of people who participate in the so-called new economy (Trigger, 1998). How much longer can such societies and a world economic system be kept operating by a monopolistic information system that propagates the view that no viable alternatives exist, or can even be imagined, to the way things are currently being done?

Unfortunately, twentieth-century efforts to build socialism foundered to no small degree as a result of the uncontrolled greed, corruption, and self-interest of those in authority. It is no accident that some of the bureaucrats of the former Soviet Union are among the most successful capitalists of post-Soviet Russia. At the same time, the welfare bureaucracies of Western societies were widely discredited because neoconservative propagandists so easily persuaded the public that these services had become arrogant and were benefiting those who managed them more than they did their intended beneficiaries. The assumption that, because human beings are essentially good, as capitalist society withered a more egalitarian way of life would replace it has not been confirmed. Socialism failed politically because it failed to create for large-scale, industrial societies mechanisms to control domination and rapacity that were equivalent to those of the hunter-gatherer anti-state.

In recent decades the anthropological left has critiqued neoconservative ideologies in Western society and elsewhere. These critiques have made anthropologists as a whole increasingly aware of the socially constituted and political aspects of their individual and collective theorizing (Patterson, 2001). Critical anthropologists have not, however, made much progress in determining how the world might be fundamentally changed. The neoconservatives have vastly outflanked both the left and the center in not only imagining the world as they wish it to be but in actually making it that way (Marchak, 1991). The challenge of the present is for progressive anthropologists to draw on their knowledge of social behavior to try to design societies of a sort that have never existed before in human history: ones that are large-scale, technologically advanced, internally culturally diverse, economically as well as politically egalitarian, and in which everyone will assume a fair share of the burdens as well as of the rewards of living on a small, rich, but fragile planet (Trigger, 1998). Ideally, these will also be societies that will not revert to neoconservative policies, as most social democracies have recently done, as soon as their work of repairing the injuries wrought by laissez-faire capitalism has been accomplished.

How, and to what extent, can large-scale, enduring egalitarian societies be fashioned? What control mechanisms are needed to keep societies both democratic and economically egalitarian? What forms of social control, performing the same role as public opinion in hunter-gatherer societies, might counter the elitist tendencies inherent in the state? What would be the costs as well as the benefits in terms of human happiness of deploying such mechanisms? Could such a society be justified as truly providing the greatest good for the greatest number? What limits, if any, are imposed by human biology on our capacity for altruism? Might a broader definition of self-interest significantly encourage the more equitable sharing of wealth in capitalist societies? Or is this notion utopian, and can a significant sharing of wealth occur only when its possessors fear that the alternative may be to lose all, as was the case during the Cold War?

These are issues that progressive anthropologists must address. As part of their forward planning, they must take account of the less flexible aspects of human nature and how these aspects might articulate with different kinds of societies. It is not sufficient only to consider cultural and social values. The goal of such research must also be not to produce technocratic knowledge but to encourage informed public discussion of alternative possibilities.

Hunter-gatherer societies do not provide a model for the future; they merely demonstrate that social and political egalitarianism was possible in societies that were small enough to be controlled by public opinion. Progressive anthropologists are challenged to shift from merely criticizing the more deplorable features of contemporary societies to using what they and other social scientists, as well as psychologists and neuroscientists, know or can learn about human beings to formulate practical and attractive alternatives. A shift in this direction might also help to rescue anthropology from its current role of playing second fiddle to cultural studies and restore it to its former central position in debates concerning the future development of a viable, as well as a more humane, global society.

Acknowledgments

I wish to thank Robin Yates for information about the Three Character Classic and to acknowledge the influence of discussions concerning the nature of inequality that I have had with my colleague Jérôme Rousseau over the course of many years. I also thank an anonymous reader for helpful comments. Work on this paper was assisted by support from my research stipend as a James McGill Professor.

References

Clastres, Pierre. 1977. *Society against the State.* New York: Urizen Books.

Coe, Michael D. 1993. *The Maya.* 5th ed. London: Thames and Hudson.

Conroy, Glenn C. 1990. *Primate Evolution.* New York: Norton.

Cowgill, George L. 1997. "State and Society at Teotihuacan, Mexico." *Annual Review of Anthropology* 26: 129–61.

Fuller, Peter. 1980. *Beyond the Crisis in Art.* London: Writers and Readers.

Geras, Norman. 1983. *Marx and Human Nature: Refutation of a Legend.* London: Verso.

Hardin, Garrett J. 1968. "The Tragedy of the Commons," *Science* 162: 1243–48.

Kenoyer, Jonathan M. 1997. "Early City-States in South Asia: Comparing the Harappan Phase and Early Historic Period." In *The Archaeology of City-States: Cross-Cultural Approaches,* ed. Deborah L. Nichols and Thomas H. Charlton. Washington, D.C.: Smithsonian Institution Press, 51–70.

Leach, Edmund R. 1954. *Political Systems of Highland Burma.* Cambridge, Mass.: Harvard University Press.

Lee, Richard B. 1979. *The !Kung San: Men, Women, and Work in a Foraging Society.* Cambridge: Cambridge University Press.

———. 1990. "Primitive Communism and the Origin of Social Inequality." In *The Evolution of Political Systems: Sociopolitics in Small-Scale Sedentary Societies,* ed. Steadman Upham. Cambridge: Cambridge University Press, 225–46.

Maisels, Charles K. 1999. *Early Civilizations of the Old World: The Formative Histories of Egypt, the Levant, Mesopotamia, India and China.* London: Routledge.

Marchak, M. Patricia. 1991. *The Integrated Circus: The New Right and the Restructuring of Global Markets.* Montreal: McGill-Queen's University Press.

Patterson, Thomas C. 2001. *A Social History of Anthropology in the United States.* Oxford: Berg.

Possehl, Gregory L. 1998. "Sociocultural Complexity without the State: The Indus Civilization." *Archaic States,* ed. Gary M. Feinman and Joyce Marcus. Santa Fe: School of American Research Press, 261–91.

Rousseau, Jérôme. 2001. "Hereditary Stratification in Middle-Range Societies." *Journal of the Royal Anthropological Institute* 7: 117–31.

Salzman, Philip C. 1999. "Is Inequality Universal?" *Current Anthropology* 40: 31–61.

————. 2001. "Toward a Balanced Approach to the Study of Equality." *Current Anthropology* 42: 281–84.

Stone, Elizabeth. 1997. "City-States and Their Cities: The Mesopotamian Example." In *The Archaeology of City-States: Cross-Cultural Approaches,* ed. Deborah L. Nichols and Thomas H. Charlton. Washington, D.C.: Smithsonian Institution Press, 15–26.

Thompson, J.E.S. 1954. *The Rise and Fall of Maya Civilization.* Norman: University of Oklahoma Press.

Toulmin, Stephen E., and June Goodfield. 1966. *The Discovery of Time.* New York: Harper and Row.

Trigger, Bruce G. 1969. *The Huron: Farmers of the North.* New York: Holt, Rinehart and Winston.

————. 1976. "Inequality and Communication in Early Civilizations." *Anthropologica* 18: 27–52.

————. 1985. "Generalized Coercion and Inequality: The Basis of State Power in Early Civilizations." *Development and Decline: The Evolution of Sociopolitical Organization,* ed. H.J. Claessen, Pieter van de Velde, and M.E. Smith. South Hadley, Mass.: Bergin and Garvey, 46–61.

————. 1990. "Maintaining Economic Equality in Opposition to Complexity: An Iroquoian Case Study." *The Evolution of Political Systems: Sociopolitics in Small-Scale Sedentary Societies,* ed. Steadman Upham. Cambridge: Cambridge University Press, 119–45.

————. 1993. *Early Civilizations: Ancient Egypt in Context.* Cairo: American University in Cairo Press.

————. 1998. *Sociocultural Evolution: Calculation and Contingency.* Oxford: Blackwell.

Chapter 2

COMMUNITY, STATE, AND QUESTIONS OF SOCIAL EVOLUTION IN KARL MARX'S *ETHNOLOGICAL NOTEBOOKS*

Christine Ward Gailey

"Despite our seeming adaptation to life in hierarchical societies, and despite the rather dismal record of human rights in many parts of the world, there are signs that humankind retains a deep-rooted egalitarianism, a deep-rooted commitment to the norm of reciprocity, a deep-rooted desire for ... the sense of community. All theories of justice revolve around these principles, and our sense of outrage at the violation of these norms indicates the depth of its gut-level appeal. That, in my view, is the secret of primitive communism."
—Richard Lee, "Demystifying Primitive Communism"

Karl Marx's last writings were concerned with a study of precapitalist social formations, both primitive communist and class-based. The *Ethnological Notebooks* were written from 1880 to 1882—that is, in the period just prior to Marx's death in 1883. Friedrich Engels used parts of the *Ethnological Notebooks* in drafting his 1884 *Origin of the Family, Private Property, and the State.* Over the years other parts have been translated, but not until 1974 was the entire work transcribed by Lawrence Krader.[1]

Why should one consider the *Ethnological Notebooks* today? I was drawn to reconsider them as a result of a graduate exam in sociology,

Notes for this section can be found on page 50.

where a well-known senior social theorist was trying to drub the candidate into embracing a stage model of social evolution. The candidate, a single mother returning to school after a decade, resisted his characterization of primitive societies as passé, albeit lamentably so. Annoyed at his badgering of this student, I intervened with a rejoinder about Marx's *Ethnological Notebooks,* which he had never attempted to read. Beyond eschewing the notion of necessary stages of social evolution, I pointed out, Marx repeatedly pointed to the viability of communal forms as lived in particular societies. Over and again Marx showed how they pose inherent opposition to state forms of control and are therefore targeted in repeated attempts by state agents to prevent their reproduction as communally organized.

Walking with me after the exam, the graduate student exclaimed, "I didn't know how to say it, but every day of my life I see how important creating a circle of sharing and caring is in getting by. If societies that are organized that way are no longer viable, then neither are we." Like that woman and millions of other mothers and care-engaged people, I am deeply implicated in practices at home and at work that must address on a daily basis the consequences of different ideologies of kinship and questions of transformative work versus labor.[2] Time and again students in my courses emphasize the importance of kinship and community as the most compelling dynamics that either deflect or reflect what is a terrifying insecurity; in their discussions, kinship and community represent the most immediate and devastating of a range of oppressive relations or pose the most sustaining resistance to them. At least a third of our students at the University of California, Riverside, are the first members of their families to have attended college. These students understand the slender thread that education provides in constructing a modicum of economic security in the midst of volatile economic cycles. They rely on networks of sustaining relationships to obtain that security with the clear and present understanding that they will owe their prosperity to others.

Social evolution as a theory passes in and out of academic fashion: in the past decade it has enjoyed a resurgence, following the "triumph" of capitalism in the wake of a collapsed Socialist bloc. In this new variation, social evolution is facilitated through the state and expressed in unfettered capitalist commerce across national boundaries: neoliberalism is its credo, and global communications technology its metaphor of interconnection. Proponents presume that globalized capitalism in this new phase will result in higher standards of living for more people, greater democratization, and therefore, social and cultural progress. A proliferation of neoliberal economic and social policies has accompanied the post-Cold War shift in corporate accumulation strategies.

As the welfare supports of the earlier phase of industrial capitalism erode under these new policies, and as international lending agencies force poorer countries to impose ever more austere conditions on their people, the global search for jobs appears increasingly to transform the citizens of one country into the guest workers, or in some instances, modern-day slaves, of others. The implications of guest-worker models of labor flows can be seen vividly in the rhetoric of the apartheid-era South African state. Prior to his tenure as prime minister, Pieter Botha declared that unemployed blacks were "superfluous appendages" without a viable role to play in the country. Working blacks were defined as "labor units": categorically kinless and metaphorically robotic. With that chilling reminder of the fascist tendencies of capitalist states, more than ever before we need to appreciate what structures and practices sustain people as more than the expendable labor units that neoliberal economics would have the vast majority of us become.

Around the world grassroots opposition to such policies takes a myriad of forms. Yet one sees in all the organizations and protests a connecting thread: women and men, children and youth, are demanding basic security and a rehumanization of daily life. Sometimes the call is to bolster existing communities and families: often this has a conservative agenda, disguised as family preservation, of defending patriarchal forms and practices. But sometimes the call is to remedy the conditions and ideologies that have turned intimate institutions and relations into locations of violence.

While many of these movements make demands of the state in specific ways—for city services, educational access, cessation of militaristic repression—none argue that either states or the corporations they serve are loci for human emancipation. Although some romanticize iconic notions of "the people" or "the community," the more feminist of these movements are keenly aware of the ways that gender hierarchies permeate familial and community structures, with injurious consequences (see, for example, the case studies in Waller and Rycenga, 2000).

From Borneo to Chiapas, one sees efforts to defend communal rights to land. In Kenya and South Africa, mothers exiled from their marital lineages because legal changes have denied them any use-rights as lineage wives to their husband's private property (Okeyo, 1980), or dispossessed because they have been infected with HIV by their husbands, are demanding that their patterns of sharing and caregiving be socially valued. These women are clear that some customary usage should be defended, but other traditions have become so distorted by the context of capitalist legal and labor policies that they compromise the very survival of the communities that espouse them.

The resilience of communal forms in the face of overarching structures of domination was a central issue in Marx's examination of literature on precapitalist societies. The final writings of Marx's corpus focused on the relationship of communities to the state in various precapitalist contexts. Considering this continuity of concern, the Marx of the *Notebooks* appears as consistent with the Marx who authored the *Grundrisse* (1857) and other earlier efforts. Louis Althusser (1969) argued that there was an earlier, more Hegelian Marx who could be distinguished from the author of his later, supposedly more scientific and revolutionary writings, but this argument overlooks the *Notebooks*. Certainly Marx's final writings suffer from the admittedly inadequate and poorly researched sources he was forced to consult, a problem he bemoaned repeatedly in his notes. But I do not think this constitutes grounds for dismissal, particularly if we are trying to discern the trajectory of his thinking about social transformation.

We are confronting a situation where state policies and a genomic imperium in the name of scientific understanding are simultaneously exacerbating and naturalizing the racialization that accompanies the neoliberal phase of capital accumulation. Capitalism in its "globalization" dress relies on innovations in communications technology, the capacity to ravage environments on an unprecedented scale, and the strangulation of alternative political forms. In this setting we can appreciate all the more how Marx in his *Notebooks* repeatedly rejects a number of theories current in his time, notably racial ranking and social evolution in the sense of necessary and sequential stages, especially stages based on subsistence and techno-environmental sophistication. But I would like to go further and risk skittering along the razor's edge of intentionality to pose this question: Why would the author of the foremost analysis and critique of the structure and operation of capitalism turn, after completing that three-volume opus, to the examination of earlier forms of societies, when his explicit aim in undertaking the study of capitalism was its dismantling?

Marx against Social Evolutionism

Marx was not Leo Tolstoy, with the peasantry posed as a simpler and more natural counterpoint to the alienated lesser nobility and urbanized elite. Marx was a revolutionary, not a primitivist. But we can see in his notes, letters, and commentaries Marx's rejection of organic models of society, particularly state societies. In contrast to many of the sources he uses and the subsequent characterization of Marx as a social evolutionist, he does not portray people living in classless social formations as backward, less intelligent, or less developed cognitively.[3]

Community, State, and Questions of Social Evolution

Instead, based on his critical reading of a number of evolutionist scholars, he attempts to associate particular forms of authority, kinship, use-rights, and subsistence strategies as historically, rather than evolutionarily, linked configurations.

Put a different way, when Marx uses the term "evolution," it is couched very carefully as historical transformation; the term "earlier" is used only in the sense of temporal priority. Marx employs the term "archaic" in the *Ethnological Notebooks* to indicate temporality, not civilizational ranking. Indeed, connotations of backwardness are rejected explicitly: the "unfreedom" of the communal group is everywhere presented as security. Every instance of "freeing up"—as with the shifts in marriage rules from Mosaic to Levitical law—is tied to changing property relations, reduced authority of women, and growing social oppression (see, for example, 137).

The first part of the *Notebooks* concerns so-called primitive societies, while the second part focuses on different forms of precapitalist class societies and state formation. One finds detailed sections on kinship and social organization taken from Lewis Henry Morgan (1963), J.F. McLennan (1876), and Sir John Lubbock (1870) in the first part, as well as a range of early travelers' accounts of the Americas and the southern Pacific Islands. Marx adopts the categories of Morgan—savagery, barbarism, and so on—but appears more concerned with particular configurations and dynamics of kinship, labor, and work relations, technology, and decision-making processes than with the author's typology. As a result Morgan's classification scheme becomes historically specific and analytical, rather than evolutionary in a progressive sense. Marx identifies certain transformations as possible, but nowhere does he postulate a necessary transition. One looks in vain for any "motors" or "triggers" of social change, such as population increase, pressure on productive resources, or technological innovation.

Marx recognizes periods of dramatic change in social organization or political economy, but these are historically, not naturally or evolutionarily determined. Radical change is the result of contradictions emerging between human agency and structural processes on the one hand, and within the structures of polity and economy on the other. He notes, for instance, that communal property cannot coexist indefinitely with patriarchal family relations because of the fundamental opposition the latter poses to the former; similarly, "common usage" or custom cannot persist unchallenged alongside state-associated law (see also Diamond, 1974). Where archaic forms persist, Marx does not depict them as "vestiges" or cultural lags, but fundamentally as evidence of resistance to the penetration of state-associated institutions. For example, Marx does not present the replacement of "common usage" by legal codes and judicial structures as evidence of societal evolution in the sense of progressive change. Instead, as he writes in the following passage, law is intrinsically repressive:

> Customary law ... is not obeyed, as enacted law is obeyed.... The actual constrain [*sic*] which is required to secure conformity with usage is conceivably small.... [Laws, to the contrary, come from] *an authority external to the small natural group* and forming no part of it, ... wholly unlike customary rule. They [laws] lose the assistance of superstition (par exemple Christian Religion. Roman Church?), probably that of opinion, certainly that of spontaneous impulse. The *force at the back of law* comes therefore to be *purely coercive force* to a degree quite unknown in societies of the more primitive type. (335, emphasis in the original)

Marx rejects the pervasive nineteenth-century classification of societies by racial typologies. In his notes on works by Sir Henry Maine and John Budd Phear, time and again he rails in parentheses about the pseudoscience inherent in such racial classification schemes: "The devil take this 'Aryan' cant!" (324) and "Aryan (! again this nonsense!) race" (335). He also rejects the notion of differential intelligence accruing to those in one type of society versus another.

In several places he scorns the ideological character of most ethnographic accounts of the time. His parenthetical remarks on one passage from Lubbock illustrate the point. Lubbock refers to a friend of Reverend Lang, who

> tried long and patiently to make a very intelligent Australian understand (sollte heissen make him believe) his existence without a body, but the black never would keep his countenance ... for a long time he could not believe ("he" is the intelligent black) that the "gentleman" (i.e., d. Pfaffen Lang silly friend) was serious, and when he did realize it (that the gentleman was an ass in good earnest), the more serious the teacher was the more ludicrous the whole affair appeared to be (Spottet Lubbock seiner selbst u. weiss doch nicht wie).[4] (349)

The *Notebooks* underscore one central dynamic in the known historical transformations of communal societies: the emergence and persistence of nonproducing classes and alienable use-rights, bolstered perforce by emerging, coercive state structures. In the *Notebooks* Marx is concerned with variations and patterns in communal societies, and in precapitalist state societies, read not as typologies but as historically specific configurations that might share certain features. In the class-based social formations, he seems particularly focused on the relationship of sovereign and state functionaries and institutions to local communities. The sections on states make distinctions with regard to property, labor, political and religious ideologies between the precapitalist states emerging from the Mesopotamian region (Assyria, Babylonia, Greece, Rome), those societies colonized by Roman-derived states (the Germanic tribes, Ireland), and what Marx calls the "great states" known in the nineteenth century in Asia (India, Ceylon, China) and Mesoamerica (Aztec). Marx's commentaries focus on studies by Phear (1880), Maine (1861), and John Austin (1832), using these studies to argue forcefully that, contrary to the beliefs of those scholars, the state is fundamentally parasitic. Nowhere in the *Notebooks* does Marx discuss the state as a progressive force in human evolution or as a force in ameliorating social problems.

In his discussions of the state, Marx focuses on the local level, from daily and seasonal routines, to variations in diet and expenditures, kinship dynamics and rituals of social reproduction. These arrangements are then contrasted in content, even if forms seem similar, to the bureaucratic, religious, and legal structures imposed from above. Moreover, Marx denies the integrative functions of the state and the effectiveness of state ideologies in providing coherence to most precapitalist class societies. We find no successful propaganda machine here, no consensus of the ruled: to the contrary, we find contradiction, power struggles within the elite class and between the state and communities, and coercion. The "tax-taking" character of most of the "great states" precluded deeper penetration by state-sponsored edicts and ideological structures. The "particular commands" of the sovereign did not constitute law but "a sudden, spasmodic, and temporary interference with ancient multifarious usage left in general undisturbed" (334). Where coherence became judicially and legislatively defined, as in the Roman Empire, Marx comments:

> the process was spread over many centuries ... a vast and miscellaneous mass of customary law was broken up and replaced by new institutions.... It (the Roman Empire) devoured, brake [sic] into pieces, and stamped the residue with its feet. (335)

In one place Marx notes a function of a precapitalist state that at first appears to have improved local conditions. Phear discusses the intervention of the Bengali state in times of food scarcity, distributing stores to villages facing famine. Marx's commentary on this passage includes his point that, in order to make ready this distribution, all available means of transportation in the region had to be impressed into state service, sometimes weeks in advance of the projected scarcity, thereby exacerbating the problem (266). The other factor in periodic scarcity in this social formation was the commodification of food staples, which Marx identifies as entwined with class formation. Speculation in food grains is a consequence and a symptom of class relations. First, the cultivators (*ryots*) had to provide part of the harvest to state-associated functionaries (*Zamindaris*) to reaffirm and retain use-rights to land. These officials would either siphon off a portion of these taxes for their own use, or require labor service of subjects on their own use-plots. Harvests would then be available for sale, where sale became necessary because of exactions from the peasantry. Second, the *ryots* had to settle debts with interest; money-lenders (often petty officials) claimed portions of the harvest regardless of the cultivators' consumption needs (256). In short, Marx dismisses Malthusian explanations of food shortages. He insists that the famines described by Phear as caused by nature and as occasions for state beneficence were politically caused or at the very least exacerbated by the interference of class and state dynamics.

The common assumption that Marx was scornful of the peasantry, seeing them solely as ignorant or reactionary—a decontextualized reading of the "sack of potatoes" metaphor in his and Engels' 1852 *Eighteenth Brumaire of Louis Bonaparte*—simply cannot be born out in the *Notebooks*. Instead, one finds a decidedly mixed reaction, keyed to the specificities of the particular society and time. On the one hand, as repository of the "customary usage" deemed by Marx to be less oppressive when associated with the absence of the state or class relations, the "local natural group" is also more egalitarian than the rest of the society. But on the other hand, it is also affected by shifts in property and labor, and can acquire characteristics based on "superstition." While he adopts the term "superstition" from Phear, Marx gives it a decidedly different spin than does Phear. Judging from his parenthetical remarks, as Marx uses it, superstition refers to belief systems as they are parodied by, but do not entirely embody, the state-promoted ideology; the formal qualities of those beliefs are presented back to the villagers as traditional religion. Superstition, in other words, reveals a powered, dialectical relationship between state and community rather than timeless and unchanging local beliefs.

There is no essentialized "peasant" here, either as reactionary or heroic. Oppression may permeate the local group, but it is not due to traditions rooted in the communal shell of previously autonomous villages. His marginal notes on Phear's description of an essentialized and ahistorical Bengali peasant show this:

A husbandman of the present day is the primitive being he always (!) has been.... He is the greatest enemy of social reform [? wäre nicht enemy of getting himself the rent to pay the Zemindarees, old or young!] and never dreams of throwing off the trammels which time or superstition has spun around him. He will not send his son to school for fear [and a very just one, too!] of being deprived of his manual assistance in the field.... The ryots *too*

Community, State, and Questions of Social Evolution 39

poor (!), too ignorant, *too disunited among themselves to effect* ... improvement. (257; Marx's emphasis)

Marx here portrays the constraints on agency posed by class relations and the state on the one hand, and on the other hand, the constraints on collective action. Contradictions between communal ownership and private use-rights, and class formation within the community create internal disunity. The passage anticipates debates nearly a century later on the role of the peasantry in social revolution. Eric Wolf appears to adopt Phear's position that extreme poverty among peasantries is inimical to revolutionary action (Wolf, 1968). Marx's exclamation point and emphasis on disunity might have served as a cautionary note, as more recent grassroots movements throughout the world bear witness.

In a section on Maine's 1875 treatise, Marx challenges Thomas Hobbes for assuming that human nature is inherently competitive, and the English analytical jurists Jeremy Bentham and Austin for claiming as scientific what is projection. Marx criticizes Maine for casting the Roman patriarchal family into prehistory (324). Each author presents a classification scheme that Marx argues merely echoes the reigning political ideology of the particular time (328–29). Marx's concern with "science" can be read as needing to ground social theory in empirically informed research. At the same time, this empirical grounding demanded continuous, critical evaluation of analytical terms used. Throughout the *Notebooks,* Marx deconstructs terms used by other authors, as we have seen in his deployment of "superstition" and "evolution."

The *Ethnological Notebooks* appear to some as a scholastic exercise, or as an indication that, toward the end of his life, Marx was "slipping a bit," as one rather orthodox Marxist put it. Yet the *Notebooks* show the same kind of attention to historical contingencies and local dynamics that inform his 1881 response to a letter from Vera Zasulich. Zasulich writes with some urgency:

> In one way or another, even the personal fate of our revolutionary socialists depends upon your answer to the question. For there are only two possibilities. Either the rural commune, freed of exorbitant tax demands, payment to the nobility and arbitrary administration, is capable of developing in a socialist direction, that is, gradually organising its production and distribution on a collectivist basis. In that case, the revolutionary socialist must devote all his strength to the liberation and development of the commune.
>
> If, however, the commune is destined to perish, all that remains for the socialist, as such, is more or less ill-founded calculations as to how many decades it will take for the Russian peasant's land to pass into the hands of

40   *The Politics of Egalitarianism*

the bourgeoisie, and how many centuries it will take for capitalism in Russia to reach something like the level of development already attained in Western Europe.... You would be doing us a very great favour if you were to set forth Your ideas on the possible fate of our rural commune, and on the theory that it is historically necessary for every country in the world to pass through all the phases of capitalist production. In the name of my friends, I take the liberty to ask You, Citizen, to do us this favour. (Quoted in Shanin, 1983: 98)

Marx writes several drafts prior to sending his lengthy reply two months later. In his drafts and final reply (Shanin, 1983: 100–126), he details the historically unique qualities of the local collective villages (*mir*) and of local communal forms elsewhere. He also discusses the process of expropriation of the peasantries and the political and social dynamics that underwrote capitalist development in Western European countries. Marx weighs what would be necessary to create capitalism in Russia, without at any time saying this would be either desirable or that Western European countries somehow provide a model to be emulated:

If capitalist production is to establish its sway in Russia, then the great majority of peasants—that is, of the Russian people—will have to be transformed into wage-laborers, and hence be expropriated through the prior abolition of their communist property. But in any event, the Western precedent would prove nothing at all [about the "historical inevitability" of this process].

He goes on to eschew any notion of a necessary stage of capitalist expropriation and development in Russia:

However, the situation of the Russian commune is absolutely different from that of the primitive communities in the West [in Western Europe]. Russia is the only European country in which communal property has maintained itself on a vast, nationwide scale. But at the same time, Russia exists in a modern historical context: it is contemporaneous with a higher culture, and it is linked to a world market in which capitalist production is predominant.... Thus, in appropriating the positive results of this mode of production, [Russia] is able to develop and transform the still archaic form of its rural commune, instead of destroying it.... If the admirers of the capitalist system in Russia deny that such a combination is possible, let them prove that Russia had to undergo an incubation period of mechanical production in order to make use of machinery! Let them explain to me how they managed, in just a few days as it were, to introduce the machinery of exchange (banks, credit companies, etc.) which was the work of centuries in the West. (Shanin, 1983: 102–3)

He talks about the historical typologies of communal forms of property, outlines how as a result of state policies and capitalist markets, the Russian *mir* has come to combine communal ownership with private use-plots and mixed labor forms, and how this set of contradictions, constructed through state intervention as well as commerce and changing production, threatens the continuity of local communities.

> What threatens the life of the Russian commune is neither a historical inevitability nor a theory; it is state oppression, and exploitation by capitalist intruders whom the state has made powerful at the peasants' expense. (Shanin, 1983: 104–5)

In another draft he outlines a model of the kind of relations and structure that such "archaic" forms as the *mir* create for the removal of the more oppressive forms of private property:

> Also favourable to the maintenance of the Russian commune (on the path of development) is the fact not only that it is contemporary with capitalist production (in the Western countries), but that it has survived the epoch when the social system stood intact. Today, it faces a social system which, both in Western Europe and the United States, is in conflict with science, with the popular masses, and with the very productive forces that it generates. (Shanin, 1983: 106)

Marx goes on to argue that capitalism "has become the arena of flagrant antagonisms, conflicts and periodic disasters" and that this "state of crisis ... will end only when the social system is eliminated through the return of modern societies to the "archaic" type of communal property" (Shanin, 1983: 106). He calls for better comprehension of historical transformations in particular locations and an appreciation of the ways the structure of the communal forms afforded less oppressive daily conditions than those of the wider feudal or later, capitalist forms:

> But at least we should be thoroughly acquainted with all the historical twists and turns. We know nothing about them.... In one way or another, this commune perished in the midst of never-ending foreign and intestine [internecine - sic] warfare. It probably died a violent death when the Germanic tribes came to conquer Italy, Spain, Gaul, and so on. The commune of the archaic type had already ceased to exist. And yet, its natural vitality is proved by two facts. Scattered examples survived all the vicissitudes of the Middle Ages and have maintained themselves up to the present day— e.g. in my own home region of Trier. More importantly, however, it so stamped its own features on the commune that supplanted it (a commune in which arable land became private property, while the forests, pastures, waste ground, etc., remained communal property), that Maurer was able to reconstruct the archaic prototype while deciphering the commune [of more recent origin] of secondary formation. Thanks to the characteristic

features inherited from the prototype, the new commune which the Germans introduced into every conquered region became the only focus of liberty and popular life throughout the Middle Ages. (Shanin, 1983: 107–8)

Moreover, he cautions Zasulich and her Marxist audience about the political agendas of various writers and the barely disguised colonialism associated with economic determinism and the "inevitability of capitalism arguments":

> One has to be on one's guard when reading the histories of primitive communities written by bourgeois authors. They do not shrink [from anything] even from falsehoods. Sir Henry Maine, for example, who enthusiastically collaborated with the English government in its violent destruction of the Indian communes, hypocritically tells us that all the government's noble efforts to maintain the communes succumbed to the spontaneous power of economic laws! (Shanin 1983: 107)

What, then, is the future of these village communities? Certainly Marx did not see them disappearing as a matter of course. Historically the expansion of capitalist relations and state control have challenged and distorted communal relations, even crushed them in some cases. But even in this kind of transformation, Marx did not posit laws of transition or development:

> But does this mean that the development of the "agricultural commune" must follow this route in every circumstance [in every historical context]? Not at all. Its constitutive form allows of the following alternative: either the element of private property which it implies gains the upper hand over the collective element, or the reverse takes place. Everything depends upon the historical context in which it is situated.... Both solutions are a priori possibilities, but each one naturally requires a completely different historical context. (Shanin, 1983: 108–9).

The *Ethnological Notebooks* and Critical Anthropology in North America

It is in the spirit of Marx's call for careful ethnohistorical accounts that we can situate one strand of North American anthropology. Stanley Diamond (1974, 1975), Eleanor Leacock (1954, 1963, 1972), Richard Lee (1992), and Tom Patterson (1981) have pointed to the importance of ethnological writings by Marx and Engels, as well as their ethnographic methodology, as in Engels's *The Condition of the Working Class in England* ([1844] 1887) and the "Enquête Ouvrière" (1880). These authors point out that in Marx there is an abiding concern with discerning conditions and societal structures and processes that facilitate emancipation and those that underwrite and reproduce forms of oppression. Rather than dividing Marx's writings into an earlier phase more imbued with German Romantic philosophy and a later phase more focused on political-economic transformations (Althusser, 1969), Diamond and Krader emphasize the continuity of Marx's attention to the primitive commune as a model, at a different level of socioeconomic integration, of an emancipatory future (Diamond, 1975: 1–6; Krader, 1975: 5, 6).

This view lends itself better to an anthropology concerned with human liberation, not one that celebrates the entrenchment of neoliberal structures, anticommunist states, and a "global interdependence" that never questions the rights of corporations, the echoes of fascism in so-called democratic forms, or the virulent effects of the normal operation of the political economy on many millions of people. What this tradition in anthropology includes is advocacy for the efforts of indigenous peoples in their efforts to defend a way of life that is structurally and in practice deeply opposed to capitalism. Leacock and Lee, for instance, worked closely with the Innu of Labrador to oppose military overflights that wreaked havoc with hunting efforts (Leacock and Lee, 1982).

Lee in particular has argued on the basis of painstaking and long-term ethnographic research that people living in communal societies enjoy a "safety net" of pooled resources, sharing, and widespread care-giving that ventures far beyond any dream of social welfare in state societies. In addition, Lee and Leacock reintroduced and defended the use of the term "primitive communism" to describe such social formations at a time when Cold War politics and neoliberal forms of postmodern discourse made any reference to the Marxist tradition in anthropology seem poignantly passé (Lee, 1992; Leacock and Gailey, 1992). But despite a number of specious attacks on his ethnology, Lee remained among a handful of anthropologists who opposed South Africa's recruitment of San men in its war against the anti-apartheid forces of the Southwest African People's Organization (SWAPO) in Namibia. In the post-apartheid era, he continues to work with the San on the issues of HIV, of poverty in the areas subject to reservations, and of how communal values and practices can address various development agendas and the racial politics that are a legacy of apartheid. This kind of engagement is far from stubborn clinging to some ossified relic of outdated theory. As in the *Ethnographic Notebooks*, Lee's effort is to discern in local communal relations confronting powerful and sometimes coercive economic and political processes the dynamics that might help produce or reproduce unoppressive social relations and relative health and prosperity.

Marginalization of the *Ethnological Notebooks*

Given the predominance of anticommunist forces inside and outside the academy, one can readily comprehend why mainstream scholars have ignored the *Ethnological Notebooks*. Nevertheless, it is worth asking why they have attracted little attention among Marxist researchers. Some reasons are readily apparent: the commentaries are in fact notes rather than essays and therefore somewhat cryptic. Compounding this frustration is Marx's habit of conversing with himself and the authors he reads in five languages. At times reading the *Notebooks* makes one feel like the street cop in "Blade Runner," having to grapple with a city-speak agglomeration of phrases drawn from English, German, French, Greek, and Latin in order to make sense of the surroundings.[5] Perhaps these difficulties are sufficient explanation. However, International Publishers, the provider of so many of Marx's writings translated into English, had the subsidies and infrastructure at the time of its heyday in the 1960s and 1970s to accomplish this, and yet it did not develop such a project. Another reason for delayed publication is the absence of an explicitly framed narrative argument. Nevertheless, one can discern arguments in the selection of passages, authors, and commentaries, and there is ample precedent for publishing notes by major authors that can be combed by scholars.

Despite their obscurity in subsequent Marxist scholarship, the *Notebooks* bring up intriguing questions. For example, why was Marx taking notes on those particular sources, and those particular passages? It helps, of course, to have a certain familiarity with the volumes on ancient legal systems, histories of archaic civilizations, and what passed for ethnography in the latter part of the nineteenth century. But if we have learned anything from the last quarter century of literary criticism, it is that reading author's intentionality is at best a creative act, at worst, projective folly. So I have tried to frame the notes chronologically: they were written after Marx and Engels' 1871 commentaries on the failure of the Paris Commune and in the same period as Marx's correspondence with Vera Zasulich, working in Russia. In the *Notebooks* we can trace elaborations on his discussion of the fatal lack of communication between the Communards and rural areas, and the relative isolation of French peasant communities, articulated almost uniquely through state vectors. We also can see a defense of historical specificity, a multiplicity of possible outcomes for a given set of dynamics, and otherwise indications of the importance of organizing—that is, of concerted human agency in determining particular pathways of change.

Many Marxist scholars have commented that Marx never addressed the problem of the transition to socialism. I do not think of Marx as a utopian philosopher, and so I would not expect him to have much sympathy with the construction of blueprints. Still, throughout Marx's works is the concept of dialectical return. This concept provides us with a clue to one of the purposes of the anthropological explorations in the *Notebooks;* the letter to Zasulich underscores the point. Clearly Marx's concept of communism involves recapitulating the kind of absence of private property and classless division of labor characteristic of primitive societies while utilizing the technologies and more widespread communication capabilities developed under capitalism. The nature of the state is central, both with regard to the historical transformations from the earlier communal societies to class-based ones, and the potential obstacles to achieving communism involved in socialist transitions.

Marx's abiding scorn for the state as a vehicle for human emancipation is, I think, at the heart of the marginalization of *The Ethnological Notebooks* in twentieth-century Marxist scholarship. Despite their wish to counter the vicious international politics of US cold warriors, it was not possible for many more ethnographically grounded scholars to ignore the repressive quality of most of the Socialist bloc states regarding local communities and the question of ethnicity in general. To do so did not mean that one upheld an imaginary capitalist West as less racist, homophobic, and repressive, particularly if one conceived of corporate policies as an invisible branch of the state.

Reading the *Notebooks,* it becomes impossible to view socialism as a telos. Socialism would be beneficial only insofar as it facilitated the achievement of a dialectical return to the communal societies of the past. But as a source of taxation, conscription, and surveillance, it could not be defended, even as Marx vilified the imperialist policies or domestic repression characteristic of the capitalist state societies he analyzed. As he argued in 1871 in relation to the Paris Commune, "But the working class cannot simply lay hold on the ready-made state-machinery and wield it for their own purpose. The political instrument of their enslavement cannot serve as the political instrument of their emancipation" (196). He went on to describe the kind of representational, accountable, and democratic governance structure that the Communards devised in Paris as a model for the nation.

The sections on the "great states" in Asia focus on the dynamics in a tribute-based mode of production, although the term is not used as such (Krader, 1975). Marx discusses the layering of use-rights, the absence of real private property, and the contrast between the assertion of ownership by the "Sovereign" (state) and the everyday possession and use by direct producers, organized for the most part in custom-oriented communities. The basic determination of what was to be produced was shaped by state demands in the form of tax-goods or labor service, but the production process was largely governed by ideologies of kinship and reciprocity, better understood by the producers than by agents of the state. The state apparatus is depicted as a growth on top and at the expense of the local communities. Marx states explicitly that the state "in all forms is an excrescence of the society" (329).[6]

The question of class formation in socialist states can be seen in a framework of dialectical return. Socialist states, where they emerged, would exhibit contradictions associated with divisions of labor, property relations, and social relations that parallel, at a different level of technical and productive capacities, earlier tribute-based states. If we consider any transition through socialism this way, the fundamentally unoppressive conditions found in primitive communism appear both as history and potentiality. Socialism would represent the rejection of private property at the root of the contradictions in capitalist relations of production. As in capitalism, in socialism the production process is largely collective, socialized.

But in socialist societies, the state claims resources on behalf of the citizenry. The state as property owner has a direct parallel in the assertions of tribute-based states throughout the ancient world. The "excrescent" state becomes, as in the "tax-taking" state societies of the precapitalist past, the basis of social contradiction. Producers in theory might own the means of production, but the degree to which they actually control the labor process and products of their labor becomes the cause for political struggle. We have seen in the actions of the early Solidarity movement in Poland[7] that this effort to actualize the rhetoric of worker control in the face of de facto state control can lead to the state's collapse. We also can see that this does not necessarily lead to communism but can result in capitalist relations and the erosion of social welfare. But Marx never saw pathways of development as inevitabilities. One always comes back to the importance of organization and the values and practices of actual, historically situated people.

The class relations in socialist settings differ markedly from those in capitalist ones. Private accumulation occurs as graft or corruption, because the privileged classes are state-associated. While private accumulation is not an automatic result of state-associated class formation, it can be. The tax-farming of archaic states can find a parallel in settings where agents enjoy a degree of autonomy in their positions and a surrounding global system that provides an incentive, the skimming or extortion destined for Swiss bank accounts. In contrast to capitalism, here wealth is a result of, rather than a basis for, class formation.

Indeed, most of the twentieth-century socialist states had been, prior to capitalist colonization or partial penetration, variations of the tribute-based mode of production, the "tax-taking" societies discussed by Marx as surviving in the nineteenth century primarily in Asia. For example,

Community, State, and Questions of Social Evolution   47

in his letters to Zasulich, Marx holds that the village-community structure had not been eliminated in Russia, although commodity production was fostering rapid class formation. Capital penetration was contributing to the dissolution of what had been a community without internal class divisions, but the resilience of the older communal form was not inevitable.

If we take these so-called Asiatic states—that is, precapitalist—"tribute-paying" social formations as a model, then classes in socialist transitions derive from relative control over labor and resources rather than ownership per se. In the tribute-paying formations, state representatives and retainers took their income from their official positions that (in theory) could not be inherited. Any accumulated wealth was expended on lifestyle items or invested in extremely limited arenas, since the state or sovereign claimed most venues. Over time the tendency could be seen, for example, in precapitalist China or the principalities in India, for the bureaucratic elites to reproduce themselves as such, with some mobility possible for the more prosperous levels of the peasantry, or for those linking their reproductive potential to the state (through military demonstrations of fealty or concubinage). The political dynamic between villages and the state in these societies was a struggle over the relative determination of production, including the distribution of products. For instance, Marx emphasizes that within the Bengali ruling class, "the contest for power ... was mainly a struggle for command of the *kachari tabils*," that is, the regional structure that administered the extraction of products and labor service, as well as accounting (284).

Pressures for deconstructing the state apparatus and bureaucratically defined class formation would depend not only on socialized production but also on the communal dynamics that persist in reproductive spheres and are enacted in daily life. In other words, the relations of pooling resources and technical rather than social divisions of labor, the nets of "sharing and caring" invoked by the UC Riverside graduate student, when combined with transformed labor relations, provide an alternative to the ideology of state as collective will.

Throughout the *Notebooks*, Marx reviles in unambiguous ways the self-serving presentation of state-associated classes as necessary for societal prosperity (329). He does not confuse the collectivities organized for purposes of extracting goods or labor—military units, work groups ordained by the state—with communal forms (334). Reading the *Notebooks* it appears impossible to hold socialism up as a guiding light. Unoppressive conditions were presented only in the context of his discussions of "primitive" communal societies. He presents political struggle—not simply technical innovation, novel property relations, or systems of labor alone—as pressing internal contradictions in a particular social formation toward transformation. The outcome of transformation is nowhere shown as predestined or as merely a logical outgrowth of existing structures. This dependence on human agency provides another clue as to why the *Notebooks* fly in the face of Second International agendas.

Marx identifies the partial dissolution of communal relations as one consequence of emerging class differences, themselves due to a myriad of conditions involving both contradictions in structure and human action. The layered social formations, such as those in Asia or Russia, that had interfered the least in the communal relations of the "local natural group" would in Marx's view require the least intensity of action to remove the primary sources of oppression. Fully capitalist societies would therefore be less likely to foster socialist transformations, since communities are—except as rearguard efforts and on the margins—effectively dissolved. In capitalist settings, the hegemony of state ideology is the most effective because it appears simultaneously as natural and as individual choice. For those Marxists who insist that capitalism is a necessary stage on the road to socialism, the *Notebooks* stress that it is not and that socialism involves a different set of oppressive relations and structural contradictions that can be glimpsed through an appreciation of dynamics in precapitalist, tribute-based states.

The emphasis on forces of production as the motor of social change and the insistence on socialism as a necessary precursor to communism—major tenets of the Second International—stand in contrast to the commentaries and concerns of the *Notebooks*. While the Second International stressed the forces of production as marshalling in a socialist society, where for an indeterminate time the state would act on behalf of the working class, Marx in the *Notebooks* stressed struggle between communities and the state over control of resources and labor. Where voices of the Second International called for the need to replace forms of community associated with earlier social stages, and the need to construct the "new man" through state agendas, Marx in his discussions of the "great Asian" states stressed the proclivity of state agents to defend state interests at the expense of local dynamism and viable kin communities, even if they had been distorted through the taxation/conscription impositions of state. Where the Second International stressed that socialism was a necessary stage prior to the withering away of the state that would usher in communism, Marx in the *Notebooks* discussed the ways in which local communities tried to retain practices despite state intervention, some of which could be characterized as communist. To develop a critical Marxism that included the *Notebooks* through the Soviet-approved publishing venues, such as International Publishers, would be to encourage criticism of the USSR on a non-Cold War basis. This was not feasible in the Cold War context or in the context of Soviet state agendas. The transcription, prepared through the monumental efforts of Lawrence Krader, was published by one of the Dutch houses that subscribe so steadfastly to the need for primary texts in research.

The Ethnological Notebooks provide a final chapter to Marx's work, one that shows the importance of local community relations in shaping long-term resistance to oppressive conditions. In efforts to ensure the continuity of a net of sharing and unalienated work (including caring), we create an emancipatory vision, episodically enacted under conditions people do not control in their daily lives. In sum, it is not surprising that a complete translation of the *Notebooks* has yet to appear. The difficulties of translation are obvious, but they are insufficient to explain the 120-year silence. But Marx's characterization of class formation in state-dominated control of property might well explain the reluctance on the part of adherents to the Second International—the development of the productive forces advocates who parallel their modernization counterparts of the right—to hear the *Notebooks'* messages. Taken together, Marx's call for the empirical study of historically transformed tribute-based states and his notion of dialectical return give us a way of framing problems of class formation in postcolonial states in general, and now the neoliberal colonization of the former Socialist bloc. The Cold War may have strangled almost all of the socialist experiments, but the kind of capitalist development, mafia and warlord activities, and fascist states it spawned in their wake require an appreciation of state-associated classes as a vehicle of accumulation.

Grass-roots movements throughout the world today that oppose the neoliberal policies of the post-Cold War are not for the most part linked to an explicit socialist agenda. What we can learn from the antimilitarist efforts of international feminist groups like those discussed in *Frontline Feminisms* (Waller and Rycenga, 2000) is a call for more or less egalitarian dynamics within groups pressing for sustainable and livable futures, the coordination of familial and community priorities with those oriented toward national and international claims, and the creative use of some traditions to inform practice and the subversion of other customary usage that has oppressive consequences.

Acknowledgments

I began thinking about this problem fifteen years ago and presented an early effort at the joint meetings of the Canadian Ethnological Society and the American Ethnological Society joint meetings in Toronto in 1985. I thank Richard Lee and Tom Patterson for suggesting I return to the issues involved for the session honoring Richard in Montreal, May 2001, and Jackie Solway for her encouragement in preparing the written version. Since I have only a reader's acquaintance of German, I want to thank Sabine Jell Bahlsen and Wolf Dieter Narr for making sure my translations were apt. Finally, I want to thank the reviewers for helping me hone the argument.

Notes

1. Unless otherwise noted, all quotations from Marx's *Notebooks* come from Lawrence Krader's 1974 translation: *The Ethnological Notebooks of Karl Marx. (Studies of Morgan, Phear, Maine, Lubbock)* Assen, Netherlands: Van Gorcum.
2. Ulysses Santamaria discusses Marx's notion of work as transformative activity, in contrast to labor, which was alienated (Santamaria, 1992). As such, it is much closer to the sense of work found in Richard Lee's discussions of foraging. Santamaria's careful treatment poses a powerful critique of the ways both socialist and capitalist proponents extol the virtues of labor productivity as social good. Feminists coming from Marxism as an intellectual home have eschewed the distinction of reproductive and productive labor as rendering what gets called "women's work" invisible (see, e.g., Hartman, [1981] 1992; Sargent, 1986).
3. Indeed, Marx reserves accusations of stupidity and backwardness for those against whom he is arguing.
4. Loosely, "Lubbock makes a fool of himself without even realizing it" (my translation).
5. I do not read Greek, for instance, and therefore have skipped those passages.
6. The comment is made in a passage criticizing Maine, Austin, and Bentham:
    "Maine ignores das viel Tiefere: dass d. scheinbare supreme selbstandige Existenz des *Staats* selbst nur *scheinbar* und dass er in allen Formen eine *excresence of society* is." ["Maine ignores the real difference: that the apparently paramount, autonomous existence of the *State* remains only an *appearance* and that it in all forms is an *excrescence of society*."] (Author's translation.)
7. The initial demands of Solidarity were printed in the United States only in *Monthly Review* and *The Village Voice*. The demands at the outset were not antisocialist, unless one considers demands consistent with communism to be antisocialist. The global context of US Cold War policies and the international lending apparatus that supported them played a decisive role in shaping the transformation of the movement.

References

Althusser, Louis. 1969. *For Marx*. Trans. Ben Brewster. New York: Vintage Books/Random House.
Austin, John. 1832. *The Province of Jurisprudence Determined*. London: J. Murray.
Bottomore, Tom B., trans. and ed. 1964. *Karl Marx: Early Writings*. New York: McGraw-Hill.

Community, State, and Questions of Social Evolution 51

Diamond, Stanley. 1974. *In Search of the Primitive: A Critique of Civilization.* New Brunswick, NJ: E.P. Dutton/Transaction Books.

———. 1975. "The Marxist Tradition as Dialectical Anthropology." *Dialectical Anthropology* 1(1): 1–6.

Engels, Friedrich. [1884] 1972. *The Origin of the Family, Private Property, and the State.* Ed. Eleanor B. Leacock. New York: International Publishers.

———. 1887. *The Condition of the Working Class in England in 1844.* Appendix written in 1886, and preface 1887, trans. Florence Kelly Wischnewetsky. New York: J.W. Lovell.

Hartman, Heidi. [1981] 1992. "The Unhappy Marriage of Marxism and Feminism: Towards a More Progressive Union." In *Feminist Philosophies,* ed. Janet Kourany, James Sterba, and Rosemarie Tong. Englewood Cliffs, NJ: Prentice-Hall, 343–55.

Krader, Lawrence. 1974. "Introduction." In *The Ethnological Notebooks by Karl Marx,* trans. and ed. Lawrence Krader. Assen, Netherlands: Van Gorcum.

———. 1975. *The Asiatic Mode of Production,* Assen, Netherlands: Van Gorcum.

Leacock, Eleanor B. 1954. "The Montagnais 'Hunting Territory' and the Fur Trade." *American Anthropologist Memoir* 78. Washington, D.C.

———. 1963. "Introduction." In *Ancient Society,* by Lewis Henry Morgan, ed. E.B. Leacock. New York: Meridian Books, i–xx.

———. 1972. "Introduction." *The Origin of the Family, Private Property, and the State,* by Frederick Engels. New York: International Publisher, 7–67.

Leacock, Eleanor B., and Richard B. Lee, ed. 1982. *Politics and History in Band Societies.* New York: Cambridge University Press.

Lee, Richard B. 1992. "Demystifying Primitive Communism." In *Civilization in Crisis: Anthropological Perspectives.* Vol. 1: Dialectical Anthropology: Essays in Honor of Stanley Diamond, ed. Christine W. Gailey. Gainesville: University Press of Florida, 73–94.

Lubbock, Sir John. 1870. *The Origin of Civilisation and the Primitive Condition of Man; Mental and Social Condition of Savages.* London: Longmans, Green, and Co.

Maine, Sir Henry Sumner. 1861. *Ancient Law: Its Connection with the Early History of Society, and Its Relation to Modern Ideas.* London: J. Murray.

Marx, Karl. [1857] 1972. *The Grundrisse,* trans. and ed. David McLellan. New York: Harper and Row.

———. [1880] 1964. "Enquête Ouvrière." *Revue Socialiste.* Reprinted in *Karl Marx: Selected Writings in Sociology and Social Philosophy,* ed. Tom B. Bottomore and M. Rubel. New York: McGraw-Hill, 203–12.

———. [1880–82] 1974. *The Ethnological Notebooks of Karl Marx (Studies of Morgan, Phear, Maine, Lubbock),* trans. and ed. Lawrence Krader. Assen, Netherlands: Van Gorcum.

Marx, Karl, and Friedrich Engels. [1871] 1971. *Writings on the Paris Commune,* ed. Hal Draper. New York: Monthly Review Press.

McLennan, John Ferguson. 1876. *Studies in Ancient History.* London: Bernard Quaritch.

Morgan, Lewis Henry. [1877] 1963. *Ancient Society, or, Researches in the Lines of Human Progress from Savagery through Barbarism to Civilization,* ed. Eleanor B. Leacock. New York: Meridian Books.

Okeyo, Achola Pala. 1980. "Daughters of the Lakes and Rivers: Colonization and the Land Rights of Luo Women." *Women and Colonization*, ed. Eleanor Leacock and Mona Etienne. New York: Praeger, 186–213.

Patterson, Thomas C. 1981. *Archaeology, the Evolution of Ancient Societies*. Englewood Cliffs, N.J.: Prentice-Hall.

Phear, John Budd. 1880. *The Aryan Village in India and Ceylon*. London: Macmillan.

Santamaria, Ulysses. 1992. "Marx and the Question of Anthropology." In *The Politics of Culture and Creativity*. Vol. 2, *Dialectical Anthropology: Essays in Honor of Stanley Diamond*, ed. Christine W. Gailey. Gainesville: University Press of Florida, 407–26.

Sargent, Lydia, ed. 1986. *The Unhappy Marriage of Marxism and Feminism: A Debate of Class and Patriarchy*. London: Pluto Press.

Shanin, Teodor, ed. 1983. *Late Marx and the Russian Road: Marx and "The Peripheries of Capitalism."* New York: Monthly Review Press, 98–126.

Waller, Marguerite, and Jennifer Rycenga, eds. 2000. *Frontline Feminisms: Women, War, and Resistance*. New York: Garland Press.

Chapter 3

SUBTLE MATTERS OF THEORY AND EMPHASIS
RICHARD LEE AND CONTROVERSIES ABOUT FORAGING PEOPLES

Thomas C. Patterson

When I think about the professional career of my friend Richard Lee, I first think about his contributions to the study of foraging societies and his commitment to the development of a critical, socially engaged, integrated anthropology. Then I think about the controversies and debates in which he has been involved over the years. This is not to say that Richard is a particularly combative person. He is feisty, perhaps, always ready and eager to engage in critically constructive dialogue and debate, but definitely not combative. He is a person who has held strong opinions at least since our days as graduate students together at Berkeley in the early 1960s. A careful look at those controversies and debates, especially at the theoretical underpinnings and matters of emphasis of their participants, is overdue. It will tell us a good deal about anthropology and its practitioners in the late twentieth century. Such an inquiry was, of course, launched in the late 1970s by feminist social critic and theorist, Donna Haraway ([1978a] 1991; [1978b] 1991; 1989), but the particular articles to which I refer and am indebted have rarely been cited by anthropologists. They certainly do not inform our understanding of controversy and debate in late twentieth-century anglophone anthropology, even though they should be required reading in courses that deal with the history of anthropological theory.

Studies of foraging societies conducted in the last half of the twentieth century were marked by an adherence to liberal social thought from Sherry Washburn's "man the hunter" (Washburn and Avis, 1958: 433–34; Washburn and Lancaster, 1968) and Sally Slocum's "woman the gatherer" ([1971] 1975), to Napoleon Chagnon's "fierce people" (1968) and Ed Wilmsen's "political economy of the Kalahari" (1989). The shared theoretical framework of these writers carries with it a number of assumptions, mostly implicit, that have not been adequately scrutinized. Early on, Richard Lee adopted a Marxist theoretical perspective that contrasted with the liberal viewpoints of his contemporaries. It is my contention that this theoretical divide, as well as the differences in emphasis and meaning between Lee and the writers building on liberal social thought, has underpinned the controversies concerned with foraging communities, their relations with surrounding societies, and their place in the modern world. Let us examine how liberal social thought underpins the writings of the authors mentioned above and how their perspectives contrasted with the positions inspired by Marxist and Marxist-feminist social theory that Lee honed and refined over the years.

From the mid-1950s onward, Sherry Washburn elaborated a complex picture of the development of human society. It was underpinned by the idea that the fundamental universal pattern underlying human life was the hunting adaptation. Washburn and Virginia Avis depicted its impact in the following way:

> Hunting not only necessitated new activities and new kinds of cooperation but changed the role of the adult male in the group.... The very same actions which caused man to be feared by other animals led to more cooperation, food sharing, and economic interdependence within the group. (1958: 433–34)

Washburn and Lancaster elaborated on this thesis in the late 1960s, writing that

> the general characteristics of man ... can be attributed to the hunting way of life.... It involves divisions of labor between male and female, sharing according to custom, cooperation among males, planning, knowledge of many species and large areas and technical skill.... Within the group of nonhuman primates, the mother and her young may form a subgroup that continues even after the young are fully grown. This grouping affects dominance, grooming, and resting patterns, and, along with dominance, is one of the factors giving order to the social relations in a group. The group is not a horde in the nineteenth-century sense, but it is ordered by positive affectionate habits and by the strength of personal dominance. Both these principles continue into human society, and dominance based on personal

achievement must have been particularly powerful in small groups living physically dangerous lives. The mother-young group must have been intensified by the prolongation of infancy. But in human society, economic reciprocity is added, and this created a whole new set of interpersonal bonds. When males hunt and females gather, the results are shared and given to the young, and the habitual sharing between a male, a female, and their offspring becomes the basis for the human family. (1968: 293–301)

In this view, "mother-young groups" and "dominance based on personal achievement" are rooted in nature. They persist into human society and become the basis for the sexual division of labor given the purported propensity of males to hunt and kill and of females to forage for plants and to care for their young.

But what is dominance, and where does it come from? Elsewhere Washburn argued that aggression was a fundamental adaptation of the entire primate order, including humans, and that social order was maintained by hormonal and neural activity and by learning:

Order within most primate groups is maintained by a hierarchy, which depends ultimately primarily on the power of males.... Aggressive individuals are essential actors in the social system and competition between groups is necessary for species dispersal and control of local populations. (Washburn and Hamburg, 1968: 282)

In other words, males engage in dominance behavior because of their propensity to hunt and kill. They form dominance hierarchies, enter into social contracts when they cooperate around hunting, and make tools to dispatch their prey. Female primates engage in less dominance behavior; they are more maternal and exhibit parental control over their young; they do not hunt, make hunting tools, or engage in the same kind of cooperative activity as males. They and their offspring are ultimately subordinate to males who order group structures and defend their members. Females are not incorporated into the group on the same basis as males, because they have different capacities. It also means that the inequalities reflected by the continually shifting pecking orders of males and by the subordination of females and their offspring are ultimately rooted in the nature of the primates themselves. In a phrase, social hierarchy and power relations are part of the natural order—something that humans acquired as part of their primate ancestry and subsequently elaborated. Slocum ([1971] 1975) remarked perceptively that this construction "gives one the decided impression that only half the species—the male half—did any evolving" (42).

As Haraway notes, Washburn's construction of primate society, nonhuman and human, refracts liberal social theory. His views were not those of Thomas Hobbes, who claimed that males and females were equal in the state of nature, and that women only became subject to men after they had children and only through the marriage contract (Pateman, 1991: 55). Washburn's views resonated with those of John Locke ([1690] 1960: 74–76), who constituted the family and the dependence of a woman and her children on her husband in the state of nature. In spite of his comments on the equality of man, Locke did not believe in the absolute equality of all men, either. In *The Second Treatise on Government*, Locke wrote that

> Though I have said ... *That all Men by Nature are equal*, I cannot be supposed to understand all sorts of *Equality; Age* or *Virtue* may give Men a just precedency; *Excellence of Parts* and *Merit* may place others above the Common Level; Birth may subject some and *Alliance or Benefits* others, to pay an observance to those whom Nature, Gratitude, or other Respects may have made due. ([1690] 1960: 54)

Thus, in Locke's view, women were naturally subordinate to men, and not all men were equal.

Slocum's conclusions contrasted with those of Washburn and Lancaster. Like Lee (1965, 1968a, 1968b), she emphasized the importance of sharing in the evolution of the human species.

> Food sharing and the family developed from the mother-infant bond. The techniques of hunting large animals were probably much later developments, after the mother-infant family pattern was established. When hunting did begin, the most likely recipients would be first their mothers, and second their siblings. In other words, a hunter would share food *not* with a wife or sexual partner, but with those who had shared food with him: his mother and siblings. ([1971] 1975: 45)

This implied social relations and a division of labor simply unimaginable to Locke, whose liberal social theory portrayed or refracted the social arrangements of an emergent agrarian capitalist regime (Wood, 1984).

Neither Washburn and Lancaster nor Slocum, nor Lee argued that sex was the basis of human sociality (Haraway, 1989: 215). This was the position adopted by Napoleon Chagnon and the sociobiologists who stressed reproduction, reproductive success, inclusive fitness, and sexual selection rather than the social relations of production, circulation, and use. Chagnon (1979a: 88) wrote that humans "behave reproductively in the context of defined social groups" and that males compete for mates. He asserted that Yanomami men claimed to fight over women (Chagnon, 1979a: 87). In his view, given the scarcity of marriageable women among the Yanomami, the

Subtle Matters of Theory and Emphasis

competition among males for mates can become a severely disruptive force in the internal ordering of large, heterogeneously composed villages. One expression that this takes is a tendency for men to represent themselves as aggressively as possible, indicating to potential competitors that affronts, insults, and cuckoldry will be immediately challenged and met with physical force. In addition, displays of masculinity, such as fighting prowess and *waiter* (ferocity) are admired by Yanomamo women, and particularly aggressive men have an advantage both in soliciting the sexual favors of women as well as depressing the temptation of other men to seduce their wives.

Aggressive men, those with power in Chagnon's view, have more children (Chagnon, Flinn and Melancon, 1979: 297). Social relations are cast in terms of a "political economy of sex" among the Yanomami in particular and human society in general that is rooted in the inequalities of men a la John Locke. Chagnon writes that

> If we consider polygamy to be a perquisite of leaders and a mark or measure of inequality, then in the world's so-called "egalitarian" societies not all men are in fact equal, at least in so far as their reproductive potential and ultimate biological success are concerned. Polygamy is widespread in the tribal world and has probably characterized human mating and reproduction for the greater fraction of our species' history.... Given that natural selection by definition entails the differential reproduction of and survival of individuals, this fact of life—this inequality—is of considerable importance. (1979b: 375)

At this point, Chagnon breaks with Locke, who was concerned with the social relations of production and property rather than with adducing evidence to support arguments about the subordination of women and control of their reproductive capacities. Locke, like Chagnon, already knew the answers to those questions. He assumed that power could not be shared equally by the husband and wife, that the presumed inferiority of women was rooted in nature, and that women were not incorporated into civil society on the same basis as men because they lacked the capacities of strength, mind, and civility to become civil individuals (Butler, 1991: 82, 85; Pateman, 1989: 52–54, 93–94).

Chagnon proceeds to develop his argument, focusing not on reproduction, reproductive fitness, and sexual selection but rather on attacking liberal and materialist conceptions of history that explained class structures and conflict in terms of control over resources. He thus continues:

> This raises the question of the utility of viewing human status differentials largely, if not exclusively, in terms of *material* resources and the relationships that individuals in different societies have to such resources. That the

relationship between people and control over strategic resources is central to understanding status differences in our own highly industrialized, materialist culture is insufficient to project these relationships back in evolutionary time and to suggest that all human status systems derive from struggles over the means and ends of production. Struggles in the Stone Age were more likely over the means and ends of reproduction. (1979b: 375)

On the one hand, to his credit, Chagnon, unlike many liberal anthropologists, recognized that the social relations definitive of modern industrial capitalism—the capitalist mode of production—were not characteristic of all societies, at all times, and at all places. On the other hand, he believed that gender relations and gender hierarchies are universal features of all societies regardless of whether they manifest kin-communal, tributary, capitalist, or socialist social relations.

Here, Chagnon, the cold warrior, was responding to critics of the Vietnam War, some of whom were influenced by Marxist social theory, and to counterculture activists who advocated viewpoints ranging from anarchism to the libertarianism of Ayn Rand. Patrick Tierney pointed this out in his book *Darkness in El Dorado* (quoted in Grandin, 2000: 12–14). He described Chagnon's portrayal of the Yanomami in the following manner:

As a Cold War metaphor, the Yanomami's "ceaseless warfare" over women proved that, even in a society without property hierarchies prevailed. Thus, Communism was unnatural because even the most classless societies had pecking orders in reproductive matters. The underlying ferocity and deceit that fueled the Yanomami's successful military strategy also offered a kind of parable: the ruthless Communists were going to win if long-haired hippies did not rejoin the march of Darwin. (2000: 42)

From the late 1960s onward, anthropologists girded in liberal social theory discussed egalitarian foraging societies in terms of the inequalities they presumed existed among their members. For some, women were naturally subordinated to men. For others, not only were women subordinated to men, but even the men themselves were arranged in pecking orders that refracted their varying abilities to attract and mate with women. During this same period, however, Richard Lee and others—notably Eleanor Leacock (1954, 1972) and Janet Siskind (1978)—continually emphasized the importance of sharing in foraging societies. In *Man the Hunter,* Lee described the group structure of the Dobe area !Kung in the early 1960s in the following way:

The "camp" is an open aggregate of cooperating persons which changes in size and composition from day to day.... The camp is a self-sufficient subsistence unit. The members move out each day to hunt and gather, and return

Subtle Matters of Theory and Emphasis

in the evening to pool the collected foods in such a way that every person present receives an equitable share. (1968a: 31)

He then proceeded to describe the gendered division of labor that existed at Dobe:

> A woman gathers on one day enough food to feed her family for three days, and spends the rest of her time resting in camp, doing embroidery, visiting other camps, or entertaining visitors from other camps.... The hunters tend to work more frequently than women, but their schedule is uneven. It is not unusual for a man to hunt avidly for a week and then do no hunting at all for two or three weeks. (37)

Finally, Lee pointed out that much of the subsistence work in the Dobe !Kung camp at this time was done by married, young, and middle-aged adults, and that the number of nonproductive young and old people was large.

> The aged hold a respected position in Bushman society and are the effective leaders of the camps.... Long after their productive years have passed, the old people are fed and cared for by their children and grandchildren. The blind, the senile, and the crippled are respected for the special ritual and technical skills they possess....
>
> Another significant feature of the composition of the work force is the late assumption of adult responsibility by adolescents. Young people are not expected to provide food regularly until they are married.... It is not unusual to find healthy, active teenagers visiting from camp to camp while their older relatives provide food for them. (36)

During the 1970s, Lee and others became increasingly more explicit about the Marxist theoretical frameworks that underpinned their research. In their introduction to the *Politics and History in Band Societies*, Leacock and Lee were quite explicit:

> As editors, our own view is that anything less than a dialectical and historical-materialist view of society ends in distortion; a view we have each elaborated elsewhere.... As we see, the strength of the Marxist approach comes to the fore at the level of synthesis. Marxist methodology resolves the conflict between generalizing and particularizing emphases, for it both enables fine-grained analyses of underlying determinant relations in specific instances and articulates these analyses with a comprehensive general theory of human history....
>
> While committed to the importance of historical and cultural specificity, a dialectical and historical-materialist approach requires the search for underlying regularities or "laws." While committed to the significance of social cohesion, the approach calls for definition of the basic disharmonies,

conflicts, or "contradictions" within socio-economic structures that impel change....

A dialectical and historical-materialist approach situates a society's center of gravity in the relations and forces of production—the ways in which people necessarily relate to each other in the course of producing and reproducing life. It necessitates both placing a society fully in the historically specific context of its relationships with its social and geographical environment, and dealing with the complex interrelations and interactions within and between the relations and forces of production on the one hand and the social and ideological superstructures on the other. (1982 : 6–7)

This dialectical and historical-materialist approach contrasted with the ones described above that were ultimately rooted in liberal social theory in general and Lockean thought in particular.

After describing the evidence for the relations between men and women in !Kung society, Lee (1982: 39–50) pointed out that these were relatively egalitarian. Age, life experience, personal qualities, and kinship were as important as gender in discussions and decision making by the group. There were headmen, but they had no real authority. One man was quite surprised to learn that other individuals in a camp where he had lived considered him to be the headman. These and other facets of everyday life among the !Kung led Lee to conclude that

> The fact that communal sharing of food resources and of power is a phenomenon that has been observed directly in recent years among the !Kung and dozens of other foraging groups is a finding that should not be glossed over lightly. Its universality among foragers lends strong support to the theory of Marx and Engels that a stage of primitive communism prevailed before the state and the break-up of society into classes....
>
> Having declared that the foraging mode of production is a form of primitive communism, it would be a mistake to idealize the foraging peoples as noble savages who have solved all the basic problems of living. Like individuals in any society, foragers have to struggle with their own internal contradictions.... The demands of the collective existence are not achieved effortlessly, but rather they require a continuing struggle to deal with one's own selfish, arrogant and antisocial impulses. The fact that the !Kung and other foragers succeed ... offers us an important insight. (1982: 55–56)

However, by the late 1970s, Lee (1979: 401–31) was indicating that the tempo of processes barely perceptible a decade or two earlier was increasing. He examined the impact of a number of the processes transforming everyday life for the !Kung: working on cattle posts, planting crops, tending herds, wage work, migrant labor, and penny capitalism. Their effects were compounded in the 1970s by the introduction of schools, increased missionary activity, changes in land tenure, armed liberation struggles in both Namibia and South Africa,

Subtle Matters of Theory and Emphasis 61

and the eventual militarization of the !Kung homelands. As the armed struggle intensified, the !Kung were enmeshed in new structures of power and social relations that were not entirely of their own making.

During the 1980s, Edwin Wilmsen and James Denbow developed a critique of Lee's work (Wilmsen, 1989; Wilmsen and Denbow, 1990). The essence of their critique is that Lee and other Marxists who make use of the concept of primitive communism or the kin-communal mode of production "do not treat forager societies as segments of large social formations" (Wilmsen, 1989: 52). He suggests that the way out of the impasse this creates is to utilize the concept of "the articulation ... of formerly colonized peoples in modern nation-states and more broadly in a world system." He proceeds to describe the world system as "a multiple cultural system that incorporates 'mini-systems' such as tribes" (52). He subscribes to Wallerstein's view that "Most entities usually described as social systems—'tribes,' communities, nation-states—are not in fact total systems" (1974: 347–48).

Wilmsen (1989: 52–53) correctly points to the close relationship of Wallerstein's notion of world system with dependency theory and the development of underdevelopment. What these perspectives have in common is that they postulate the existence of a single world economy, an international system of production and distribution, held together by unequal exchange. The developed industrial countries have siphoned capital, raw materials, and labor from the underdeveloped countries that far exceeded the value of the finished goods the latter were forced to import. In the process, the social formations of the periphery were distorted and transformed. The current world system "is capitalist through and through" and "one that intensified or invented 'precapitalist' modes of production to articulate with" (Wilmsen, 1989: 53).

World systems theory and dependency theory are internal critiques of the classical and neoclassical economic models of development and modernization that were popular in the mid-twentieth century. Like some of the structural Marxist arguments cited with approval by Wilmsen, they are rooted in liberal rather than Marxist social thought. These liberal theories give precedence to exchange and the market rather than to production and the ways in which surplus goods and labor are pumped out of society. They assume that all production is for exchange rather than use and that capitalist social relations are natural. These theories locate the single motor for development—exchange—in the industrial capitalist countries rather than in the underdeveloped periphery; they assert that peoples on the periphery lack agency and the capacity to shape their own history in circumstances not entirely of their own choosing. These theories largely ignore both the violence of articulation and the myriad forms of resistance devised by communities threatened with encapsulation by industrial capitalist states. In a phrase, the analyses that liberal social theorists produce are functionalist rather than dialectical.

Thus, the crux of Wilmsen's and Denbow's critique is that they do not like dialectical analyses that challenge the primacy of exchange relations, the dominance of the West, and the inevitability of capitalist expansion across the face of the globe. They imply that people have always been the way they are today, and, further, since human nature is fixed, they cannot change. This brings us back full circle, through the writings of classical economists such as James Steuart and Adam Smith, to the views of Hobbes and Locke, the founders of modern liberal thought.

Acknowledgments

This essay was prepared for a symposium "The Art and Politics of Anthropology," organized by Christine Gailey and me for the joint meeting of the American Ethnological Society and the Canadian Anthropological Society in Montreal, May 3–6, 2001. I want to thank Christine Gailey and Wendy Ashmore for their constructive comments.

References

Butler, Melissa. 1991. "Early Liberal Roots of Feminism: John Locke and the Attack on Patriarchy." In *Feminist Interpretations and Political Theory*, ed. Mary Lyndon Shanley and Carole Pateman. University Park, Penn.: Pennsylvania State University Press, 74–94.

Chagnon, Napoleon A. 1968. *Yanomamö: The Fierce People*. New York: Holt, Rinehart and Winston.

———. 1979a. "Mate Competition, Favoring Close Kin, and Village Fissioning among the Yanomamö Indians." In *Evolutionary Biology and Human Social Behavior: An Anthropological Perspective*, ed. Napoleon A. Chagnon and William Irons. North Scituate, Mass.: Duxbury Press, 86–131.

———. 1979b. "Is Reproductive Success Equal in Egalitarian Societies." In *Evolutionary Biology and Human Social Behavior: An Anthropological Perspective*, ed. Napoleon A. Chagnon and William Irons. North Scituate, Mass.: Duxbury Press, 374–401.

Chagnon, Napoleon A., Mark V. Flinn, and Thomas F. Melancon. 1979. "Sex-Ratio Variation among the Yanomamö Indians." In *Evolutionary Biology*

Subtle Matters of Theory and Emphasis 63

and Human Social Behavior: An Anthropological Perspective, ed. Napoleon A. Chagnon and William Irons. North Scituate, Mass.: Duxbury Press, 290–320.

Grandin, Greg. 2000. "Coming of Age in Venezuela." *The Nation* 271 (19), 12–17.

Haraway, Donna. [1978a] 1991. "Animal Sociology and a Natural Economy of the Body Politic: A Political Physiology of Dominance." *Simians, Cyborgs, and Women: The Reinvention of Nature.* New York: Routledge, 7–20.

———. [1978b] 1991. "The Past Is the Contested Zone: Human Nature and Theories of Production and Reproduction in Primate Behaviour Studies." In *Simians, Cyborgs, and Women: The Reinvention of Nature.* New York: Routledge, 21–42.

———. 1989. "Remodeling the Human Way of Life: Sherwood Washburn and the New Physical Anthropology, 1950–1980." In *Primate Visions: Gender, Race, and Nature in the World of Modern Sciences.* New York: Routledge, 186–230.

Leacock, Eleanor B. 1954. *The Montagnais "Hunting Territory" and the Fur Trade.* American Anthropological Association Memoir, no. 78. Menasha, Wisc.

———. 1972. "Introduction." *The Origin of the Family, Private Property, and the State,* by Friedrich Engels. New York: International Publishers, 7–67.

Leacock, Eleanor B., and Richard B. Lee. 1982. "Introduction." In *Politics and History in Band Societies,* ed. Eleanor Leacock and Richard Lee. Cambridge: Cambridge University Press: 1–20.

Lee, Richard B. 1965. "Subsistence Ecology of !Kung Bushmen." PhD Dissertation, University of California, Berkeley. Ann Arbor, Mich.: University Microfilms International.

———. 1968a. "What Hunters Do for a Living, or, How to Make Out on Scarce Resources. *Man the Hunter,* ed. Richard B. Lee and Irven DeVore. Chicago, Ill.: Aldine, 30–48.

———. 1968b. "Analysis of Group Composition." *Man the Hunter,* ed. Richard B. Lee and Irven DeVore. Chicago, Ill.: Aldine, 152.

———. 1979. *The !Kung San: Men, Women, and Work in a Foraging Society.* Cambridge: Cambridge University Press.

———. 1982. "Politics, Sexual and Non-sexual, in an Egalitarian Society." *Politics and History in Band Societies,* ed. Eleanor B. Leacock and Richard B. Lee. Cambridge: Cambridge University Press, 37–60.

Locke, John. 1690 [1960]. *Two Treatises of Government,* ed. Peter Laslett. Cambridge: Cambridge University Press.

Pateman, Carole. 1989. *The Sexual Contract.* Stanford, Calif.: Stanford University Press.

———. 1991. "God Hath Ordained to Man a Helper": Hobbes, Patriarchy and Conjugal Right." In *Feminist Interpretations and Political Theory,* ed. Mary Lyndon Shanley and Carole Pateman. University Park, Penn.: Pennsylvania State University Press, 52–73.

Siskind, Janet. 1978. "Kinship and Mode of Production." *American Anthropologist* 89(4): 860–72.

Slocum, Sally. [1971] 1975. "Woman the Gatherer: Male Bias in Anthropology." In *Toward an Anthropology of Women*, ed. Rayna Rapp Reiter. New York: Monthly Review Press, 36–50.

Tierney, Patrick. 2000. *Darkness in El Dorado: How Scientists and Journalists Devastated the Amazon*. New York: W.W. Norton.

Wallerstein, Immanuel. 1974. *The Modern World-System*, Vol. 1, *Capitalist Agriculture and the Origins of the European World-Economy of the Sixteenth Century*. New York: Academic Press.

Washburn, Sherwood L., and Virginia Avis. 1958. "Evolution of Human Behavior." In *Behavior and Evolution*, ed. Anne Roe and George Gaylord Simpson. New Haven: Yale University Press, 421–36.

Washburn, Sherwood L., and David Hamburg. [1968] 1972. "Aggressive Behavior in Old World Monkeys and Apes." In *Primate Patterns*, ed. Phyllis Dolhinow. New York: Holt, Rinehart and Winston, 276–96.

Washburn, Sherwood L., and C.S. Lancaster. 1968. "The Evolution of Hunting." In *Man the Hunter*, ed. Richard B. Lee and Irven DeVore. Chicago, Ill.: Aldine, 293–303.

Wilmsen, Edwin N. 1989. *Land Filled with Flies: A Political Economy of the Kalahari*. Chicago, Ill.: University of Chicago Press.

Wilmsen, Edwin N., and James R. Denbow. 1990. "Paradigmatic History of San-speaking Peoples and Current Attempts at Revision." *Current Anthropology* 31(5): Chicago: 489–524.

Wood, Neal. 1984. *John Locke and Agrarian Capitalism*. Berkeley: University of California Press.

Chapter 4

"THE ORIGINAL AFFLUENT SOCIETY": FOUR DECADES ON

Jacqueline Solway

Introduction

At the 1966 "Man the Hunter" conference, Marshall Sahlins first advanced his provocative conception of hunter–gatherers[1] as "The Original Affluent Society." Eventually published in 1968 in extended form in *Les Temps Modernes* and as the lead essay in his important book, *Stone Age Economics* ([1972] 2004), Sahlins drew on recent hunter-gatherer ethnography, especially Lee's work on the !Kung San, to argue that hunters and gatherers experience reasonable material security and consequently are not perpetually on the edge of starvation. Taking the point further, and offering a clever twist on Galbraith's recently published book, *The Affluent Society*, he proposed that foragers might well be the original affluent society because of the relative ease with which they satisfy their wants.

The argument of original affluence was far more than empirical. Sahlins theorized the absence of scarcity and in doing so challenged a basic assumption of formalist anthropological economics—and of neoclassical economics upon which it is predicated. If the economy, as neoclassical economics assumes, is a relation between ends and means, Sahlins asks, must the ends always be unlimited and the means lim-

Notes for this section can be found on page 75.

ited? Are humans inexorably doomed to material deprivation, or is an alternative possible in which scarcity is not ubiquitous? Neoclassical economics takes unlimited ends for granted. But Sahlins proposes the Zen possibility that hunters and gatherers could have both limited means and limited ends. Therefore wants can be satisfied; and data emerging at the time from foraging societies indicated that they could be satisfied with modest work effort. While Sahlins challenges the very basis of neoclassical economics in subsequent chapters of *Stone Age Economics*, in "The Original Affluent Society" he accepts its depiction of the economy as a means-end relationship but contests the universal applicability of the assumption that ends are infinite. Sahlins states that "economic man" is a "bourgeois construction," and not a "natural construction"; the possibility exists that people have no need to "suppress desires that were never broached" (13). In following chapters he revives the formalist-substantivist debate in anthropological economics, arguing in support of the substantivist position that the economy constitutes a category of culture. The economy represents the "material life process of society" (Sahlins, 1972: xii) and not a means-end calculation predicated upon omnipresent scarcity (as the formalist position maintains).

"The Original Affluent Society" In and Outside the Academy

The significance of Sahlins's piece lies not only in its inventiveness and analytic power, but also in its ability to stimulate critical reflection and scholarship, spawn controversy, and attract attention in academia and beyond. Ranking in status with concepts such G. Hardin's "Tragedy of the Commons," B. Anderson's "Imagined Communities," and E.P. Thompson's "Moral Economy,"[2] Sahlins's "The Original Affluent Society" has become part of academic thought and popular imagination. It has proven a remarkably malleable term, enabling its users to read it selectively and to impart meanings to it not necessarily intended by its author.[3] Academic debates have tended to remain truer to Sahlins's argument, especially its empirical component, than have the nonacademic. Some of the academic debates, especially within the cultural anthropology of hunter-gatherer or forager studies, will be reviewed below.

"The Original Affluent Society," although born of academic discourse, has had an interesting life outside the ivory tower. Common popular readings (and some academic) offer a romantic view of hunter gatherers that take Sahlins's term literally to indicate that foragers lived, and live, in a carefree state untroubled by any material want, a point that Sahlins was careful not to make. Rather, he proposed that foragers are free of the constant menace of market scarcity in spite of the fact that forager economies operate under serious constraints (1972: 2). Nonetheless, some nonacademic groups have elevated "The Original Affluent Society" to something approaching cult status, the anthropological equivalent of an "urban legend." Organizations promoting ecological sustainability and advocating a return to nature, antimaterialism, and communalism find in the "The Original Affluent Society" a rationale and a vision for their utopic dreams and positions.[4]

Amongst the strongest endorsements of Sahlins's theoretical argument within the academy but outside of anthropology is that of John Gowdy, an environmental economist whose book *Limited Wants, Unlimited Means* (1998) accepts Sahlins's proposal on ideological principle and brings together a number of articles to provide elaboration. For Gowdy, foragers offer a "blueprint for survival" (1999: 397); they not only demonstrate the absence of economic scarcity but also illustrate that people can live in egalitarian (gender and socioeconomic) societies with high levels of social and ecological harmony. In general, however, academic debate has centered more around the purported empirical basis of "The Original Affluent Society" than its theoretical foundation, which is harder to prove or disprove. As Sahlins himself stated, "The decisive differences between formalism and substantivism, as far as their acceptance is at issue, if not so far as their truth, are ideological" (1972: xiii).

As noted above, Sahlins's theoretical proposition that societies can have limited ends does not readily lend itself to testing; this and the fact that "The Original Affluent Society" is written in such a complex, clever, and persuasive manner led Nurit Bird-David to observe that the work has been resistant to conventional critical scrutiny. It rapidly became part of anthropological oral tradition, which put it further outside the zone of questioning. Its appeal also lay in the fact that it accorded with the zeitgeist of the era—the 1960s—a time of social unrest, dissent, and utopic yearnings. Foragers resonated with prevalent countercultural sentiments that sought an alternative and gentler way of being in the world than the "military-industrial" complex that was then the target of so much protest. It became, in Bird-David's words, virtually a "sacred text," especially in cultural anthropology, and thus largely unquestioned by cultural anthropologists for two decades (1992: 26).

Ecological anthropologists, especially more biologically oriented evolutionary ecologists, were amongst the first to critically scrutinize "The Original Affluent Society." Researchers employed optimal foraging theory to test aspects of the empirical basis of Sahlins's hypothesis.

In particular, by adopting a more inclusive definition of work than did Sahlins and Lee, upon whose data Sahlins's argument relies heavily, they challenged the notion of underutilized labor amongst foragers. They broadened the category of work to include not just food procurement but also food processing (Hawkes and O'Connell, 1981). New data from foraging societies analyzed in light of the expanded definition of work suggested that foragers enjoyed less leisure and were thus less "affluent" than Sahlins proposed. Optimal foraging strategy analysts raised important questions, provided valuable data, and offered a means by which data from different societies (or "populations" in their terms) could be compared.

But there are definite limits on the extent to which optimal foraging theory advances or offers a critique of the argument and substance of "The Original Affluent Society," as it is based on fundamentally different premises. Sahlins's analysis is not only explicitly culturalist but it also problematizes the economists' basic assumption of maximization. Optimal foraging theory, however, assumes economic maximization as a given, not in the market choices that actors make, but in the labor saving "strategies" that individual members of species or "populations" take to gain the most valuable food (generally of highest caloric content) for the least effort (Hawkes and O'Connell, 1981). Therefore the argument for decreased affluence based on greater labor expenditure only addresses part of Sahlins's hypothesis. The more important theoretical question arguably relates to the nature of ends and their cultural construction. In addition, as Eric Alden Smith emphasizes, the theory is predicated upon methodological individualism in which "social and ecological processes at the level of groups and populations can be analyzed most fruitfully as the result of actions and motives of the component individuals..." (1991: 225). In this view, the role of culture is likened to that of genes; both are categorized as "inherited instructions" (Smith, 1991: 225) that influence but are not profoundly formative of behavior (as a culturalist analysis would assert). Therefore, in its fundamental assumption of scarcity and maximization, its demotion/reduction of culture from social fact to inherited instructions and its utilitarianism, optimal foraging theory veers far from Sahlins's analysis and intention. Optimal foraging theorists attempted to "prove" original affluence through positivist methods; Sahlins was skeptical of the possibilities of proving or disproving "The Original Affluent Society"; the best he hoped for was that his analysis might "explain matters better than the competing theoretical model" (1972: xiii). However, his combination of culturalist and ecological quantitative analyses opened a door and allowed evolutionary ecologists to go where others had yet feared to tread.

Original Affluence under the Lens of Cultural Anthropology

Alan Barnard and James Woodburn were amongst the first cultural anthropologists to critically examine Sahlins's thesis. In their introduction to the second volume emerging from the 1986 "Hunter-Gatherer Conference," they maintain that the argument for original affluence has "stood up well to twenty years of additional research" (1991:11) if two provisos are taken into account. First, original affluence more appropriately characterizes foragers with "immediate-return" systems than those with "delayed-return"; and second, the definition of material wants must be given sharper delineation. The distinction between delayed and immediate-return, developed by Woodburn in a series of essays (in particular 1982, 1991), presents an important refinement to "The Original Affluent Society." Briefly put, in economies of immediate-return systems "people usually obtain an immediate yield for their labor, use this yield with minimal delay and place minimal emphasis on property relations" in contrast to delayed-return systems, "in which people place more emphasis on property rights, rights which are usually but not always linked with delayed return on labor" (1991: 11). Foragers with delayed return systems are infrastructurally similar to 'Neolithic' societies and can easily assimilate agricultural and pastoral subsistence strategies, which are based upon delayed-return. Property relations are more stringent in delayed-return societies than in immediate-return. In delayed-return societies property relations bind people in committed, future-oriented relations that connect people to specific others via the mediation of things. Although not absent amongst immediate-return foragers, property relations are relatively unelaborated and connect people to numerous others with less specific material obligations. Not all foragers have immediate-return systems. The Australian Aborigines, owing to their elaborate ritual life and social organization, which is built upon a complex system of binding and dependent relationships with attendant obligatory material exchange, have a delayed-return system.

According to Barnard and Woodburn (1991:12), foraging societies with immediate-return systems such as the San and Hazda of East Africa and others in sub-Saharan Africa are "almost always able to meet their nutritional needs very adequately without working long hours." Low production targets and widespread sharing ensure the health and welfare of all, even the weak and vulnerable. Gowdy takes the point a step further in asserting that affluence lies "in the absence of a link between individual production and economic security" (1998: xxii). As a generalization, this may be an overstatement, but it does capture the intense pressure to share that is so widely reported for many foraging societies (Lee, 1991; c.f. Wilmsen, 1989). Woodburn and Barnard are careful to distinguish the intense sharing practiced by immediate-return foragers from gift giving. The latter entails greater calculation of reciprocal obligation.

Immediate-return societies exhibit many of the qualities that Sahlins identifies as typifying original affluence. They tend to be nomadic with flexible group composition, they have few material possessions and tools, and what they have can be readily acquired or manufactured with resources that are widely available. In addition to the intense sharing discussed above, societies with immediate-return are noted (and are "notorious") for their marked prodigality, what Sahlins refers to as a "peculiarity" that renders hunter-gatherers "uneconomic man" (1972: 12–13). Immediate-return hunter-gatherers tend to be disparaged by their nonforaging neighbors for consuming what they have at the moment with "no thought for the morrow."[5] To these qualities Woodburn would add a certain lack of fixity in social relations in the sense that, while people have wide ranging kinship relations, they are not bound or dependent upon "specific other people for their access to basic requirements" (1991: 34). They can easily satisfy their needs and, more importantly, do so without indebting themselves in any fundamental way to specific others.

Both Sahlins and Woodburn observe that foragers today do not live in a world of foragers, and those remaining are often relegated to the most marginal environments. Sahlins (1972: 38) suggests further that most contemporary foragers, save for a few examples such as the Australian Aborigines, appear to lack a layer of superstructure, of ritual and exchange cycles, that may have been eroded in the early phases of colonialism. Woodburn notes the fact that immediate-return contemporary foraging societies are encapsulated and stigmatized by their neighbors. This leads him to speculate on the nature and origins of immediate-return: is it a response or possibly a defensive strategy in light of encapsulation or a sui generis phenomenon? However, Woodburn is hesitant to draw any conclusion given the incomplete nature of the historical evidence.

In their second proviso, Barnard and Woodburn query the definition of material wants. It is too simple to suggest that foragers merely have limited material wants. As the authors have observed and have experienced in the field, foragers often desire more than what they have, for example, of special foods such as honey or of gifts from anthropologists. But the point is that they do not work longer hours to obtain them (unless one considers beseeching anthropologists work—perhaps an argument could be made). More to the point, forager production targets are set low; desire may exist, but fulfilling it is not tied

"The Original Affluent Society": Four Decades On 71

to production. Individuals are under little or no pressure to exert additional effort to produce goods beyond what they deem necessary for the satisfaction of their culturally-defined basic needs (Barnard and Woodburn, 1991: 12). Satisfying desire is sought through an almost coercive requirement to share—what the authors refer to as "demand sharing" (12) rather than through increased subsistence labor.

Bird-David (1992: 25–47) tackled "The Original Affluent Society" head on. As noted earlier, she attributes an almost "sacred text" quality to the manner in which it has been treated in cultural anthropology. Apart from the awe inspired by its clever prose, she maintains that it deflected conventional academic scrutiny largely as a result of three features. First, it advanced quantitative data to support its case, thereby shrouding its argument in the authority of hard science. However, in contradiction to its purportedly scientific approach, and this is her second point, it tried to make its case by relying upon markedly "unscientific" concepts such as "Zen" that even stretched the bounds of humanist discourse. Critics and commentators were put off. How could one count and compare a "Zen" way to affluence? Third, she argues that Sahlins finessed his potential critics by acknowledging the problems of generalizing broadly through time and space from scant data, but nonetheless proceeded to do so despite his own cautionary stance. Combined, these gave the work a certain authority and resilience that Bird-David claims was ill-gotten.

Perhaps her most serious accusation is that Sahlins violates his own anthropological precepts by substituting "practical reason" for cultural analysis. In doing so, Bird-David argues, he sloppily blurs cultural and ecological-rationalist argumentation by lapsing into the latter when he lacked the material or discipline to sustain the former. Thus by attributing foragers' leisure to their trust in the bounty of the environment—an ecological, not a cultural, proposition in her view — he fails to heed his own advice laid out in *Culture and Practical Reason* (1976).[6]

Despite Bird-David's criticisms, she is quick to concede that Sahlins "had a point" (25), especially with reference to immediate-return foragers, a distinction she retains from Woodburn. She endeavors to rehabilitate the argument for original affluence by proposing a culturalist basis for it. Instead of crediting affluence to confidence in environmental abundance, she offers a cultural metaphor through which she argues hunter-gatherers perceive not just each other but their environment as a whole, including its "social," "natural," and "spiritual" components. These are part of an animate and seamless "cosmic economy of sharing" in which all participants are morally bound to share (28). Therefore, hunter-gatherers achieve abundance not through simple trust or confidence in the environmental bounty that is "out there" and ontologically distinct from themselves, but rather the environment is assimilated into a larger world of "giving and taking" in which foragers themselves are amongst its many members. Foragers' confidence resides in that "world" and the fact that their needs will be met through its networks of sharing, in which they are enmeshed.

Bird-David, like Sahlins, "has a point," and there are ways in which her notion of a "cosmic economy of sharing" constitutes an advance by offering a more thorough cultural basis to affluence. But when she extends the point further and offers a new metaphor, her case weakens. She attempts to find another metaphor or "cognitive model" to "evoke the way in which these hunter-gatherers relate to their environment" (32). She proposes the concept of a bank not only to capture the bounty "out there" but the capacity for this wealth to increase. The bank metaphor, or cognitive model, to follow Bird-David's usage, also highlights or captures the complex coexistence of seemingly contradictory or paradoxical regimes of ownership, use, and benefit of both banks and most immediate return hunter-gatherer systems. In both entities there exists a complex mix of collective and private principles of ownership, access, and use with regard to the unit's assets or resources. However, the bank metaphor introduces distortions as well. Banks imply deposits, investments, and a highly individuated economy (Endicott, 1992: 38). Moreover, adopting the bank metaphor entails the imposition of not only a Western model (Grinker, 1992: 39) but one that has little or no cultural resonance for the societies for whom it is meant to provide an aid in cultural translation (Gudeman, 1992: 39).

Edwin Wilmsen (1989) offers amongst the most stinging critiques of original affluence. Taking the Zhu (San) as his primary example (one of the two key case studies upon which Sahlins based his article), he argues that the notion of primitive affluence, like so many other tropes for foraging societies, is not only a misguided, overly romantic projection upon so-called simpler societies, but through rhetorical sleight of hand, it stands to harm those it describes by obfuscating the real nature of their contemporary poverty and disempowerment. Further, by representing foragers as innocent, happy-go-lucky individuals oblivious to their exploitation, it does additional damage by portraying them as lacking the wherewithal (sophistication, political savvy) to recognize, negotiate, and take their place in the contemporary world. He challenges original affluence on many fronts. For instance, he claims that the Zhu do not simply reap "natural abundance" without thought, planning, and social organization. But this is a somewhat spurious argument that entails a convenient misreading of original affluence, a concept that was never meant to imply that foragers produce in the absence of social and cultural rules and organization.

Wilmsen questions one of the key material components of affluence by attributing the Zhu's small stature to nutritional deprivation (1989: 304). His conclusions are in contrast to those of Lee, who prefers to see the San's small size as a positive or, at minimum, a neutral adaptation to a hunting and gathering way of life in a hot climate (1979: 289). Lee asks, is bigger necessarily better (290)? Both Wilmsen and Lee agree that the San experience seasonal weight loss, but so do many rural peoples; and the San's is moderate compared to many others. In addition, both acknowledge that San grow taller when they switch to an agro-pastoral diet, but their respective interpretations of the evidence are at variance. A clear resolution is difficult to establish and implies a value judgment. However, despite one's favored interpretation, relative stature does not undermine the argument for original affluence in the sense of the San being able to meet their self-defined nutritional needs and in the more important sense of addressing the theoretical possibility of limited ends.

With his 2000 article "The Darker Side of 'The Original Affluent Society,'" David Kaplan became one of the most recent scholars to cast a critical gaze towards Sahlins's piece. To his great surprise, he finds that despite some serious reservations, the anthropological world has largely endorsed Sahlins's point. Further, he notes that the "lesson" of original affluence has enjoyed such unquestioned success that it is virtually de rigueur for introductory texts to portray hunter-gatherers as leading idyllic lives.

Kaplan calls into question the data upon which Sahlins based his argument. Citing specialists in the field, he asserts that the Australian Fish Creek study, one of Sahlins's two central examples, was based upon a contrived study. The study consisted of a small group of missionary station residents, adults only, who were persuaded by the anthropologist to participate in an experiment of living on bush resources. In addition, the study was of extremely short duration—too short to prove any case for abundance. It is interesting to note in this regard that Jon Altman (1992), a specialist in the Australian case who has specifically addressed Sahlins's use of the Fish Creek data, arrives at a different conclusion. Despite the study's limitations, he accepts Sahlins's notion of abundance but qualifies it to argue that, while Australian foragers may not have experienced the leisure in the precontact period that Sahlins suggests, it is likely that they worked no harder or longer than people in modern industrial societies (36). Kaplan grants more authority to Lee's ethnographic study of the San but nonetheless combs through wider San ethnography to find evidence to contradict Lee's conclusions of ready and adequate subsistence.

Kaplan's questioning of both the methodological basis, especially the definition of and distinction between "wants" and "needs," and his skepticism regarding the legitimacy of the argument's empirical evidence raise valid concerns. However, the vehemence with which Kaplan pursues his objective of overturning original affluence renders him guilty of the same ideological crimes that he attributes to those he wishes to contradict. Like most ethnography, data on foraging societies is necessarily limited by the restricted duration of the ethnographer's fieldwork, by the fact that hunter-gatherer societies no longer live in a "world of hunters," and by the fact that many forager ethnographies attempt to reconstruct a previous mode of subsistence. All ethnographic data is refracted through the interpretative lens of the ethnographer and bears a subjective imprint; forager ethnography is no exception. Some emphasize complaint and longing, while others take the same as the banter of everyday life (see Rosenberg, 1997). Moreover, when Kaplan asserts that foragers experience "nagging hunger" (how does he know this, when even experts in the field disagree?), high infant mortality rates, and periodic shortages, his point loses its thunder when one realizes that the same is true, if not worse, for many rural societies, especially those in the world's poorer countries. As noted above, even Wilmsen and Lee who quarrel about the general well-being of the San, agree that their seasonal weight loss is less than that of many rural peoples.[7]

There are additional issues of interpretation. Do hunter-gatherers set production targets low because they are satisfied with their lot, at least the lot that can be acquired through local production (not through access to anthropologists' "stuff"), or because they are reconciled to the fact that any increased product will be lost due to the pressure to share—Woodburn's demand sharing? Surely these are questions of philosophic conjecture, not of time-motion studies, input-output analysis, cost-benefit calculations, or other utilitarian and behaviorist-oriented analyses. Kaplan argues that hunter-gatherer studies "provide an illustration of how ideological yearnings can exert a powerful influence on how we handle ethnographic data" (302). But cannot the same be said of many anthropological interpretations, including his own?

"The Original Affluent Society" is a brilliant idea, perhaps all the more brilliant for the fact that its propositions do not lend themselves to ready proof or disproof. Those who have tried to dismiss Sahlins's argument as romantic illusion or as empirical hoax have been unsuccessful in removing it from our imagination. Put forward to provoke and challenge some of the most basic assumptions of modern thought— that "primitive" wo/man worked long and hard to provide a meager existence, that affluence is achieved through greater consumption, and concomitantly, that humans are, by their nature and by the nature of society, doomed to suffer deprivation and scarcity—"The Original

Affluent Society" continues to engage anthropologists and the wider public; it is good to think about. What more could we ask from a great idea?

Acknowledgements.

I wish to thank Marshall Sahlins for reading a draft of this essay. Aram Yengoyan provided me with critical points to ponder in preparing this essay and Michael Lambek read and critiqued an earlier draft.

Notes

1. "Hunter-gatherer" is a contested term. At the "Man the Hunter" conference, it became abundantly clear that gathering supplied proportionately more food in most hunter-gathering societies than did hunting. New appellations, such as gatherer-hunter and forager, emerged. In this essay, the term "forager" is used interchangeably with "hunter-gatherer."
2. E. P. Thompson, in reflecting on "moral economy," wrote: "In any case, if I did father the term 'moral economy' upon current academic discourse, the term has long forgotten its paternity. I will not disown it, but it has come of age and I am no longer answerable for its actions." (1991: 351).
3. As evidence of the widespread currency of "The Original Affluent Economy," a search on the website Amazon.com (12 September 2004) revealed that over 2000 books include the term in their text.
4. Consider, for example, the catchphrase "Earth Crash Earth Spirit: Healing ourselves and a dying planet" (available at: http://eces.org/articles/000790.php). Many websites include abridged and editorialized versions of "The Original Affluent Society." See for example: http://www.primitivism.com/original-affluent.htm; http://www.ecoaction.org/dt/affluent.html; http://www.insurgentdesire.org.uk/sahlins.htm; and http://www.animana.org/tab1/11originalaffluentsociety.shtml
5. See Day, Papataxiarchis, and Stewart (1999) for a fascinating attempt to generalize the concept of immediate-return beyond hunting and gathering societies (and outside the constraints imposed by the evolutionary and technological associations that are part and parcel of our imagination of hunter gatherers) to others such as Hungarian Rom, London prostitutes, and wage-hunters in urban Japan. In a book entitled *Lilies of the Field*, they open with a quotation from Matthew 6:28–29, 34 "Consider the Lilies of the field, how they grow; they toil not, neither do they spin: ... Take no thought for the morrow: for the morrow shall take for the things of itself..." (1). Lilies maintain a present orientation and like the "affluent hunter-gatherers" who depend upon an unconditional if not mystical "confidence" in their environment's bounty, take a "natural" abundance for granted (1).
6. In all fairness to Sahlins, he published *Culture and Practical Reason* a decade after the "Man the Hunter" conference where he first proposed his ideas on original

affluence and four years after *Stone Age Economics*, which contained the final version. If Sahlins conflated ecological and cultural discourse as Bird-David contends, he certainly was in step with much of American anthropology at the time, which was heavily influenced by Steward's and White's neoevolutionism. Furthermore, it is problematic to fault someone for violating a precept that they had yet to articulate. In retrospect, he might have offered the same criticism of his former work.

7. Similarly Kaplan exposes his argument to logical fallacy with spurious propositions. For example, to "prove" that the !Kung actually work very long hours, he quotes Wiessner to say that "if the hours spent in the business of social relations are added to these [hours spent in the food quest], a 14-hour work week can quickly become a 40-hour one" (319). Of course, the same is true of all societies. Surely if "keeping one's social relationships in good working order" (319) was added to our official work day, we would appear more beleaguered than we already are.

References

Altman, Jon. 1992. "Comment on Beyond 'The Original Affluent Society'." *Current Anthropology* 33(1): 35–36.

Anderson, Benedict. 1991. *Imagined Communities*. London: Verso.

Barnard, Alan, and James Woodburn. 1991. "Introduction." In *Hunter and Gatherers 2: Property, Power and Ideology*, ed. T. Ingold, D. Riches, and J. Woodburn. New York: Berg.

Bird-David, Nurit. 1992. "Beyond 'The Original Affluent Society': A Culturalist Reformulation." *Current Anthropology* 33(1): 25–47.

Day, Sophie, Evthymios Papataxiarchis, and Michael Stewart, eds. 1999. *Lilies of the Field: Marginal People Who Live for the Moment*. Boulder: Woodview.

Endicott, Kirk. 1992. "Comment on Beyond 'The Original Affluent Society'." *Current Anthropology* 33(1): 38–39.

Gowdy, John, ed. 1998. *Limited Wants, Unlimited Means*. Washington, D.C.: Island Press.

———. 1999. "Hunter Gatherers and the Mythology of the Market." *The Cambridge Encyclopedia of Hunters and Gatherers*, ed. R. B. Lee and R. Daly. Cambridge and New York: Cambridge University Press.

Grinker, Richard R. 1992. "Comment on Beyond 'The Original Affluent Society'." *Current Anthropology* 33(1): 39.

Gudeman, Steve. 1992. "Comment on Beyond 'The Original Affluent Society'." *Current Anthropology* 33(1): 39–40.

Hardin, Garret. 1968. "The Tragedy of the Commons." *Science* 162(13): 1243–48.

Hawkes, K., and James O'Connell. 1981. "Affluent Hunters? Some Comments in Light of the Alyawara Case." *American Anthropologist* 84: 622–26.

Kaplan, David. 2000. "The Darker Side of the 'Original Affluent Society'." *Journal of Anthropological Research* 56: 301–24.

Lee, Richard B. 1979. *The !Kung San: Men, Women and Work in a Foraging Society*. Cambridge: Cambridge University Press.

———. 1991. "Reflections on Primitive Communism." In *Hunters and Gatherers*. Vol. 1: *Ecology, Evolution, and Social Change*, ed. Tim Ingold, David Riches, and James Woodburn. London: Berg.

Rosenberg, Harriet. 1997. "Complaint Discourse, Aging, and Care Giving among the Ju/'hoansi of Botswana." In *The Cultural Context of Aging: Worldwide Perspectives*, ed. Jay Sokolovsky. Westport, Conn.: Bergin and Garvey.

Sahlins, Marshall. 1968a. "Notes on the Original Affluent Society." In *Man the Hunter*, ed. R.B. Lee and I. DeVore. Chicago: Aldine.

———. 1968b. "La Première société d'abondance." *Les Temps Modernes* 268: 641–80.

———. 1972. *Stone Age Economics*. Chicago: Aldine.

———. 1976. *Culture and Practical Reason*. Chicago: Aldine.

Smith, Eric Alden. 1991. "Risk and Uncertainty in the 'Original Affluent Society': Evolutionary Ecology of Resource-sharing and Land Tenure." In *Hunter and Gatherers 1:History, Evolution and Social Change*, ed. T. Ingold, D. Riches, and J. Woodburn. New York: Berg.

Thompson, E.P. 1971. "The Moral Economy of the English Crowd in the Eighteenth Century." *Past and Present* 50: 76–136.

———. 1991. *Customs in Common*. London: Penguin.

Wilmsen, Edwin. 1989. *Land Filled with Flies*. Chicago: University of Chicago Press.

Woodburn, James. 1982. "Egalitarian Societies." *Man* 17: 431–51.

———. 1991. "African hunter-gatherer social organization: Is it best understood as a product of encapsulation?" In *Hunter and Gatherers 1:History, Evolution and Social Change*, ed. T. Ingold, D. Riches, and J. Woodburn. New York: Berg.

Websites

Earth Crash Earth Spirit.
   The Original Affluent Society. http://eces.org/articles/000790.php. retrieved 11 September 2004.

Primitivism.
   The Original Affluent Society. http://www.primitivism.com/original-affluent.htm, retrieved 11 September 2004.

Eco-Action.org.
   The Original Affluent Society. http://www.ecoaction.org/dt/affluent.html. retrieved 11 September 2004

Insurgent Desire: The Online Green Anarchy Archive.
   http://www.insurgentdesire.org.uk/sahlins.htm. retrieved 11 September 2004.

The Animana Pages: where the turtle's voice is heard upon the land.
   The Original Affluent Society. http://www.animana.org/tab1/11originalaffluentsociety.shtml. retrieved 11 September 2004.

Chapter 5

THE ORIGINAL
AFFLUENT SOCIETY[1]

Marshall Sahlins

If economics is the dismal science, the study of hunting and gathering economies must be its most advanced branch. Almost universally committed to the proposition that life was hard in the paleolithic, our textbooks compete to convey a sense of impending doom, leaving one to wonder not only how hunters managed to live, but whether, after all, this was living? The specter of starvation stalks the stalker through these pages. His technical incompetence is said to enjoin continuous work just to survive, affording him neither respite nor surplus, hence not even the "leisure" to "build culture." Even so, for all his efforts, the hunter pulls the lowest grades in thermodynamics—less energy/capita/year than any other mode of production. And in treatises on economic development he is condemned to play the role of bad example: the so-called "subsistence economy."

The traditional wisdom is always refractory. One is forced to oppose it polemically, to phrase the necessary revisions dialectically: in fact this was, when you come to examine it, the original affluent society. Paradoxical, that phrasing leads to another useful and unexpected conclusion. By the common understanding, an affluent society is one in which all the people's material wants are easily satisfied. To assert that the hunters are affluent is to deny then that the human condition is an ordained tragedy, with man the prisoner at hard labor of a perpetual disparity between his unlimited wants and his insufficient means.

Note for this section can be found on page 96.

For there are two possible courses to affluence. Wants may be "easily satisfied" either by producing much or desiring little. The familiar conception, the Galbraithean way, makes assumptions peculiarly appropriate to market economies: that man's wants are great, not to say infinite, whereas his means are limited, although improvable: thus, the gap between means and ends can be narrowed by industrial productivity, at least to the point that "urgent goods" become plentiful. But there is also a Zen road to affluence, departing from premises somewhat different from our own: that human material wants are finite and few, and technical means unchanging but on the whole adequate. Adopting the Zen strategy, a people can enjoy an unparalleled material plenty—with a low standard of living.

That, I think, describes the hunters. And it helps explain some of their more curious economic behavior: their "prodigality" for example—the inclination to consume at once all stocks on hand, as if they had it made. Free from market obsessions of scarcity, hunters' economic propensities may be more consistently predicated on abundance than our own. Destutt de Tracy, "fish-blooded bourgeois doctrinaire" though he might have been, at least compelled Marx's agreement on the observation that "in poor nations the people are comfortable," whereas in rich nations "they are generally poor."

This is not to deny that a preagricultural economy operates under serious constraints, but only to insist, on the evidence from modern hunters and gatherers, that a successful accommodation is usually made. After taking up the evidence, I shall return in the end to the real difficulties of the hunting-gathering economy, none of which are correctly specified in current formulas of paleolithic poverty.

Sources of the Misconception

"Mere subsistence economy," "limited leisure save in exceptional circumstances," "incessant quest for food," "meagre and relatively unreliable" natural resources, "absence of an economic surplus," "maximum energy from a maximum number of people"—so runs the fair average anthropological opinion of hunting and gathering.

The aboriginal Australians are a classic example of a people whose economic resources are of the scantiest. In many places their habitat is even more severe than that of the Bushmen, although this is perhaps not quite true in the northern portion.... A tabulation of the foodstuffs which the aborigines of northwest central Queensland extract from the country they inhabit is instructive.... The variety in this list is impressive, but we must not be deceived into thinking that variety indicates plenty, for the available quantities of each element in it are so

The Original Affluent Society 81

slight that only the most intense application makes survival possible (Herskovits, 1958: 68–69).

Or again, in reference to South American hunters:

> The nomadic hunters and gatherers barely met minimum subsistence needs and often fell far short of them. Their population of one person to 10 or 20 square miles reflects this. Constantly on the move in search of food, they clearly lacked the leisure hours for nonsubsistence activities of any significance, and they could transport little of what they might manufacture in spare moments. To them, adequacy of production meant physical survival, and they rarely had surplus of either products or time (Steward and Faron, 1959: 60; cf. Clark, 1953: 27f.; Haury, 1962: 113; Hoebel, 1958: 188; Redfield, 1953: 5; White, 1959).

But the traditional dismal view of the hunters' fix is also preanthropological and extra-anthropological, at once historical and referable to the larger economic context in which anthropology operates. It goes back to the time Adam Smith was writing, and probably to a time before anyone was writing. Probably it was one of the first distinctly neolithic prejudices, an ideological appreciation of the hunter's capacity to exploit the earth's resources most congenial to the historic task of depriving him of the same. We must have inherited it with the seed of Jacob, which "spread abroad to the west, and to the east, and to the north," to the disadvantage of Esau who was the elder son and cunning hunter, but in a famous scene deprived of his birthright.

Current low opinions of the hunting-gathering economy need not be laid to neolithic ethnocentrism, however. Bourgeois ethnocentrism will do as well. The existing business economy, at every turn an ideological trap from which anthropological economics must escape, will promote the same dim conclusions about the hunting life.

Is it so paradoxical to contend that hunters have affluent economies, their absolute poverty notwithstanding? Modern capitalist societies, however richly endowed, dedicate themselves to the proposition of scarcity. Inadequacy of economic means is the first principle of the world's wealthiest peoples. The apparent material status of the economy seems to be no clue to its accomplishments; something has to be said for the mode of economic organization (cf. Polanyi, 1947, 1957, 1959; Dalton, 1961).

The market-industrial system institutes scarcity, in a manner completely unparalleled and to a degree nowhere else approximated. Where production and distribution are arranged through the behavior of prices, and all livelihoods depend on getting and spending, insufficiency of material means becomes the explicit, calculable starting point of all economic activity. The entrepreneur is confronted with alternative investments of a finite capital, the worker (hopefully) with alternative choices of remunerative employ, and the consumer.... Consumption is a double tragedy: what begins in inadequacy will end in deprivation. Bringing together an international division of labor, the market makes available a dazzling array of products: all these Good Things within a man's reach—but never all within his grasp. Worse, in this game of consumer free choice, every acquisition is simultaneously a deprivation, for every purchase of something is a foregoing of something else, in general only marginally less desirable, and in some particulars more desirable, that could have been had instead....

That sentence of "life at hard labor" was passed uniquely upon us. Scarcity is the judgment decreed by our economy—so also the axiom of our Economics: the application of scarce means against alternative ends to derive the most satisfaction possible under the circumstances. And it is precisely from this anxious vantage that we look back upon hunters. But if modern man, with all his technological advantages, still hasn't got the wherewithal, what chance has this naked savage with his puny bow and arrow? Having equipped the hunter with bourgeois impulses and Paleolithic tools, we judge his situation hopeless in advance.

Yet scarcity is not an intrinsic property of technical means. It is a relation between means and ends. We should entertain the empirical possibility that hunters are in business for their health, a finite objective, and that bow and arrow are adequate to that end.

But still other ideas, these endemic in anthropological theory and ethnographic practice, have conspired to preclude any such understanding.

The anthropological disposition to exaggerate the economic inefficiency of hunters appears notably by way of invidious comparison with neolithic economies. Hunters, as Lowie put it blankly, "must work much harder in order to live than tillers and breeders" (1946: 13). On this point evolutionary anthropology in particular found it congenial, even necessary theoretically, to adopt the usual tone of reproach. Ethnologists and archaeologists had become neolithic revolutionaries, and in their enthusiasm for the Revolution spared nothing denouncing the Old (Stone Age) Regime. Including some very old scandal. It was not the first time philosophers would relegate the earliest stage of humanity rather to nature than to culture. ("A man who spends his whole life following animals just to kill them to eat, or moving from one berry patch to another, is really living just like an animal himself" [Braidwood, 1957: 122].) The hunters thus downgraded, anthropology was free to extol the Neolithic Great Leap Forward: a main technological advance that brought about a "general availability of leisure through release from purely food-getting pursuits" (Braidwood, 1957:5; cf. Boas, 1940: 285)....

Another specifically anthropological source of paleolithic discontent develops in the field itself, from the context of European observa-

The Original Affluent Society

tion of existing hunters and gatherers, such as the native Australians, the Bushmen, the Ona, or the Yahgan. This ethnographic context tends to distort our understanding of the hunting-gathering economy in two ways.

First, it provides singular opportunities for naiveté. The remote and exotic environments that have become the cultural theater of modern hunters have an effect on Europeans most unfavorable to the latter's assessment of the former's plight. Marginal as the Australian or Kalahari desert is to agriculture, or to everyday European experience, it is a source of wonder to the untutored observer "how anybody could live in a place like this."...

The surviving food collectors, as a class, are displaced persons. They represent the paleolithic disenfranchised, occupying marginal haunts untypical of the mode of production: sanctuaries of an era, places so beyond the range of main centers of cultural advance as to be allowed some respite from the planetary march of cultural evolution, because they were characteristically poor beyond the interest and competence of more advanced economies. Leave aside the favorably situated food collectors, such as Northwest Coast Indians, about whose (comparative) well-being there is no dispute. The remaining hunters, barred from the better parts of the earth, first by agriculture, later by industrial economies, enjoy ecological opportunities something less than the later-paleolithic average. Moreover, the disruption accomplished in the past two centuries of European imperialism has been especially severe, to the extent that many of the ethnographic notices that constitute the anthropologist's stock in trade are adulterated culture goods. Even explorer and missionary accounts, apart from their ethnocentric misconstructions, may be speaking of afflicted economies (cf. Service, 1962). The hunters of eastern Canada, of whom we read in the *Jesuit Relations,* were committed to the fur trade in the early seventeenth century. The environments of others were selectively stripped by Europeans before reliable report could be made of indigenous production: the Eskimo we know no longer hunt whales, the Bushmen have been deprived of game, the Shoshoni's pinon has been timbered and his hunting grounds grazed out by cattle. If such peoples are now described as poverty-stricken, their resources "meagre and unreliable," is this an indication of the aboriginal condition—or of the colonial duress?

The enormous implications (and problems) for evolutionary interpretation raised by this global retreat have only recently begun to evoke notice (Lee and Devore, 1968). The point of present importance is this: rather than a fair test of hunters' productive capacities, their current circumstances pose something of a supreme test. All the more extraordinary, then, the following reports of their performance.

"A Kind of Material Plenty"

Considering the poverty in which hunters and gatherers live in theory, it comes as a surprise that Bushmen who live in the Kalahari enjoy "a kind of material plenty," at least in the realm of everyday useful things, apart from food and water:

> As the !Kung come into more contact with Europeans—and this is already happening—they will feel sharply the lack of our things and will need and want more. It makes them feel inferior to be without clothes when they stand among strangers who are clothed. But in their own life and with their own artifacts *they were comparatively free from material pressures.* Except for food and water (important exceptions!) of which the Nyae Nyae !Kung have a sufficiency—but barely so, judging from the fact that all are thin though not emaciated—they all had what they needed or could make what they needed, for every man can and does make the things that men make and every woman the things that women make.... *They lived in a kind of material plenty* because they adapted the tools of their living to materials which lay in abundance around them and which were free for anyone to take (wood, reeds, bone for weapons and implements, fibers for cordage, grass for shelters), or to materials which were at least sufficient for the needs of the population.... They borrow what they do not own. With this ease, they have not hoarded, and the accumulation of objects has not become associated with status (Marshall, 1961: 243–44, emphasis mine).

Analysis of hunter-gatherer production is usefully divided into two spheres, as Mrs. Marshall has done. Food and water are certainly "important exceptions," best reserved for separate and extended treatment. For the rest, the nonsubsistence sector, what is here said of the Bushmen applies in general and in detail to hunters from the Kalahari to Labrador—or to Tierra del Fuego....

In the nonsubsistence sphere, the people's wants are generally easily satisfied. Such "material plenty" depends partly upon the ease of production, and that upon the simplicity of technology and democracy of property.... Add in the liberal customs of sharing, for which hunters are properly famous, and all the people can usually participate in the going prosperity, such as it is.

But, of course, "such as it is": this "prosperity" depends as well upon an objectively low standard of living. It is critical that the customary quota of consumables (as well as the number of consumers) be culturally set at a modest point....

For most hunters, such affluence without abundance in the nonsubsistence sphere need not be long debated. A more interesting question is why they are content with so few possessions—for it is with them a policy, a "matter of principle" as Gusinde says (1961: 2), and not a misfortune.

The Original Affluent Society 85

Want not, lack not. But are hunters so undemanding of material goods because they are themselves enslaved by a food quest "demanding maximum energy from a maximum number of people," so that no time or effort remains for the provision of other comforts? Some ethnographers testify to the contrary that the food quest is so successful that half the time the people seem not to know what to do with themselves. On the other hand, *movement* is a condition of this success, more movement in some cases than others, but always enough to rapidly depreciate the satisfactions of property. Of the hunter it is truly said that his wealth is a burden. In his condition of life, goods can become "grievously oppressive," as Gusinde observes, and the more so the longer they are carried around. Certain food collectors have canoes and a few have dog sleds, but most must carry themselves all the comforts they possess, and so only possess what they can comfortably carry themselves. Or perhaps only what the women can carry: the men are often left free to react to the sudden opportunity of the chase or the sudden necessity of defense. As Owen Lattimore wrote in a not too different context, "the pure nomad is the poor nomad." Mobility and property are in contradiction....

...This modesty of material requirements is institutionalized: it becomes a positive cultural fact, expressed in a variety of economic arrangements. Lloyd Warner reports of the Murngin, for example, that portability is a decisive value in the local scheme of things. Small goods are in general better than big goods. In the final analysis "the relative ease of transportation of the article" will prevail, so far as determining its disposition, over its relative scarcity or labor cost. For the "ultimate value," Warner writes, "is freedom of movement"... (1964: 136–37).

Here then is another economic "peculiarity"—I will not say it is general, and perhaps it is explained as well by faulty toilet training as by a trained disinterest in material accumulation: some hunters, at least, display a notable tendency to be sloppy about their possessions. They have the kind of nonchalance that would be appropriate to a people who have mastered the problems of production, even as it is maddening to a European:

> They do not know how to take care of their belongings. No one dreams of putting them in order, folding them, drying or cleaning them, hanging them up, or putting them in a neat pile. If they are looking for some particular thing, they rummage carelessly through the hodgepodge of trifles in the little baskets. Larger objects that are piled up in a heap in the hut are dragged hither and yon with no regard for the damage that might be done them. The European observer has the impression that these [Yahgan] Indians place no value whatever on their utensils and that they have completely forgotten the effort it took to make them. Actually, no one clings to

his few goods and chattels which, as it is, are often and easily lost, but just as easily replaced.... The less they own, the more comfortable they can travel, and what is ruined they occasionally replace. Hence, they are completely indifferent to any material possessions (Gusinde, 1961: 86–87).

The hunter, one is tempted to say, is "uneconomic man." At least as concerns nonsubsistence goods, he is the reverse of that standard caricature immortalized in any *General Principles of Economics*, page one. His wants are scarce and his means (in relation) plentiful. Consequently he is "comparatively free of material pressures," has "no sense of possession," shows "an undeveloped sense of property," is "completely indifferent to any material pressures," manifests a "lack of interest" in developing his technological equipment.

In this relation of hunters to worldly goods there is a neat and important point. From the internal perspective of the economy, it seems wrong to say that wants are "restricted," desires "restrained," or even that the notion of wealth is "limited." Such phrasings imply in advance an Economic Man and a struggle of the hunter against his own worse nature, which is finally then subdued by a cultural vow of poverty. The words imply the renunciation of an acquisitiveness that in reality was never developed, a suppression of desires that were never broached. Economic Man is a bourgeois construction—as Marcel Mauss said, "not behind us, but before, like the moral man." It is not that hunters and gatherers have curbed their materialistic "impulses"; they simply never made an institution of them. "Moreover, if it is a great blessing to be free from a great evil, our [Montagnais] Savages are happy; for the two tyrants who provide hell and torture for many of our Europeans, do not reign in their great forests,—I mean ambition and avarice ... as they are contented with a mere living, not one of them gives himself to the Devil to acquire wealth" (LeJeune, 1897: 231).

We are inclined to think of hunters and gatherers as poor because they don't have anything; perhaps better to think of them for that reason as *free*. "Their extremely limited material possessions relieve them of all cares with regard to daily necessities and permit them to enjoy life" (Gusinde, 1961: 1).

Subsistence

When Herskovits was writing his Economic Anthropology (1958), it was common anthropological practice to take the Bushmen or the native Australians as "a classic illustration of a people whose economic resources are of the scantiest," so precariously situated that "only the most intense application makes survival possible." Today the "classic"

The Original Affluent Society 87

understanding can be fairly reversed—on evidence largely from these two groups. A good case can be made that hunters and gatherers work less than we do; and, rather than a continuous travail, the food quest is intermittent, leisure abundant, and there is a greater amount of sleep in the daytime per capita per year than in any other condition of society.

Some of the substantiating evidence for Australia appears in early sources, but we are fortunate especially to have now the quantitative materials collected by the 1948 American-Australian Scientific Expedition to Arnhem Land. Published in 1960, these startling data must provoke some review of the Australian reportage going back for over a century, and perhaps revision of an even longer period of anthropological thought. The key research was a temporal study of hunting and gathering by McCarthy and McArthur (1960), coupled to McArthur's analysis of the nutritional outcome....

One must have serious reservations about drawing general or historical inferences from the Arnhem Land data alone. Not only was the context less than pristine and the time of study too brief, but certain elements of the modern situation may have raised productivity above aboriginal levels: metal tools, for example, or the reduction of local pressure on food resources by depopulation. And our uncertainty seems rather doubled than neutralized by other current circumstances that, conversely, would lower economic efficiency: these semi-independent hunters, for instance, are probably not as skilled as their ancestors. For the moment, let us consider the Arnhem Land conclusions as experimental, potentially credible in the measure they are supported by other ethnographic or historic accounts.

The most obvious, immediate conclusion is that the people do not work hard. The average length of time per person per day put into the appropriation and preparation of food was four or five hours. Moreover, they do not work continuously. The subsistence quest was highly intermittent. It would stop for the time being when the people had procured enough for the time being, which left them plenty of time to spare. Clearly in subsistence as in other sectors of production, we have to do with an economy of specific, limited objectives. By hunting and gathering these objectives are apt to be irregularly accomplished, so the work pattern becomes correspondingly erratic.

In the event, a third characteristic of hunting and gathering unimagined by the received wisdom: rather than straining to the limits of available labor and disposable resources, these Australians seem to *underuse* their objective economic possibilities.

> The quantity of food gathered in one day by any of these groups could in every instance have been increased. Although the search for food was, for the women, a job that went on day after day without relief ... they rested

quite frequently, and did not spend all the hours of daylight searching for and preparing food. The nature of the men's food-gathering was more sporadic, and if they had a good catch one day they frequently rested the next.... Perhaps unconsciously they weigh the benefit of greater supplies of food against the effort involved in collecting it, perhaps they judge what they consider to be enough, and when that is collected they stop (McArthur, 1960: 92).

It follows, fourthly, that the economy was not physically demanding. The investigators' daily journal indicates that the people pace themselves; only once is a hunter described as "utterly exhausted" (McCarthy and McArthur, 1960: 150f.). Neither did the Arnhem Landers themselves consider the task of subsistence onerous....

In any case, the dietary intake of the Arnhem Land hunters was adequate—according to the standards of the National Research Council of America....

The failure of Arnhem Landers to "build culture" is not strictly from want of time. It is from idle hands.

So much for the plight of hunters and gatherers in Arnhem Land. As for the Bushmen, economically likened to Australian hunters by Herskovits, two excellent recent reports by Richard Lee show their condition to be indeed the same (Lee, 1968: 1969). Lee's research merits a special hearing not only because it concerns Bushmen, but specifically the Dobe section of !Kung Bushmen, adjacent to the Nyae Nyae about whose subsistence—in a context otherwise of "material plenty"—Mrs. Marshall expressed important reservations....

Despite a low annual rainfall (6 to 10 inches), Lee found in the Dobe area a "surprising abundance of vegetation." Food resources were "both varied and abundant," particularly the energy-rich mangetti nut "so abundant that millions of the nuts rotted on the ground each year for want of picking" (all references in Lee, 1969: 59). His reports on time spent in food-getting are remarkably close to the Arnhem Land observations....

The Bushman figures imply that one man's labor in hunting and gathering will support four or five people. Taken at face value, Bushman food collecting is more efficient than French farming in the period up to World War II, when more than 20 percent of the population were engaged in feeding the rest.... the ratio of food producers to the general population is actually 3 : 5 or 2 : 3. *But*, these 65 percent of the people "worked 36 percent of the time, and 35 percent of the people did not work at all"! (Lee, 1969: 67).

For each adult worker, this comes to about two and one-half days labor per week. ("In other words, each productive individual supported herself or himself and dependents and still had $3^{1}/_{2}$ to $5^{1}/_{2}$ days available for other activities.") A "day's work" was about six hours; hence

The Original Affluent Society   89

the Dobe work week is approximately 15 hours, or an average of 2 hours 9 minutes per day. Even lower than the Arnhem Land norms, this figure however excludes cooking and the preparation of implements. All things considered, Bushmen subsistence labors are probably very close to those of native Australians.

Also like the Australians, the time Bushmen do not work in subsistence they pass in leisure or leisurely activity. One detects again that characteristic paleolithic rhythm of a day or two on, a day or two off— the latter passed desultorily in camp. Although food collecting is the primary productive activity, Lee writes, "the majority of the people's time (four to five days per week) is spent in other pursuits, such as resting in camp or visiting other camps" (1969: 74).... "The conclusion can be drawn that the Bushmen do not lead a substandard existence on the edge of starvation as has been commonly supposed" (1969: 73)....

... in Africa the Hadza have been long enjoying a comparable ease, with a burden of subsistence occupations no more strenuous in hours per day than the Bushmen or the Australian Aboriginals (Woodburn, 1968). Living in an area of "exceptional abundance" of animals and regular supplies of vegetables (the vicinity of Lake Eyasi), Hadza men seem much more concerned with games of chance than with chances of game. During the long dry season especially, they pass the greater part of days on end in gambling, perhaps only to lose the metal-tipped arrows they need for big game hunting at other times. In any case, many men are "quite unprepared or unable to hunt big game even when they possess the necessary arrows." Only a small minority, Woodburn writes, are active hunters of large animals, and if women are generally more assiduous at their vegetable collecting, still it is at a leisurely pace and without prolonged labor (cf. 1966: 51). Despite this nonchalance, and an only limited economic cooperation, Hadza "nonetheless obtain sufficient food without undue effort." Woodburn offers this "very rough approximation" of subsistence-labor requirements: "Over the year as a whole probably an average of less than two hours a day is spent obtaining food" (1968: 54).

Interesting that the Hadza, tutored by life and not by anthropology, reject the neolithic revolution in order to *keep* their leisure. Although surrounded by cultivators, they have until recently refused to take up agriculture themselves, "mainly on the grounds that this would involve too much hard work."...

The hunter's attitude towards farming introduces us, lastly, to a few particulars of the way they relate to the food quest. Once again we venture here into the internal realm of the economy, a realm sometimes subjective and always difficult to understand; where, moreover, hunters seem deliberately inclined to overtax our comprehension by customs so odd as to invite the extreme interpretation that either these people are fools or they really have nothing to worry about. The former would be a true logical deduction from the hunter's nonchalance, on the premise that his economic condition is truly exigent. On the other hand, if a livelihood is usually easily procured, if one can usually expect to succeed, then the people's seeming imprudence can no longer appear as such. Speaking to unique developments of the market economy, to its institutionalization of scarcity, Karl Polanyi said that our "animal dependence upon food has been bared and the naked fear of starvation permitted to run loose. Our humiliating enslavement to the material, which all human culture is designed to mitigate, was deliberately made more rigorous" (1947: 115). But our problems are not theirs, the hunters and gatherers. Rather, a pristine affluence colors their economic arrangements, a trust in the abundance of nature's resources rather than despair at the inadequacy of human means. My point is that otherwise curious heathen devices become understandable by the people's confidence, a confidence which is the reasonable human attribute of a generally successful economy....

Certainly, hunters quit camp because food resources have given out in the vicinity. But to see in this nomadism merely a flight from starvation only perceives the half of it; one ignores the possibility that the people's expectations of greener pastures elsewhere are not usually disappointed....

A more serious issue is presented by the frequent and exasperated observation of a certain "lack of foresight" among hunters and gatherers. Oriented forever in the present, without "the slightest thought of, or care for, what the morrow may bring" (Spencer and Gillen, 1899: 53), the hunter seems unwilling to husband supplies, incapable of a planned response to the doom surely awaiting him. He adopts instead a studied unconcern, which expresses itself in two complementary economic inclinations.

The first, prodigality: the propensity to eat right through all the food in the camp, even during objectively difficult times, "as if," LeJeune said of the Montagnais, "the game they were to hunt was shut up in a stable" (LeJeune 1897) ...

Sympathetic writers have tried to rationalize the apparent impracticality. Perhaps the people have been carried beyond reason by hunger: they are apt to gorge themselves on a kill because they have gone so long without meat—and for all they know they are likely to soon do so again. Or perhaps in making one feast of his supplies a man is responding to binding social obligations, to important imperatives of sharing. LeJeune's experience would confirm either view, but it also suggests a third. Or rather, the Montagnais have their own explanation. They are not worried by what the morrow may bring because as

The Original Affluent Society 91

far as they are concerned it will bring more of the same: "another feast." Whatever the value of other interpretations, such self-confidence must be brought to bear on the supposed prodigality of hunters....

Rethinking Hunters and Gatherers

Constantly under pressure of want, and yet, by travelling, easily able to supply their wants, their lives lack neither excitement or pleasure (Smyth, 1878, vol. 1,: 123).

Clearly, the hunting-gathering economy has to be revaluated, both as to its true accomplishments and its true limitations. The procedural fault of the received wisdom was to read from the material circumstances to the economic structure, deducing the absolute difficulty of such a life from its absolute poverty. But always the cultural design improvises dialectics on its relationship to nature. Without escaping the ecological constraints, culture would negate them, so that at once the system shows the impress of natural conditions and the originality of a social response—in their poverty, abundance.

What are the real handicaps of the hunting-gathering *praxis?* Not "low productivity of labor," if existing examples mean anything. But the economy is seriously afflicted by the *imminence of diminishing returns.* Beginning in subsistence and spreading from there to every sector, an initial success seems only to develop the probability that further efforts will yield smaller benefits. This describes the typical curve of food-getting within a particular locale. A modest number of people usually sooner than later reduce the food resources within convenient range of camp. Thereafter, they may stay on only by absorbing an increase in real costs or a decline in real returns: rise in costs if the people choose to search farther and farther afield, decline in returns if they are satisfied to live on the shorter supplies or inferior foods in easier reach. The solution, of course, is to go somewhere else. Thus the first and decisive contingency of hunting-gathering: it requires movement to maintain production on advantageous terms.

But this movement, more or less frequent in different circumstances, more or less distant, merely transposes to other spheres of production the same diminishing returns of which it is born. The manufacture of tools, clothing, utensils, or ornaments, however easily done, becomes senseless when these begin to be more of a burden than a comfort. Utility falls quickly at the margin of portability. The construction of substantial houses likewise becomes absurd if they must soon be abandoned. Hence the hunter's very ascetic conceptions of material welfare: an interest only in minimal equipment, if that; a valuation of smaller things over bigger; a disinterest in acquiring two or more of most goods; and the like. Ecological pressure assumes a rare form of concreteness when it has to be shouldered. If the gross product is trimmed down in comparison with other economies, it is not the hunter's productivity that is at fault, but his mobility.

Almost the same thing can be said of the demographic constraints of hunting-gathering. The same policy of *débarassment* is in play on the level of people, describable in similar terms and ascribable to similar causes. The terms are, cold-bloodedly: diminishing returns at the margin of portability, minimum necessary equipment, elimination of duplicates, and so forth—that is to say, infanticide, senilicide, sexual continence for the duration of the nursing period, etc., practices for which many food-collecting peoples are well known. The presumption that such devices are due to an inability to support more people is probably true—if "support" is understood in the sense of carrying them rather than feeding them. The people eliminated, as hunters sometimes sadly tell, are precisely those who cannot effectively transport themselves, who would hinder the movement of family and camp. Hunters may be obliged to handle people and goods in parallel ways, the draconic population policy an expression of the same ecology as the ascetic economy. More, these tactics of demographic restraint again form part of a larger policy for counteracting diminishing returns in subsistence. A local group becomes vulnerable to diminishing returns—so to a greater velocity of movement, or else to fission—in proportion to its size (other things equal). Insofar as the people would keep the advantage in local production, and maintain a certain physical and social stability, their Malthusian practices are just cruelly consistent. Modern hunters and gatherers, working their notably inferior environments, pass most of the year in very small groups widely spaced out. But rather than the sign of underproduction, the wages of poverty, this demographic pattern is better understood as the cost of living well.

Hunting and gathering has all the strengths of its weaknesses. Periodic movement and restraint in wealth and population are at once imperatives of the economic practice and creative adaptations, the kinds of necessities of which virtues are made. Precisely in such a framework, affluence becomes possible. Mobility and moderation put hunters' ends within range of their technical means. An undeveloped mode of production is thus rendered highly effective. The hunter's life is not as difficult as it looks from the outside. In some ways the economy reflects dire ecology, but it is also a complete inversion.

Reports on hunters and gatherers of the ethnological present—specifically on those in marginal environments—suggest a mean of three to five hours per adult worker per day in food production. Hunters keep bankers' hours, notably less than modern industrial workers

The Original Affluent Society 93

(unionized), who would surely settle for a 21–35 hour week. An interesting comparison is also posed by recent studies of labor costs among agriculturalists of neolithic type. For example, the average adult Hanunoo, man or woman, spends 1,200 hours per year in swidden cultivation (Conklin, 1957: 151); which is to say, a mean of three hours twenty minutes per day. Yet this figure does not include food gathering, animal raising, cooking, and other direct subsistence efforts of these Philippine tribesmen. Comparable data are beginning to appear in reports on other primitive agriculturalists from many parts of the world. The conclusion is put conservatively when put negatively: hunters and gatherers need not work longer getting food than do primitive cultivators. Extrapolating from ethnography to prehistory, one may say as much for the neolithic as John Stuart Mill said of all labor-saving devices, that never was one invented that saved anyone a minute's labor. The neolithic saw no particular improvement over the paleolithic in the amount of time required per capita for the production of subsistence; probably, with the advent of agriculture, people had to work harder.

There is nothing either to the convention that hunters and gatherers can enjoy little leisure from tasks of sheer survival. By this, the evolutionary inadequacies of the paleolithic are customarily explained, while for the provision of leisure the neolithic is roundly congratulated. But the traditional formulas might be truer if reversed: the amount of work (per capita) increases with the evolution of culture, and the amount of leisure decreases. Hunters' subsistence labors are characteristically intermittent, a day on and a day off, and modern hunters at least tend to employ their time off in such activities as daytime sleep. In the tropical habitats occupied by many of these existing hunters, plant collecting is more reliable than hunting itself. Therefore, the women, who do the collecting, work rather more regularly than the men, and provide the greater part of the food supply. Man's work is often done. On the other hand, it is likely to be highly erratic, unpredictably required; if men lack leisure, it is then in the Enlightenment sense rather than the literal. When Condorcet attributed the hunter's unprogressive condition to want of "the leisure in which he can indulge in thought and enrich his understanding with new combinations of ideas," he also recognized that the economy was a "necessary cycle of extreme activity and total idleness." Apparently what the hunter needed was the *assured* leisure of an aristocratic *philosophe*.

Hunters and gatherers maintain a sanguine view of their economic state despite the hardships they sometimes know. It may be that they sometimes know hardships because of the sanguine views they maintain of their economic state. Perhaps their confidence only encourages prodigality to the extent the camp falls casualty to the first untoward circumstance. In alleging this is an affluent economy, therefore, I do not deny that certain hunters have moments of difficulty. Some do find it "almost inconceivable" for a man to die of hunger, or even to fail to satisfy his hunger for more than a day or two (Woodburn, 1968: 52). But others, especially certain very peripheral hunters spread out in small groups across an environment of extremes, are exposed periodically to the kind of inclemency that interdicts travel or access to game. They suffer—although perhaps only fractionally, the shortage affecting particular immobilized families rather than the society as a whole (cf. Gusinde, 1961: 306–7).

Still, granting this vulnerability, and allowing the most poorly situated modern hunters into comparison, it would be difficult to prove that privation is distinctly characteristic of the hunter-gatherers. Food shortage is not the indicative property of this mode of production as opposed to others; it does not mark off hunters and gatherers as a class or a general evolutionary stage....

Above all, what about the world today? One-third to one-half of humanity are said to go to bed hungry every night. In the Old Stone Age the fraction must have been much smaller. *This* is the era of hunger unprecedented. Now, in the time of the greatest technical power, is starvation an institution. Reverse another venerable formula: the amount of hunger increases relatively and absolutely with the evolution of culture.

This paradox is my whole point. Hunters and gatherers have by force of circumstances an objectively low standard of living. But taken as their *objective*, and given their adequate means of production, all the people's material wants usually can be easily satisfied. The evolution of economy has known, then, two contradictory movements: enriching but at the same time impoverishing, appropriating in relation to nature but expropriating in relation to man. The progressive aspect is, of course, technological. It has been celebrated in many ways: as an increase in the amount of need-serving goods and services, an increase in the amount of energy harnessed to the service of culture, an increase in productivity, an increase in division of labor, and increased freedom from environmental control. Taken in a certain sense, the last is especially useful for understanding the earliest stages of technical advance. Agriculture not only raised society above the distribution of natural food resources, it allowed neolithic communities to maintain high degrees of social order where the requirements of human existence were absent from the natural order. Enough food could be harvested in some seasons to sustain the people while no food would grow at all; the consequent stability of social life was critical for its material enlargement. Culture went on then from triumph to triumph, in a kind of progressive contravention of the biological law of the minimum,

The Original Affluent Society   95

until it proved it could support human life in outer space—where even gravity and oxygen were naturally lacking.

Other men were dying of hunger in the market places of Asia. It has been an evolution of structures as well as technologies, and in that respect like the mythical road where for every step the traveller advances his destination recedes by two. The structures have been political as well as economic, of power as well as property. They developed first within societies, increasingly now between societies. No doubt these structures have been functional, necessary organizations of the technical development, but within the communities they have thus helped to enrich they would discriminate in the distribution of wealth and differentiate in the style of life. The world's most primitive people have few possessions, *but they are not poor.* Poverty is not a certain small amount of goods, nor is it just a relation between means and ends; above all it is a relation between people. Poverty is a social status. As such it is the invention of civilization. It has grown with civilization, at once as an invidious distinction between classes and more importantly as a tributary relation—that can render agrarian peasants more susceptible to natural catastrophes than any winter camp of Alaskan Eskimo.

All the preceding discussion takes the liberty of reading modern hunters historically, as an evolutionary base line. This liberty should not be lightly granted. Are marginal hunters such as the Bushmen of the Kalahari any more representative of the paleolithic condition than the Indians of California or the Northwest Coast? Perhaps not. Perhaps also Bushmen of the Kalahari are not even representative of marginal hunters. The great majority of surviving hunter-gatherers lead a life curiously decapitated and extremely lazy by comparison with the other few. The other few are very different. The Murngin, for example: "The first impression that any stranger must receive in a fully functioning group in Eastern Arnhem Land is of industry...

And he must be impressed with the fact that with the exception of very young children ... there is no idleness" (Thomson, 1949a: 33–34). There is nothing to indicate that the problems of livelihood are more difficult for these people than for other hunters (cf. Thomson, 1949b). The incentives of their unusual industry lie elsewhere: in "an elaborate and exacting ceremonial life," specifically in an elaborate ceremonial exchange cycle that bestows prestige on craftsmanship and trade (Thomson, 1949a: 26, 28, 34f., 87 passim). Most other hunters have no such concerns. Their existence is comparatively colorless, fixed singularly on eating with gusto and digesting at leisure. The cultural orientation is not Dionysian or Apollonian, but "gastric," as Julian Steward said of the Shoshoni. Then again it may be Dionysian, that is, Bacchanalian: "Eating among the Savages is like drinking among the drunkards of Europe. Those dry and ever-thirsty souls would willingly end their lives in a tub of malmsey, and the Savages in a pot full of meat; those over there talk only of drinking, and these here only of eating" (LeJeune, 1897: 249).

It is as if the superstructures of these societies had been eroded, leaving only the bare subsistence rock, and since production itself is readily accomplished, the people have plenty of time to perch there and talk about it. I must raise the possibility that the ethnography of hunters and gatherers is largely a record of incomplete cultures. Fragile cycles of ritual and exchange may have disappeared without trace, lost in the earliest stages of colonialism, when the intergroup relations they mediated were attacked and confounded. If so, the "original" affluent society will have to be rethought again for its originality, and the evolutionary schemes once more revised. Still this much history can always be rescued from existing hunters: the "economic problem" is easily solvable by paleolithic techniques. But then, it was not until culture neared the height of its material achievements that it erected a shrine to the Unattainable: *Infinite Needs.*

Note

1. This article is reprinted with the permission of the author with homage to Richard Lee. Solway abridged the essay and in the process removed from the original much of the supporting data, the footnotes, as well as all of the graphs, charts, and figures. Routledge as part of their *Routledge Library Editions: Anthropology and Ethnography* republished *Stone Age Economics* in 2004.

References

Boas, Franz. 1940. *Race, Language and Culture.* New York: Free Press.
Bonwick, James. 1870. *Daily Life and Origin of the Tasmanians.* London: Low and Merston.
Braidwood, Robert J. 1957. *Prehistoric Men.* 3d ed. Chicago: Chicago Natural History Museum Popular Series, Anthropology, Number 37.
Clark, Graham. 1953. *From Savagery to Civilization.* New York: Schuman.
Conklin, Harold C. 1957. *Hanunoo Agriculture.* Rome: Food and Agriculture Organization of the United Nations.
Dalton, George. 1961. "Economic Theory and Primitive Society." *American Anthropologist* 63: 1–25.
Gusinde, Martin. 1961. *The Yamana.* 5 vols. New Haven, Conn.: Human Relations Area Files. (German Edition 1931).

Haury, Emil W. 1962. "The Greater American Southwest." In *Courses toward Urban Life*, ed. J. Braidwood and G. R. Willey. Chicago: Aldine.

Herskovits, Melville J. 1958. *Economic Anthropology*. New York: Knopf.

Hoebel, E. Adamson. 1958. *Man in the Primitive World*. 2d ed. New York: McGraw-Hill.

Lee, Richard. 1968. "What Hunters Do for a Living, or, How to Make Out on Scarce Resources." In *Man the Hunter*, in R. Lee and I. DeVore. Chicago: Aldine.

———. 1969. "!Kung Bushman Subsistence: An Input-Output Analysis." In *Environment and Cultural Behaviour*, ed. A. Vayda. Garden City, N.Y.: Natural History Press.

Lee, Richard B., and Irven DeVore, ed. 1968. *Man the Hunter*. Chicago: Aldine.

LeJeune, le Pere Paul. 1897. "Relation of What Occurred in New France in the Year 1634." In *The Jesuit Relations and Allied Documents*, ed. R.G. Thwaites. Vol. 6. Cleveland: Burrows. (First French edition, 1616.)

Lowie, Robert H. 1946. *An Introduction to Cultural Anthropology*. 2d ed. New York: Rinehart.

Marshall, Lorna. 1961. "Sharing, Talking, and Giving: Relief of Social Tensions Among !Kung Bushmen." *Africa* 31: 321–49.

McArthur, Margaret. 1960. "Food Consumption and Dietary Levels of Groups of Aborigines Living on Naturally Occurring Foods." In *Records of the Australian-American Scientific Expedition to Arnhem Land*, ed. C.P. Mountford. Vol. 2: *Anthropology and Nutrition*. Melbourne: Melbourne University Press.

McCarthy, Frederick D., and Margaret McArthur. 1960. "The Food Quest and the Time Factor in Aboriginal Economic Life." In *Records of the Australian-American Scientific Expedition to Arnhem Land*, ed. C.P. Mountford. Vol. 2: *Anthropology and Nutrition*. Melbourne: Melbourne University Press.

Polanyi, Karl. 1947. "Our Obsolete Market Mentality." *Commentary* 3: 109–17.

———. 1957. "The Economy as Instituted Process." In *Trade and Market in the Early Empires*, ed. K. Polanyi, C. Arensberg, and H. Pearson. Glencoe: The Free Press.

———. 1959. "Anthropology and Economic Theory." In *Readings in Anthropology*, ed. M. Fried. Vol. 2. New York: Crowell.

Redfield, Robert. 1953. *The Primitive World and its Transformations*. Ithaca, N.Y.: Cornell University Press.

Service, Elman R. 1962. *Primitive Social Organization*. New York: Random House.

Smyth, R. Brough. 1878. *The Aborigines of Victoria*. 2 vols. Melbourne: Government Printer.

Spencer, Baldwin, and F.J. Gillen. 1899. *The Native Tribes of Central Australia*. London: Macmillan.

Steward, Julian H., and Louis C. Faron. 1959. *Native Peoples of South America*. New York: McGraw-Hill.

Thomson, Donald F. 1949a. *Economic Structure and the Ceremonial Exchange Cycle in Arnhem Land*. Melbourne: Macmillan.

———. 1949b. "Arnhem Land: Explorations Among an Unknown People." *The Geographical Journal* 113: 1–8, 114, 54–67.

Warner, W. Lloyd. 1964. *A Black Civilization* (Harper "Torchback" from the edition of 1958; first edition 1937). New York: Harper & Row.

White, Leslie A. 1959. *The Evolution of Culture.* New York: McGraw-Hill.

Woodburn, James. 1966. "The Hazda" (film available from the anthropological director, Department of Anthropology, London School of Economics).

———. 1968. "An Introduction to Hazda Ecology." In *Man the Hunter,* ed. R. Lee and I. DeVore. Chicago: Aldine.

Chapter 6

ON THE POLITICS OF BEING JEWISH IN A MULTIRACIAL STATE

Karen Brodkin

My offering to this volume honors a part of Richard Lee's commitment to social justice that we share as North American Jews. I want to consider a question we both have wrestled with as socially engaged scholars: What kind of Jewishness do Jews create when they pursue social justice in North America today?

When people come together to engage in collective political action, they also gather together to construct themselves as political agents. Part of this process involves analyzing the ways in which the particular uniting issue is important to each of them. This requires explaining the parts of one's social being or the social identities through which we make our most powerful connection to the issue. Often such connections are constructions of we-ness: racism or sexism is directed against us; homophobia hurts us, etc.

However, many who participate in various movements for social justice are not part of the obvious "we." Neither scholars nor activists any longer take ethnic identity for granted as monolithic or as natural and primordial attachments. We are becoming increasingly self-conscious about issues of identity, memory, and history. The fields most attentive to issues of social identities—ethnic studies, women's studies, lesbian and gay studies—have taken the lead in deconstructing the process of identity formation, its situationally specific dimensions, the struggles over constructions of "authenticity," and the analysis of ways that they interpenetrate and constitute one another. Identity

Notes for this section can be found on page 112.

making involves more or less strategic selections, interpretations, and deployments of shared stories and images in order to explain oneself to self and to others. I find Paul Kroskrity's (1993) concept of "repertoire of identities" a helpful way to think about identity making as an open process. By repertoire of identities he means the panoply of identities people are given and those they embrace, the full potential of resources they have for constructing social selves. The study then becomes one of understanding why people deploy the identities they do in any specific situation.

If constructing one's connection to an issue involves strategic construction of one's situational identities, then it is also the case that the ways participants construct their identities also shapes how a political movement is framed and the directions it takes. For example, unions have a history of presenting their issues in terms of class, ostensibly to unite workers across racial and gender lines. When nonwhite and/or female workers connect to such struggles, they are constrained not to deploy their racial or gender identities, rather to identify through class. However, as Daniel Letwin (1995) and Mike Honey (1993) have shown for race, this meant that militant union priorities in the South were those of white workers. Strategies of identity construction were deeply implicated in struggles over issue construction. Here, a class construction of issues encouraged nonwhite workers to connect, but the racial specificity of the actual issues undercut that connection.

A focus on how participants who do not have a seemingly natural connection to the issue construct themselves politically can help unpack the reciprocal constitution of issues and actors. Under consideration here is how North American Jews, who mainly occupy a position of class and racial privilege, construct themselves as political actors when they connect to today's movements for social justice that are centered on the priorities of low-income people of color. To answer this question, I will examine the story (and the changes over the last two generations in the way it is told) of the 1911 fire at the Triangle Shirtwaist Factory in New York's Lower East Side. My argument is that feminist tellings of the tale provide a bridge for Jewish women and men to construct their Jewishness as linking them "naturally" to struggles for social justice.

Jews have a long history of participation in progressive social movements, but quite often not as Jews. Naomi Seidman has given them a name, "vicarious Jews." By this she means Jews who enact their Jewish sense of "otherness," of being marginal and not of the mainstream, in defense of the rights of others who have been oppressed and marginalized. It is a long, noble Jewish tradition, she tells us, ranging from Freud and Marx to Jews in the US Civil Rights and feminist movements, and queer theorists. Richard Lee's activism, beginning in the 1960s against the Vietnam War, his work from the 1970s with anti-apartheid groups in solidarity with South Africa, and his work with the Innu of Labrador from the 1980s, all make him a vicarious Jew in good standing.

Seidman argues that the reason for vicarious Jewishness, or Jewishness by other means, is that the discourse of ethnoracial politics in North America equates claims to ethnic identity with claims to racial and ethnic oppression. Jews who recognize this are understandably reluctant to present their activism as specifically Jewish. To do so, they fear, might lead others to think that they are claiming that they are oppressed because they are Jewish, or that they are claiming that discrimination against Jews in North America today is like discrimination against peoples of color. Thus, Seidman notes, "In the absence of a particularist Jewish political affiliation that could also satisfy the progressive universalist agenda with which Jewish politics has been historically linked, adopting the particularist position of another group paradoxically becomes a distinctively Jewish act" (1998: 261).

The process of self-construction is social and performative as well as situational, so that it should be possible to look at other ways that progressive Jews may constitute their Jewishness. By what social performances do Jewish activists engage with Jewish politics? With non-Jewish activists? What do the ways Jewish activists construct themselves to each other, and to others in their movement, tell us about their understandings of the movement and themselves?

Self-constructions of Jewish activists today need to be set against the backdrop of Jewish politics since the mid-1960s. Those politics, especially around Israel and around race in the United States, have become increasingly conservative, as has the public face of politics in the United States more generally. Most Jewish organizations that filed amicus briefs around Bakke and DeFunis in their cases against affirmative action policies at the University of California and Washington medical schools opposed affirmative action, while only two, the National Council of Jewish Women and the Union of American Hebrew Congregations filed in support of it (Greenberg, 1998: 72, 86). From 1967 on there was a massive rise in Jewish support for Israel, and rising condemnation of "Zionism" as imperialism by activists of color and third world activists. In this atmosphere, many Jews who, like Melanie Kaye/Kantrowitz (1996), opposed Israeli policies found themselves accused of being self-hating Jews by Jews, and racists by anti-imperialists of color for arguing that Israel had a right to exist. The social space for progressive Jewishness on these key issues was small in the 1970s, and no doubt produced a fair number of vicarious Jews (Brettschneider, 1996). However, some Jews have struggled to articulate a progressive Jewish identity and to make space for it in the landscape of Jewishness.

In recent years, that space has grown considerably larger, particularly with respect to race and racism, though it remains considerably less so with respect to Israel.[1] Today, however, growing numbers of North American Jews, Richard Lee among them, are speaking out for peace, for Israel to withdraw from the West Bank and Gaza, including the Jewish settlements, and for the establishment of a Palestinian state in those territories. In his 2002 keynote address at the meetings of the Canadian Anthropology Society, Lee described Israel's systematic destruction of the infrastructure of Palestinian civil society, including its books and computers and the health and educational records they contained. He argued that willful destruction of a social infrastructure deserved to be considered a crime against humanity and for anthropologists to make that case.

In this paper I will discuss the ways North American Jews in the last decade have drawn upon a Jewish cultural heritage of collective memories—historical events, stories, and images—to explain, justify, connect to, or model specifically antiracist and progressive Jewish identities. Peter Novick framed his inquiry into the Holocaust as a study of collective memory. He points out that collective memory and a historical consciousness are almost antithetical. The former expresses "some eternal or essential truth about the group—usually tragic. A memory once established comes to define that eternal truth, and, along with it, an eternal identity, for the members of the group" (1999: 4). The collective memory of the Holocaust, as Novick shows in his book, remains a powerful organizer of a conservative Jewish identity and political performance.

Are there comparable collective memories that are shared among progressive and vicarious Jews—things by which they constitute, perform their political identities, things that at once distinguish them from and connect them to a larger palette of Jewishness? There are indeed. The story of the Triangle Factory fire has resurfaced in recent years to perform this role. Many young women garment workers died from the fire or from jumping out of the windows to escape it. The factory had no fire escapes, and the doors had been locked to prevent workers from leaving their machines. On a scale much smaller than recollections of the Holocaust, the story of the Triangle Factory fire is a collective memory, a constituent part of many Jews' repertoire of identities. It performs identity work in its present feminist telling when it is deployed to make the claim that part of an eternal Jewish identity is progressive—or, to paraphrase Gloria Steinem, progressive is what Jewish looks like. The gendered version of this story is also part of a larger discourse of Jews as workers who suffered in sweatshops, built unions, and fought for worker justice. This discourse is deployed to explain to non-Jews why American Jews, who are a pretty affluent bunch, have a "natural" solidarity with oppressed workers and with people who are racially oppressed. When American Jews perform this representation for themselves, it carries an additional prescriptive message—and therefore Jews "should" side with the oppressed.

This discourse is part of a larger conversation—often a debate—about the politics of being Jewish in a multiracial and racist society. By constructing the iconographic American Jewish subject as an oppressed woman worker, this discourse calls into question the ethnic authenticity of Jewish garment bosses, and by implication, challenges the icon of the upwardly mobile entrepreneurial Jew, and the Jews as model minorities. But it also sidesteps a confrontation with Jewish deployment of the Holocaust in support of conservative politics with respect to Israel. Jews fight it out in part with contrasting stories, contrasting representations and memories.

But not all stories and representations work equally well, and the sides are not equal—or even always clearly opposed. The struggle is a "war of position" in the sense that Gramsci used it to refer to the continual ideological struggle in which creating and deploying representations is part of a larger effort to transform a society's prevailing "common sense" into a revolutionary common sense. Images as images can be used in a variety of ways. But images have histories of use that limit the ways one can use them. For example, it is still possible to find a political mix of Jews, none of whom are working class, to identify with the image of Jewish garment workers, and to take political stands against present-day sweatshops that exploit Latin American and Asian workers even when the bosses are Jews. But even Jews who support a Palestinian state cannot appeal to the image of homeless Holocaust survivors to persuade other Jews to support that goal (although that image may now be gaining some purchase). The image of the Jewish worker has long been a staple of progressive and socialist Jewish narratives. The homeless Holocaust survivor has already been integrated into powerful narratives in support of Israel as a Jewish state. The power of a collective representation lies largely in its ability to perform identity work—to evoke recognizable and positive forms of Jewishness—for a broader swath of American Jews than those ideologically committed to the position. It is the "work" the representation performs, or that a variety of Jews perform with it, that gives it its hegemonic position.

Let me now turn to my argument that the work the feminist representation of Jewish garment workers has been doing of late, at least in Los Angeles, has been to carve out space for progressive Jewishness for men as well as women.

The story of the Triangle Factory fire has always been an important part of my (admittedly small) personal repertoire of secular Jewish identity. Together with stories about feisty young women garment workers, I have carried it with me to explain to myself why I feel connected to progressive (in the sense of politically left leaning) causes, from the civil rights and antiwar movements in the 1960s and 1970s, to more diffuse feminist, racial, and economic justice issues in the last decades.

The story of the Triangle Factory fire has also loomed large in progressive and Jewish circles in Los Angeles in recent years. For example, in the mid-1990s, Jewish members of Common Threads, a women's group supporting garment worker organizing in Los Angeles, and The Jewish Committee Against Sweatshops in Los Angeles often invoked the image of the 1911 fire in a way that merged it with images of heroic young women garment workers and union organizing. For the latter group, that connection was especially important in its support of the Smithsonian's controversial sweatshop exhibit hosted at the Los Angeles Museum of Tolerance. Interestingly, this was the only US museum to house it as a visiting exhibition, although it did so uncomfortably. In a similar vein, a 1998 Women's History Month program by the Feminist Center of the American Jewish Congress made the Triangle Factory fire its focus. Rose Friedman, then a 102-year-old survivor of the fire, spoke. Other speakers, including me, linked it to ongoing sweatshop issues and to Jews' historic responsibility to continue fighting sweatshops now as we had when sweatshop workers were predominantly Jewish. And in 2000, the theatrical fundraiser for the Sholem community, a progressive community of secular Jews in Los Angeles, "Bread and Roses," was described as being about "one Jewish family's involvement in American labor history, including the tragedy of the 1911 Triangle Shirtwaist fire, union organizing and in the garment industry, and contemporary labor struggles" (Sholem flyer).

Since the late 1980s, there also has been something of a mini-flood of books about the Triangle Factory fire. A search turned up some twelve books on the subject published since 1961. Several of the authors of these works report that they were told the story as children, and some of these indicated that they heard the story from survivors, their children or grandchildren (Bogen, 1993: 13; Goldin, 1992: 54; Stein, 1961: 217–18). Besides Leon Stein's important 1961 book and a 1971 children's story, the rest were published after 1983, with seven titles appearing since 1992.[2] Especially in the children's books and works of fiction that dominate the recent treatments, the heroines are feisty young women who tend to be unionists; additionally, unions are portrayed sympathetically as workers' weapons against such tragedies (Baker, 1999; Goldin, 1992; Llewellyn, 1986: 10, 35, 48). Embedded in these tellings is a moral lesson about American Jews' relationship to other ethnic groups in the United States: that Jews have an ethical responsibility to align themselves with the struggles of nonwhite peoples and the oppressed, even though American Jews are not now numerous among the economically or ethnically oppressed. Jews as a people have an obligation to fight for social justice—or this is what being Jewish should look like.

This is not the same moral lesson I heard in the story when my mother and aunt told it to me in the early 1950s. In the memory that remains with me, I picture my aunt Fannie or my mother taking me to the garment district on a day in Manhattan—for shopping and lunch at the Automat. They pointed out the Triangle Factory building and told the story of the fire, the locked doors, the girls jumping and burned to death, the greed of the garment bosses, the indifference of the city authorities. It was a vivid story, told as if they had been there, even though they were not. And either they showed me the wrong building or I confused the Flatiron Building at 23rd Street with the Triangle Factory. Nevertheless, the lesson I took away from this version is consistent with that of Leon Stein's 1961 book, that tragedy resulting from greed is the result of business left unchecked, and that impoverished Jews could not expect justice from the courts. Yet, despite the fact that Stein started as a garment cutter and went on to write for the International Ladies Garment Workers Union, there is remarkably little in his book about union struggles or heroic young women. This is consistent with John McClymer's observation (1998) that his documentary history was the first analysis to link fully the story of the 1909/10 "Uprising of Twenty Thousand"—the enormous and seemingly spontaneous walkouts and rallies by largely young women garment workers in support of unionization—with the story of the fire. It would appear then that the emphasis in the telling of this story has changed in the last several decades from one in which women are tragic victims of capitalist greed to one in which they are active fighters for social justice against that greed.

How do we account for the changes in the telling between the 1950s and the 1990s? And what is it about this story as it is presently told that makes it loom so large in the performance of progressive Jewishness? I suspect that the deployment of the linked stories of the Triangle Factory fire and union justice is doing important identity work in constructing a progressive Jewish identity.

This work is done among Jews, and by Jews, for an audience extending beyond Jews. As an example of the former, at the first meeting of the Los Angeles Progressive Jewish Alliance in 1999, Rabbi Steve Jacobs invoked the Triangle Factory fire to indicate Jews' connection to other oppressed peoples and our continued moral responsibility to economic and social justice. Turning outward to an audience that was not Jewish, progressive Jews (and others) used the example of the Triangle Factory fire as a prominent part of an occupational safety and health curriculum developed in the Labor and Occupational Safety and Health program at UCLA for working-class African American and Latino high school students. In a Jewish context, the shared memory linked being Jewish to experiencing oppression and the "natural" or consequent obligation to fight alongside anyone being oppressed. In a non-Jewish context, the work of the image was to explain to others why Jews, who are perceived as a particularly well-off group in Los Angeles, are likely to side with those fighting oppression.

The relationship between progressive Jewish identity and the Triangle Factory fire story also offers one answer to the "Jewish question" in post-World War II America: How have Jews reconciled their history of poverty and oppression with their present mainstream acceptance and affluence? What does it mean to be Jewish in a society that has accorded them the privileges formerly reserved for the white Protestant mainstream and has allowed them extraordinary economic success in the last fifty years? I think of this tension as wrestling with whiteness, an issue of some importance in recent Jewish critical scholarship. But why should the fire story, with its backdrop of working-class identity, resonate so strongly with today's Jews, to explain why they are (or should be) "naturally" progressive, especially about ethnoracial issues?

I suspect that it is the centrality of women in the story's telling today. More than victims, women are active subjects, fighters against their own oppression and that of others. Told this way, I believe the story makes a Jewish feminist bridge to other contemporary struggles. It is easy to understand why progressive Jewish women might embrace the identities presented in this story. Less obvious is what a story whose central characters are strong women does for the identities of Jewish men. To understand that, we need to examine the background from which it emerged—namely, the changing situation of Jews in postwar America.

Gender and Wrestling with Whiteness

Postwar America was good for the Jews. As I have argued elsewhere (1998), in this period institutionalized barriers fell in higher education, in many occupations, and in where Jews could live. Anti-Semitism fell from fashion (even as racism did not), and Jews were arguably embraced as one of America's most visible and favored ethnic groups. But postwar America was also deeply sexist. Its prosperity and opportunities were reserved for men. Women's prescribed access to the good life was through marriage.

Jews responded to this goodness in varied and complex ways. They seized them, but they also struggled to understand the meanings for their newfound success: Why us? How could one be simultaneously Jewish and mainstream American? In part because racial segregation in the United States remained legal and deeply institutionalized in practice, answers to the question of "why Jews" were racially charged, especially with regard to African Americans. And in part because white America in the 1950s and 1960s was deeply masculinist (more people probably experienced "traditional" middle-class patriarchal domesticity than ever before or since), the mainstream offered very different things to Jewish men and Jewish women. The active subjects—those who spoke publicly and wrote, and those about whom they spoke—of Jewish attempts to understand the secrets of their success were men. Jewish women appeared in their relationship to Jewish men, seldom in their own right. When Jewish men pondered the causes and consequences of Jewish success, they pondered it as stories about the virtues of Jewish masculinity and the impact of worldly success on men. Even if what was good for Jewish men was supposed to be good for Jewish women, it was far from clear even to Jewish men what was good for them.

An important celebratory story was told by an influential cohort of Jewish public intellectuals, including Nathan Glazer, Norman Podhoretz, Daniel Bell, and Irving Kristol. They updated and elaborated a theme in the American Jewish repertoire of identities that Jews were better Americans than mainstream white Protestants. The version prevalent in the early twentieth century stressed Jewish commitment to American ideals of democracy and social justice by pointing to Jews' antidiscrimination efforts in concert with African Americans (Diner, 1977). The version developed in the 1950s and 1960s created the concept of a model minority as an ethnic culture that has what it takes to help its members succeed in mainstream America. Jews embodied this model minority. In this case, purportedly Jewish traits of strong families, deferred gratification, hard work, and sticking together were deployed to explain—to Jews and non-Jews—the steep upward rise of Jewish educational and occupational attainments and income. Where the earlier story of Jews-as-better-Americans highlighted Jews' cultural passion for democracy, this story emphasized the Weberian connection between the Protestant ethic and worldly success for both Jews and WASPs. The moral of both stories was to urge mainstream white Americans to embrace and emulate Jews as one of themselves. The particular irony of the post-World War II version was that it persuaded Jews and non-Jews alike that Jews were exemplary Protestants, and that Jewishness was an exemplary cultural way to be white Americans. However, the ways in which the newer celebratory story explained Jews' extraordinary success in comparison to African Americans—linking persistent African American poverty to an inferior culture rather than to persistent and institutionalized discrimination—set the stage for conflict between the two groups and for tension between Jews and other peoples of color in the United States.

A different, less celebratory story that was deeply anxious about the negative consequences of upward mobility and patriarchal domesticity for Jewish masculinity was told by postwar Jewish writers like Phillip Roth and Herman Wouk. Were Jewish men losing their souls in the quest for material affluence and middle-class domesticity? By casting Jewish women as obstacles to Jewish men's ability to combine Jewish authenticity and mainstream affluence without pain, they ignited a gender war between Jewish women and men that continues to play a role in the formation of Jewish identities today.

Both the celebratory story and the anxious masculinist story (and the same writer might tell both stories) presented Jewish identities that were politically conservative by the racial and gendered standards of the late-1960s onward. To the extent that they were borne out in conservative Jewish politics, they explained Jewishness in a way that was conservative with regard to race and gender, and presented Jews to non-Jews in the same way. The celebratory story and its invidious contrasts have been keystones of Jewish organizational conservatism, including that of opposition to affirmative action. This much bigger story is beyond the scope of this chapter. However, it is worth noting that the celebratory embrace and presentation of Jewish identity as prefiguratively white, Protestant middle class, and as a model minority group has been an impediment to understanding Jewishness as progressive, especially when it comes to racial justice, by a non-Jewish, nonwhite public.

There was a gender issue as well. The virtues and rewards Jewish intellectuals claimed for themselves as good Jewish sons also depended upon showing how similar Jewish culture was to 1950s white gender ideals. What were the ways in which Jewish identity was presented as specifically male? What baggage came with those presentations? If Jewish intellectuals and artists embraced the models of male success, they did so with a strong dose of ambivalence about the masculinity it entailed. Jewish men's ambivalence revolved around the promise and the reality of patriarchal domesticity upon which so much of 1950s white masculinity depended. Norman Podhoretz analyzed the ways his childhood construction of African American men was implicated in his anxiety and ambivalence toward his own white Jewish manhood. Even as he appreciated his good grades and his mother's solicitousness, he wished he had the tough, independent masculinity of the bad black boys and feared being called a sissy.

Riv Ellen Prell has insightfully unpacked male ambivalence in Jewish fiction as being about the rebellions of Jewish sons against the second-generation, hard-working, middle-class breadwinning domestic Jewish life. Both Prell and Paula Hyman have analyzed Jewish fiction to show how Jewish men expressed their ambivalence about mainstream masculinity by projecting their anxieties onto Jewish women. In these works, Jewish women appear inadequate because they refuse to be self-denying mothers and deferential helpmates. Jewish women are presented as stereotypic mothers who henpecked their husbands and made their sons neurotic. Somewhat later, they became Jewish American Princesses (JAPs), defective lovers and wives who forsook Jewishness and sensuality for unfettered materialism—the crasser the better. They are also distinctly less up to the task than Jewish men of gracefully managing to combine an authentic Jewish soul with mainstream prosperity. The subtext here is that were it not for the inadequacies of their mothers and wives, Jewish men would have it all. Hyman argues that although the tension around assimilation was not new, its particular gendering was a postwar product. As part of their responsibility for preserving Jewish culture, Jewish mothers were supposed to make sure their sons became nice Jewish boys and married nice Jewish girls. But some boys did not want to be so nice and Jewish, and some even aspired to non-Jewish trophy wives as visible and seductive symbols of their masculinity and their success in entering the white mainstream. Prell argues that Jewish American princesses are Jewish men's projective nightmares about their own whiteness. Where Jewish mothers hovered and smothered and guilt-tripped their sons into forsaking the hard-earned pleasures of white middle-class masculine materialism, JAPs were the metastasizing cancer of that materialism. Perhaps they emerged a decade or two later because they reflected anxieties that came from several decades of life in mainstream consumer culture.

For Jewish women, the mainstream was even more of a mixed blessing than it was for men, since the rewards and their identities were contingent mainly upon their relationships with Jewish men. Regardless of how Jewish women felt at the time about the ways they were portrayed, their available responses were limited. Before the women's movement came along, feminist perspectives that asserted a woman's right to personhood over and above her relationship to fathers, husbands, and sons were not readily available. Absent the concept of a woman's entitlement to an identity in her own right, Jewish women had no social place from which to effectively critique Jewish misogyny. Instead they were constrained to talking back from within a male-centered framework. Thus, Zena Smith Blau (1969) defended Jewish mothers against negative stereotyping by inverting the stereotype: Yes, Jewish mothers controlled their sons through love and guilt; yes, this might make them neurotic, but this motherly control was also responsible for teaching the Jewish virtues that made these men so successful. Betty Friedan, author of the 1963 classic *The Feminist Mystique*, from which the rebirth of the feminist movement is often dated, was among the few women who did have access to feminist ideas in the 1950s. As a labor journalist for the United Electrical Workers, she knew about left labor ideas and women's struggles for equal pay for equal work. But she wrote as a white middle-class suburban woman, not as a radical, not as a Jew. For Friedan, as for Blau, there was no Jewish place to stand in which to engage Jewish misogyny. The anger and the desire to speak out is still there. When I spoke to a largely community audience at San Diego State University's Jewish Studies Program in 1999, women in their seventies still spoke angrily of Philip Roth's "male chauvinism," suggesting the longevity of the Jewish gender wars.

These linked stories, the celebratory and the anxious, are still with us. But the political context within which Jews are constructing their identities has changed. On the one hand, the celebratory story of Jews as model minorities has had by now a long association with conservative Jewish social politics, particularly around race. Peter Novick has argued that the story of the Holocaust and its "lessons" came to be used within this political field by conservative Jewish organizations in order to become players in a discourse of victim politics and to legitimate their opposition to such "special treatment" efforts. The power of the Holocaust, together with the almost canonical status of the Jewish success story, provided a framework for a hegemonic sense of Jewish identity that was fairly conservative and that left little space for American Jews to advance alternative politics as specifically Jewish politics, especially when it came to race.

On the other hand, the feminist movement opened up a conceptual and discursive space for Jewish women to critique the male dominance of post-World War II Jewishness and from there, to rethink Jewish identity more generally. Although Jewish women arguably have been overrepresented among feminists, specifically Jewish feminism has been a long time coming. It has only flowered in the last decade. Jewish feminist scholars, nurtured in women's studies programs and feminist committees of their professional associations through the 1970s, produced powerful critiques of postwar Jewish stories and identities in the 1980s and 1990s. They have also begun to recover and rethink the past to develop alternative stories that underpin new identities for Jewish women. Their work is restoring working-class Jewish women's personhood, agency, and sexuality. It shows their central roles in Jewish community, leftist and labor politics, as well as the historical persistence of Jewish women's voices and agency in popular culture. In the process they also have produced analyses that rehistoricize American Jewish culture. By so doing, they challenge the ahistorical "lessons" embedded in the old stories. They show us Jewish identities of the past that did not conform to the timeless ones presented in the Jewish stories of the 1950s and 1960s, and they help us to understand how and why the palette of Jewish identities has changed (among others, see Antler, 1995; 1998; Ewen, 1985; Hyman, 1980; 1995; Kessler-Harris, 1976; 1979; 1982; Moore, 1981; 1992; 1994; Orleck, 1995; Prell, 1993; 1996; 1999; and Simon, 1982).

When Lions Write History

The new telling of the Triangle Factory fire story embodies these feminist critiques, and by so doing may well be performing identity work about Jewishness in relation to the wider world, as well as about its constructions of womanhood and manhood. With respect to identity work around gender, the telling presents an alternative range of Jewish womanly virtues, such as assertiveness, dreams of personhood, sensuality, political entrepreneurship, leftist activism, and political theorizing, that figure most positively. As Susannah Heschel (1998: 113) has argued, Jewish women have a particular vantage point—as a minority within a minority. Where Jewish men may well have an outsider sensibility, it is largely one of memory; but for Jewish women, their second-class gender status within the Jewish community provides them with a lived outsider vision that helps to animate a progressive politics. By opening up Jewish women's identities in ways that emphasize social justice activism as Jewish, these tellings also give men a platform from which to rethink the repertoire of alternatives of Jewish masculinity embedded in the old stories—hardworking materialist and paterfamilias, or personally rebellious and somewhat irresponsible luftmensch. Neither the nice Jewish boy nor the luftmensch is an identity for changing an imperfect world. The representations and discourses of Jewishness surrounding the Holocaust and Israel present another range of masculinities. The discourse and politics of "never again" play off anti-Semitic stereotypes of effeminized Jewish men, and docile, timid Jews being herded to the gas chambers, the ultimate victim, the ultimate nonagent. The conservative discourse of "never again" organizes a wide swath of Jews around its message of military strength and evocation of the old counter-representation of muscular and male Zionism in the service of righteousness (or self-righteousness). Until the growth of the Refusenick movement of military reservists in Israel, this story was too fully occupied by the Jewish right to have room for a progressive Jewish masculinity to retell the story. However, Jewish feminists' reinterpretations of particular pasts have made progressive social activist identities visible and again available. As such,

112   *The Politics of Egalitarianism*

the story of the Triangle Factory fire may serve as a place for Jewish men as well as women to rethink the relationship of Jewishness to contemporary North American society. All these stories or collective memories are part of a larger dialogue within the Jewish community about the meaning of being Jewish today, about the nature of our connections, contradictions, and affiliations, about our commitment to social stasis or social transformation. In that dialogue, I suggest, stories and how they are told are part of the repertoire with which we think, that we deploy sometimes strategically, sometimes unselfconsciously. They are cultural tools, the dramatic repertoire of argument and display for reshaping Jewishness to adapt to changing times and changing politics.

Notes

1. Nevertheless, there were Jews who struggled to create a place within Jewishness to develop alternatives to the right-wing positions on Israel promoted by much of the Jewish organizational lobby and to make a place for Jewishness as antiracist in the wider society. On the early 1970s, see Porter and Dreier, 1973. More recently there has been much more critical Jewish scholarship on race and racism, and a rise in progressive and antiracist Jewish activism. A few examples include works by Melanie Kaye/Kantrowitz (1996), Marla Brettschneider (1996a, 1996b), Adams and Bracey (1999); Salzman, Back, and Sorin (1992); Kleeblatt (1996); David Biale et al. (1998).
2. A good bibliography of garment worker unionization and the Triangle Factory fire can be found in McClymer, 1998; 173–78. I thank Deborah Dash Moore for suggesting that I look at children's books on the fire. I conducted an online book search by subject and title words in OCLC, the University of California libraries, the Santa Monica and Los Angeles public libraries, and Amazon.com. Of twelve books, half were children's, five of the six published since 1989 (the sixth in 1971). Two were fictional, and two were poetry, leaving only two scholarly studies of the fire, one published in 1961, the other in 1998.

References

Adams, Maurianne, and John Bracey, ed. 1999. *Strangers and Neighbors: Relations between Blacks and Jews in the United States.* Amherst: University of Massachusetts Press.

Antler, Joyce. 1995. "Between Culture and Politics: The Emma Lazarus Federation of Jewish Women's Clubs and the Promulgation of Women's History, 1944–1989." In *U.S. History as Women's History: New Feminist Essays*, ed. L. Kerber, A. Kessler-Harris, and K. Sklar. Chapel Hill: University of North Carolina Press, 267–95.

———, ed. 1998. *Talking Back: Images of Jewish Women in American Popular Culture.* Hanover: University Press of New England for Brandeis University Press.

Baker, Kevin. 1999. *Dreamland.* New York: Harper Collins.

Bell, Daniel. 1964. "Plea for a 'New Phase' in Negro Leadership." *New York Times Magazine,* May 31, 11–15.

Biale, David, Michael Galchinsky, and Susannah Heschel, ed. 1998. *Insider/Outsider: American Jews and Multiculturalism.* Berkeley and Los Angeles: University of California Press.

Blau, Zena Smith. 1969. "In Defense of the Jewish Mother." In *The Ghetto and Beyond,* ed. Peter Rose. New York: Random House, 57–68.

Bogen, Nancy. 1993. *Bobe Maye: A Tale of Washington Square.* New York: Twickenham Press.

Brettschneider, Marla. 1996 a. *The Narrow Bridge: Jewish Voices on Multiculturalism.* New Brunswick: Rutgers University Press.

Brettschneider, Marla. 1996b. Cornerstones of Peace: Jewish Identity Politics and Democratic Theory. New Brunswick: Rutgers University Press.

Brodkin, Karen. 1998. *How Jews Became White Folks and What that Says About Race in America.* New Brunswick: Rutgers University Press.

DeAngelis, Gina. 2000. *The Triangle Shirtwaist Company Fire of 1911.* Philadelphia: Chelsea House.

Diner, Hasia. 1977. *In the Almost Promised Land: American Jews and Blacks, 1915–1935.* Westport: Greenwood Press.

Ewen, Elizabeth. 1985. *Immigrant Women in the Land of Dollars: Life and Culture on the Lower East Side, 1890–1925.* New York: Monthly Review Press.

Fell, Mary. 1983. *Triangle Fire: A Poem.* New York: Shadow Press.

Friedan, Betty. 1963. *The Feminine Mystique.* New York: Norton.

Glazer, Nathan. [1964] 1967. "Negroes and Jews: The New Challenge to Pluralism." In *The Commentary Reader.* New York: Atheneum, 388–98.

Glazer, Nathan, and Daniel Moynihan. 1963. *Beyond the Melting Pot.* Cambridge: MIT Press.

Goldin, Barbara Diamond, and James Watling. 1992. *Fire! The Beginnings of the Labor Movement.* New York: Viking.

Greenberg, Cheryl. 1998. "Pluralism and Its Discontents: The Case of Blacks and Jews." In *Insider/Outsider,* Biale, et al. 55–87.

Heschel, Susannah. 1998. "Jewish Studies as Counterhistory." In *Insider/Outsider,* Biale, et al. 101–15.

Honey, Michael K. 1993. *Southern Labor and Black Civil Rights: Organizing Memphis Workers.* Urbana and Chicago: University of Illinois Press.

Hyman, Paula E. 1980. "Immigrant Women and Consumer Protest: The New York City Kosher Meat Boycott of 1902." *American Jewish History* 70: 91–105.

———. 1995. *Gender and Assimilation in Modern Jewish History: The Roles and Representations of Women.* Seattle: University of Washington Press.

Kaye/Kantrowitz, Melanie. 1996. "Stayed on Freedom: Jew in the Civil Rights Movement and After." In *The Narrow Bridge: Jewish Views on Multiculturalism,* ed. Maria Brettschneider. New Brunswick: Rutgers University Press.

Kent, Zachary. 1989. *The Story of the Triangle Factory Fire.* Chicago: Children's Press.

114   *The Politics of Egalitarianism*

Kessler-Harris, Alice. 1976. "Organizing the Unorganizable: Three Jewish Women and Their Union." *Labor History* 17(1): 5–23.

———, ed. 1979. *The Open Cage: An Anzia Yezierska Collection.* New York: Persea Books, 77–104.

———. 1982. *Out to Work.* New York: Oxford University Press.

Kleeblatt, Norman, ed. 1996. *Too Jewish?: Challenging Traditional Identities.* New York: The Jewish Museum and New Brunswick: Rutgers University Press.

Kristol, Irving. 1965. "A Few Kind Words for Uncle Tom." *Harpers,* February, 98–104.

———. 1966. "The Negro Today Is Like the Immigrant Yesterday." *New York Times,* September 11. Available at: http://www.nytimes.com.

Kroskrity, Paul V. 1993. *Language, History, and Identity: Ethnolinguistic Studies of the Arizona Tewa.* Tucson: University of Arizona Press.

Letwin, Daniel. 1995. "Interracial Unionism, Gender, and 'Social Equality' in the Alabama Coalfields, 1878–1908." *Journal of Southern History* 61(3): 519–54.

Littlefield, Holly, and Mary O'Keefe Young. 1996. *Fire at the Triangle Factory.* Minneapolis: Carolhoda Books.

Llewellyn, Chris. 1987. *Fragments from the Fire: The Triangle Shirtwaist Company Fire of March 25, 1911.* New York: Viking Penguin.

McClymer, John F. 1998. *The Triangle Strike and Fire.* Fort Worth: Harcourt Brace.

Moore, Deborah Dash. 1981. *At Home in America: Second Generation New York Jews.* New York: Columbia University Press.

———. 1992. "On the Fringes of the City: Jewish Neighborhoods in Three Boroughs." In *The Landscape of Modernity: Essays on New York City, 1900–1940,* ed. David Ward and Olivier Zunz. New York: Russell Sage Foundation.

———. 1994. *To the Golden Cities: Pursuing the American Jewish Dream in Miami and L.A.* Toronto and New York: Maxwell MacMillan.

Naden, Corinne. 1971. *The Triangle Shirtwaist Fire, March 25, 1911: The Blaze That Changed an Industry.* New York: F. Watts.

Novick, Peter. 1999. *The Holocaust in American Life.* Boston: Houghton Mifflin.

Orleck, Annelise. 1995. *Common Sense and a Little Fire: Women and Working-Class Politics in the United States, 1900–1965.* Chapel Hill: University of North Carolina Press.

Podhoretz, Norman. [1963] 1992. "My Negro Problem—and Ours." In *Bridges and Boundaries: African Americans and American Jews,* Jack Salzman, Adina Back, and Gretchen Sorin, ed. New York: George Braziller, 108–17.

Porter, Jack Nusan, and Peter Dreier, ed. 1973. *Jewish Radicalism: A Selected Anthology.* New York: Grove Press.

Prell, Riv-Ellen. 1993. "The Begetting of America's Jews: Seeds of American Jewish Identity in the Representations of American Jewish Women." *Journal of Jewish Communal Service* 699 (2/3) (winter/spring): 4–23.

———. 1996. "Why Jewish Princesses Don't Sweat: Desire and Consumption in Postwar American Jewish Culture." In *Too Jewish?: Challenging Traditional Identities,* ed. Norman Kleeblatt. New Brunswick: Rutgers University Press.

On the Politics of Being Jewish in a Multiracial State　　115

————. 1998. "Cinderellas Who (Almost) Never Become Princesses: Subversive Representations of Jewish Women in Postwar Popular Novels." In *Talking Back: Images of Jewish Women in American Popular Culture*, ed. Joyce Antler. Hanover, N.H.: University Press of New England for Brandeis University Press, 123–38.

————. 1999. *Fighting to Become Americans: Jews, Gender and the Anxiety of Assimilation*. Boston: Beacon Press.

Salzman, Jack, Adina Back, and Gretchen Sullivan Sorin, ed. 1992. *Bridges and Boundaries: African Americans and American Jews*. New York: George Braziller and The Jewish Museum.

Seidman, Naomi. 1998. "Fag-Hags and Bu-Jews: Toward a (Jewish) Politics of Vicarious Identity." In *Insider/Outsider*, Biale. 254–69.

Sherrow, Victoria. 1995. *The Triangle Fire*. Brookfield, Conn.: Millbrook Press.

Simon, Kate. 1982. *Bronx Primitive: Portraits in a Childhood*. New York: Harper and Row.

Stein, Leon. 1961. *The Triangle Fire*. New York: Carroll and Graf/ Quicksilver.

PART II

The Kalahari Then and Now

Chapter 7

THE LION/BUSHMAN RELATIONSHIP IN NYAE NYAE IN THE 1950S
A RELATIONSHIP CRAFTED IN THE OLD WAY

Elizabeth Marshall Thomas

This paper concerns the relationship of the hunter-gatherer people of the Kalahari Desert, the Ju/wa[1] Bushmen or Ju/wasi, to some of the predators who also lived there, the lions. The observations derive from work done in the Nyae Nyae area of the Kalahari between 1951 and 1990, but mostly between 1951 and 1956, during which time I spent over two years in Nyae Nyae. Other members of our group were there much longer. No seasonal variation in the human-predator relationship was observed. The observations herein are mine unless otherwise noted.[2]

In the 1950s, as a member of the Peabody Harvard Southwest Africa Expeditions, I was privileged to observe certain groups of Bushmen including the Ju/wasi of Nyae Nyae as these people interfaced with the local population of lions. I had never before lived among either Bushmen or wild lions, and, taking the behavior of both for granted, I assumed that it typified such behavior everywhere.

Because the people had no protection against lions, I assumed that none was needed. The people slept on the ground, without fences or walls or large, intimidating fires, surely as our ancestors had slept ever since they moved from the forests to the savannah. If lions came to the

Notes for this section can be found on page 128.

120 *The Politics of Egalitarianism*

Bushmen camps at night, the people would stand up and sometimes shake burning branches at the lions. They would also speak to them loudly in steady, commanding tones, telling them to leave.[3] On most occasions that we observed nocturnal visits by lions, the lions stayed around for a short time, but soon enough they faded into the darkness beyond the firelight and then left, as requested.[4]

Nor did people take special precautions against lions when walking in the bush, other than to pay attention to their surroundings, as the Bushmen do anyway. If the people came upon a lion while traveling, they would move slowly away at an oblique angle and continue un-molested, on their way. The technique of moving slowly away at an oblique angle was not confined to people. On one occasion, a lion whom we encountered moved away from us in that manner—slowly, at an oblique angle.

In contrast to lions, leopards posed a real danger to people. Al-though during the 1950s none of the people among whom we worked was killed by an animal (although someone was seriously bitten by a poisonous snake), later on in the 1980s I learned of several people killed by leopards. I was present when a leopard attempted a nocturnal raid on a Bushmen encampment, presumably with a dog or a person in mind as a victim. Even so, the people seemed to have no special feel-ings for leopards, treating them as a dangerous nuisance; at the same time, though, they respected lions more than any other animal, even according to lions some of the same attributes they accorded to the //gauasi, the spirits of the dead. As during trance-dances, people in a trance would confront the //gauasi; so too would they confront lions, running out into the darkness while in trance for the purpose of en-countering lions, whom they would then vilify verbally. It was my strong impression that on these occasions lions were not actually pre-sent, at least not very often, but were believed to be aware of the trance-dancers just the same.

However, although the Bushmen treated lions as they treated no other animal, they also manifested so little actual, visible fear of them that they would sometimes take their kills. I witnessed one such occa-sion; when attracted by vultures sitting in a tree, a group of four Bush-men hunters went to investigate and found the red bones of a lion's kill (a hartebeest) lying near some bushes. They looked around for a minute or two. The lions were resting in the bushes and did not seem to notice the hunters. After brief consideration, despite the fact that the vultures were still in the tree, presumably in fear of the lions, the hunters simply walked up to the carcass and took it in an unhurried, deliberate manner.

In another instance, Bushmen hunters had shot a wildebeest with a poisoned arrow and were tracking him, but when they finally caught up to him, he was so consumed by the poison that he was lying down. However, a large pride of about thirty lionesses and a black-maned lion had found him first. Although the wildebeest could still toss his horns, some of the lionesses were starting to close in on him, watched by the others, including the lion, who stayed in the background. Seeing all this, the Bushmen approached the nearest two lionesses cautiously and very gently eased them away by speaking respectfully, saying "Old Ones, this meat is ours," and tossing lumps of dirt so that the lumps landed in front of the lionesses without hitting them. The two lionesses did not seem happy about this, and one of them growled, but amazingly, both of them averted their eyes. Turning their faces sideways, they soon moved back into the bushes. Eventually they turned tail and bounded off. Soon, the other lions followed them, and the Bushmen killed and butchered the wildebeest. (When twenty years later I naively tried the dirt-throwing technique to try to move a lioness in Etosha National Park, she stared at me with real hostility, and then, far from turning her face appeasingly, she charged me.)

In later years, John Marshall and Claire Ritchie (1984) made a survey of causes of death among the Bushmen—a survey that covered about 100 years and included about 1,500 deaths. Of those, only two could definitely be attributed to lions, and one was a paraplegic girl who, because she moved by dragging herself in a seated position, was probably in extra danger.[5]

All lion populations are not the same in their treatment of our species. On the contrary, in many areas near Nyae Nyae, including Etosha National Park, the lions indulge in occasional, opportunistic man-eating (several years ago, a German tourist became the victim of two lions who found him asleep on the ground near the tourist center). According to park authorities, the man-eating habits of the Etosha lions discouraged SWAPO guerrillas from entering Namibia through the park. In contrast, the lions of northern Uganda, terrorized by the Ugandan army, took pains to avoid people at all costs, to the point that they were seldom seen and were virtually never heard roaring. What then was the secret of the Bushmen and the lions sharing their land in their relatively pleasant relationship (which might best be characterized as a truce)?

Perhaps the single most important factor in this relationship was that, like all the other animals present, the Bushmen lived entirely from the savannah, without fabric or manufactured items (except that they were slowly replacing their bone arrowheads with arrowheads made of wire, which while being a change of material was not a change in technology, as the form of the arrows and the ways of using them remained the same). The people had no domestic plants or animals, including cattle and dogs. The importance of this cannot be overstated, as it kept the people on a more equal footing with other species. When in later years these very people acquired cattle and dogs, the relationship with lions changed markedly, as might be expected. The lions were seen, often rightly, as threats to the cattle, and the dogs did their best to keep predators of all species far away from the villages. The people were no longer what they had once been—one of many species of mammal of the African plain—but were an entity apart, complete with animal slaves and agricultural interests, all of which put them in direct conflict with many kinds of wild animals, but especially with the large predators.

But in the 1950s (perhaps not surprisingly, since both the people and the lions were midsized to large social animals and also hunters), the people and the lions had certain similarities, beginning with land use and group size. Bushmen grouped themselves into bands numbering about 15 to 25 people above the age of infancy (averaging maybe 22 or 23 people). These would be the people who lived together in one place at any given time, although they would have considered themselves as members of a much larger unit (in one part of Nyae Nyae, the larger unit consisted of approximately 150 people) spread over a large area. The concepts of territorial rights as visualized by the Bushmen have been dealt with comprehensively elsewhere. Suffice it to say here that these people believed themselves to control the area in human terms, so that residence rights were enjoyed by some, the "owners," but not by just anybody. On rare occasions—during droughts, for instance, when a few deep, permanent waterholes were the only source of water—large groups of people would assemble. Yet all these people would have the right to be there, the right having been acquired through kinship or marriage.[6]

In Nyae Nyae, many of the people we knew lived in places to which women had the primary birth-rights, or n!ore. For example, the n!ore for a certain permanent waterhole and the surrounding land with its hunting and gathering potentials pertained to an elderly widow, her two married daughters and their children, her married granddaughter, her two adult nieces (the daughters of her husband's deceased sister) and the children of these women, including the elderly widow's unmarried adolescent son. The women's husbands also had every right to live at this waterhole and were of course among the most important members of the group, but their n!ore was not for the same area. Their birth-rights were for other places, which they had left to join their wives. Similarly, the elderly widow's older son did not live at this particular site, nor did her nephew—the brother of her two nieces—although these men would, like their mothers and sisters, have held the n!ore. These men, both adults, lived elsewhere with their wives.[7]

The lions would have had a somewhat similar arrangement. Certain aspects of lion society that were not understood in the 1950s are widely understood today, such as the fact that a lion territory is held by a pride of lionesses, a pride that might be composed of related females—mothers and daughters, sisters, aunts, and nieces. This seemed not unlike the human arrangement. The males of the pride also bore a certain similarity to the human hunter-gatherer males. The young males, the sons and brothers of the pride members, stay with the pride until they reach maturity, at which time they disperse to find females of their own. Any adult males who may be present are not related to any of the pride members (except to any cubs they may have fathered) but have come from elsewhere to live among the females and to help defend the territory from rivals. (Here the similarity with people ends, as the male lions of a pride can expect eventually to be ousted by other males, who battle with them for the company of the lionesses. The winning males take over the females and their territory, sometimes killing the infants of the defeated rivals. The people of course do nothing of the kind.)

In Nyae Nyae during the 1950s, lions were normally seen in groups of five or six, but in the place we knew best, the area around Gautscha Pan, approximately thirty lions evidently owned the area with respect to other lions. On what seemed to us like rare occasions (such as the time, mentioned earlier, that the lions tried to take the hunters' wildebeest), this group of thirty would assemble in one place. No human being knew why this group of lions assembled when it did. But even when the group seemed to be scattered, the individuals appeared to keep in touch by calling and answering as they moved about at night. If strange lions had tried to occupy the territory, the resident lions almost certainly would have tried to drive them off.

Water was probably the single most important of the territorial requirements for both the people and the lions, and probably it was the water that held the people and the lions to their places. Unlike many other animals (most savannah antelopes, for instance, are water-independent), both people and lions need water to cool themselves, so a water source is especially important in a hot, dry climate. However, both species can and do live without actually drinking water, as each can get liquid from other sources—a certain wild melon, the rumen of antelopes, watery roots, and the like. But if people or lions are to get their liquid from such other sources, their groups must be significantly smaller. Lions living without water per se usually live singly or at most as a pair. The only group of people we encountered who were living without water numbered only eleven, about half the size of an optimal group. However, both lions and people, being social, vastly prefer the so-called optimal group-size. They have several likely reasons for this—both species practice a certain of division of labor, including team hunting, cooperative foraging, and cooperative child care. Territorial defense is also undertaken as a group activity, whereby conspecifics are repelled, probably more frequently in the case of lions. But there are historical instances where Bushmen drove off or tried to drive off strangers whom they perceived as intruders.

Lions and people preferred group life to solitary life, so in the Nyae Nyae area both species formed groups roughly similar in size, but not in number. A residential group of Bushmen would be larger in number than a residential group of lions, but more or less the same in mass. Counting everyone except nursing babies, I estimate the average weight of an individual in a group of Bushmen to be about 80 lb., and the average weight of a lion at about 300 lb., or in other words, taken together, each group might weigh about 2,000 lb. And this probably pertains to the meat requirement (if not, in the case of the Bushmen, to the total food requirement), in that a meal of meat big enough to satisfy a group of Bushmen would equally well satisfy a group of lions.

Probably for that reason, the hunting preferences of both species appeared to be closely related to group size. Both species hunted the same prey, with strong preference for large antelopes. Both species hunted in a very similar manner, the primary method being to stalk the prey, then strike. A few Bushmen hunters were also able to course game—one man in particular could and often would run down an antelope, traveling long distances just as African hunting dogs would do. Yet as far as the Bushmen were concerned, stalking an animal cat-style, getting as close as possible, then shooting it with a poisoned arrow, was by far the most common method of hunting. And just as the bow hunters needed to be fairly close to the victim, so did the lions, who struck by making a short dash of lightning speed, then leaping on the victim. Not having to course the victim, gaining no special benefit from poor physical condition on the part of the victim, neither the lions nor the human hunters made a point of selecting sick, old, or weak animals as prey. For a bow-hunter, the closer the target, the better, and for a cat (because they grow winded very quickly), the shorter the rush, the better. Therefore, all else being equal, when stalking herd animals as potential prey, both kinds of hunters tended to select the nearest animal as victim. And the distance that a lion can effectively rush is about the same as a bow-shot.

How can two species who are so very similar, and with such similar needs, habits, and methods, drink from the same waterhole and lay claim to the same territory without coming into conflict? The answer is that they lived in a manner that could sustain a truce, retaining certain lifestyle patterns, probably quite consciously. Most notably, they used the same area at different times of day, spreading out all over the area to forage for roughly twelve hours, and then retreating to a very small, restricted area to rest for another twelve hours. Because Nyae Nyae was at about 20 degrees south latitude, days and nights were about the same length, without pronounced seasonal variation. Thus, throughout the year, both species had equal time to forage. The people used the hours of daylight, and the lions used the night.

I think it safe to assume that the arrangement was intentional by both parties. It is true that people tend to be diurnal, and the Bushmen of course were no exception—they needed daylight to forage, but they virtually never went about at night for any reason, by which they were different from people in many other African communities who go about at night regularly despite lions and snakes.

As for the lions, we erroneously think of them as nocturnal. If they are, it is usually because their hunting lands have poor cover. Then, lions must hunt at night; if the grass is very short, they must hunt when the moon is down. But in the Gautscha area, the cover was such that the lions could have been active by day if they chose, just as some lions are elsewhere—in the nearby Etosha National Park, for example, and other game parks, where lions often hunt by day. We never saw daylight hunting by lions in Nyae Nyae. In fact, although we ranged almost continuously on foot and in vehicles throughout most of Nyae Nyae, where we frequently saw all the other fauna of that vast and pristine wilderness, we hardly ever saw lions in the daytime.

In any situation where animals avoid people, or where dangerous animals decline to attack or eat people, we assume that human technology is responsible. Fire and weapons, we think, will keep wild animals at bay. Not so. The Kalahari animals evolved in the presence of fires and are no more afraid of them than we are, and for an excellent reason—in the low-density growth that covers a savannah, wildfires do not get very hot and are not very dangerous. Midsize to large mammals pay little attention to them, stepping casually over the flames if the fire comes near.

Even so, it is often said that campfires discourage lions and other predators. And indeed, the Bushmen attributed much importance to nighttime fires and tried every day to gather enough fuel to last the night—something that the people did very purposefully and specifically. One of the stars was known as the Firewood Star, which, when it rose, would indicate whether or not a fuel supply was adequate. But the role of campfires in discouraging predators was mainly to cast light. If predators came, their eyes would shine in the firelight, thus betraying their presence, and the people could immediately take precautionary steps. One of these steps was to build up the campfires to cast even more light so that the people could spot all the predators, not just the nearest, but any that might be lurking in the background, too. Sometimes, as mentioned earlier, the people shook burning branches at visiting lions, but this was not so much a threat, not so much to say, "See this? I'll hit you with it," than it was a device to make the bearer seem more formidable. Virtually all other mammals, also many birds and reptiles, do something similar, such as raising the hair or otherwise puffing up to appear larger.

I believe there to be yet another reason why nighttime fires might have helped the people to avoid conflicts with predators. If the fires revealed the animals to the people, they also revealed the people to the animals. This could be very helpful to animals passing through the wide area near a camp that would be impregnated with human odor, which the wind would be carrying in all directions. Odor, while giving much information in great detail, would not usually be as specific as a sharp visual impression. Hence a campfire, visible from a distance, would be more reliable than odors. Any animal who wished to mind its own business and not get mixed up with our dangerous species needed only to keep away from the firelight.

As for the weapons, the Bushmen essentially did not have any. In places such as East Africa, pastoralists used to carry 10-foot spears and body-length shields to use against lions. But the Bushmen carried spears that were less than four feet long, perfectly adequate for their intended use—dispatching a wounded antelope who would not fight back—but very risky to use against a lion, because a Bushman's spear was about the same length as a lion's reach. A hunter could throw his spear from a distance, but then what? Unless he dropped the lion instantly—not an easy thing to do—his spear would be gone, and right in front of him would be an angry, wounded lion.

Then there were the Bushmen arrows, poisoned with one of the deadliest poisons ever known to humankind. A lion or anyone else shot with a poisoned arrow would most certainly die. Not from the arrow itself, which is basically a little dart too small and lightweight to cause serious injury.[8] The poison is the lethal factor, but the process is slow—one to four days, more or less, largely depending on the size of the victim—during which time the injured party could inflict a tremendous amount of damage on its tormentors. It is hard to imagine a worse scenario than a group of relatively defenseless people, without tall trees to climb, without protective clothing, without strong shelters to get into, without shields, without guns, without long spears, trying to cope with a wounded lion for, say, 12 to 48 hours.

Bushmen spears and poisoned arrows were surely not designed as weapons. Yes, they have been used as weapons, but so have pitchforks in the hands of embattled farmers. The Bushmen spears and poisoned arrows are essentially hunting tools, for which they are as elegant as they are well-suited. As weapons, they are second rate at best, no good for launching an attack or dispatching any enemy quickly.

They serve as a deterrent, however, and a powerful one. One drop of poison in the blood is certain death—there is no antidote. A poisoned arrow says, as clearly as a hydrogen bomb, don't mess with me or you'll regret it. Perhaps this explains why, unlike so very many peoples, African and otherwise, the Bushmen had no shields or any other item that could serve as a shield. In contrast to some of the East African pastoralists, for instance, who kept different kinds of spears and shields for different kinds of agonistic encounters (human or animal, alienated kinsmen or enemy tribesmen), the Bushmen preferred to conduct themselves in such a way that they did not need combat weapons. Their even-tempered manner and their phenomenal deterrent were enough. Many other animals behave similarly. Most animals, particularly the carnivores, practice all sorts of maneuvers to divert and allay aggression from conspecifics, and even from other species. And in fact, the Bushmen spent much of their time and energy in peace-keeping, with an emphasis on sharing—all to keep a lid on things.

In the 1950s, the Bushman/lion truce existed only in the interior of Nyae Nyae. It exists no longer, and even in those days it did not exist at the surrounding cattle posts such as Cho//ana and /Kai /Kai, where lions hunted the cattle and where people hunted the lions, or on the South African farmlands, or in most game parks. The truce existed only under certain conditions when a hunter-gatherer people had a technology so stable that they were integrated with the other resident populations (the Kalahari animals seemed to know the charge distance of a lion or the flight distance of an arrow, for instance, but they did not know the range of a bullet, hence they fell easy prey to anybody with a rifle) and when the people were without domestic animals. Cattle seriously interfere with indigenous populations of water-independent antelope, thus decreasing the lions' food supply, so that sooner or later, resident lions are almost forced to prey on cattle, which invariably puts an end to any human-animal truce. The truce also requires a lion population of high stability, where the behavioral response to human beings—a response that is handed down from generation to generation in lions and is not innate or genetically programmed—can be maintained. Many animals, lions among them, learn certain responses by watching their elders, but for this to happen the teaching tool—in this case, the hunter-gatherers—must of course be physically present. In nearby Etosha National Park, the human hunter-gatherers had been assiduously removed, so that a generation of lions grew up without ever experiencing human beings, except for the park rangers and the tourists in their cars. The Etosha lions were incredibly dangerous. Not knowing just what you were, they would go to great pains to find out, so that in certain areas of the park they seemed to be always sneaking around behind you, trying to catch you.

128 *The Politics of Egalitarianism*

Mainly because of the lions, all persons not associated with the park management were absolutely prohibited from leaving their cars, in contrast to the people of Nyae Nyae who, for as long as anyone could remember, perhaps for as long as human beings had lived on the savannah, lived in continuous association with lions but walked everywhere freely, and at night slept on the ground.

In Nyae Nyae in the 1950s, the lions knew about people. The people knew about lions. Their relationship was stable, as are those of many other species, and seemed to have endured indefinitely, perhaps for many thousands of years.

Notes

1. A word with many spellings—also Zhu/hwa, Ju/hoan, Zhu/hoan, and many more. Ju/wa is singular, Ju/wasi is plural. Some but not all of the people discussed here were Ju/wasi, so I include the terms Bushman and Bushmen, especially when implications go beyond any specific group.

2. The observations are drawn from my field notes and supported by photographs and films take by other members of our group. This paper is more or less a condensed version of Thomas (1990, 1994). I hope eventually to present the material in still greater detail in a book now in preparation, to be called *The Old Way*.

3. This, incidentally, is the recommended method for dealing with mountain lions in places such as the state parks and national forests in Colorado, where hikers may encounter mountain lions on the trails. One is advised to stand up (but never to squat or sit down) to make oneself look bigger by raising one's arms and if possible by holding aloft one's coat or camera, and to speak in a deep, commanding tone. The technique differs from the Bushmen's only in that the Colorado hikers are advised to say, "Bad cat! Bad cat!" whereas the Bushmen would address the lions respectfully, saying, "Old Lions, we respect you, but now you must go."

4. One night, however, a single lioness positioned herself between our camp and the Bushmen's camp (the two camps were about 50 feet apart) and stayed for about half an hour, roaring loudly and continuously at us. No one knew what she wanted, so everyone kept still, awaiting developments. Eventually this lioness left.

5. Additional lion-related incidents were mentioned in Marshall and Ritchie (1984). For example, they note that a man was killed by lions in 1980 (long after the Bushman/lion truce had come to an end). They also note a man who was mauled by a lion, supposedly in 1929, and two people who disappeared in the bush and were assumed, whether rightly or wrongly, to have been eaten by lions.

6. A detailed account of these people's territorial rights is offered in L. Marshall (1976: 71–79, 184–87).

7. N!ore is explained extensively in L. Marshall (1976: 184–87).

8. A Bushman arrow weighs about $\frac{1}{4}$ oz. and is shot from a bow with about a 25 lb. pull. To kill a deer-sized animal with an unpoisoned arrow requires a much heavier, longer arrow and a much more potent bow—one with a 50 or 60 lb. pull, minimally.

References

Marshall, J., and C. Ritchie. 1984. *Where Are the Bushmen of Nyae Nyae? Changes in a Bushman Society, 1958–1981.* Communication No. 9. Cape Town: University Center for African Studies.

Marshall L. 1976. *The !Kung of Nyae Nyae.* Cambridge: Harvard University Press.

Thomas, E.M. 1990. "The Old Way." *The New Yorker,* 15 October 1990.

———. 1994. *The Tribe of Tiger.* New York: Simon and Schuster.

Chapter 8

THE KALAHARI PEOPLES FUND
THE ACTIVIST LEGACY OF THE HARVARD
KALAHARI RESEARCH GROUP

Megan Biesele

Introduction: Activism as an Outgrowth of Long-Term Field Research

In 2001, Richard Lee and I wrote a paper for a volume on long-term ethnographic research (Kemper et al., 2002) entitled "Local Cultures and Global Systems: The Ju/'hoansi-!Kung and their Ethnographers Fifty Years On." In it, we detail research over five decades, a period that has seen the Ju/'hoansi drawn increasingly into the world system. Lee's successive editions of *The Dobe !Kung* (1984 and 1993) outline the challenges facing the Ju/'hoansi in these decades, including the demands of the cash economy, poverty, class formation, bureaucratic and media manipulation, militarization, and dispossession.

The responses of the Ju/'hoansi to these daunting challenges make a fascinating and encouraging story. By way of perspective on the changes that have occurred, I start with some recent news. On 28 March 2001, Telecom Namibia finished installing telecommunications infrastructure in Tjum!kui, Namibia, only some 50 kilometers across the border from Dobe, Botswana. Namibian President Sam Nujoma and Tsamkxao =Oma, first chairperson of the Ju/'hoansi's Nyae Nyae Farmers' Cooperative, spoke on the telephone that day from Tjum!kui to New York. Since then it has been possible for the Kalahari Peoples Fund (KPF) in the United States to have regular email contact with the

Notes for this section can be found on page 145.

Tsumkwe (Tjum!kui) Junior Secondary School and other entities in Tjum!kui via the Otjozondjupa Regional Council. Likewise, the world of electronic information on the Internet is now within the reach of Ju/'hoan students, leaders, and communities. This instant communication is a far cry from what Richard Lee would have experienced when he began his fieldwork in the area in the 1960s, when the turnaround time for a letter mailed from then South West Africa to North America took at least six weeks.

Starting with the Marshall expeditions in the 1950s and taken as a whole, the long-term research in the Dobe-Tjum!kui area contextualized and eventually documented the Ju/'hoan determination to take control of their resources, assert their political and human rights, and affect the way they were represented to a world largely ignorant of their way of life. As the Marshall studies were succeeded by those of the Harvard Kalahari Research Group (HKRG) and of the University of New Mexico Department of Anthropology, it became increasingly clear that integrated interdisciplinary research was the best way to encompass the complex and rapidly changing realities of Ju/'hoan life. Collaborative work on ethnography, ecological adaptation, world view, and acculturation formed the backdrop to a comprehensive understanding of both traditional Ju/'hoan lifeways and their role in ongoing internal and external negotiations.

History of the Kalahari Peoples Fund

When I began conducting fieldwork in 1970, I was privileged to work with Lorna Marshall and to be among the first wave of HKRG graduate students. Believing interdisciplinary understanding must prominently include the expressive forms through which people understand and comment on their lives, I convinced Richard Lee and Irven DeVore to include me in the HKRG. I have written elsewhere (1990; 1994b; 1997) of the way research in Ju/'hoan expressive forms led me directly to what the people were most enthusiastic about: their present problems and their future.

I discussed these problems extensively with colleagues in the field and on my return to Harvard in 1972, asking how we as anthropologists could hope to be of help. At that time I found in my graduate school few sympathizers (beyond HKRG colleagues) for my nascent activism, with the exception of those who founded Cultural Survival, Inc. Luckily, many of my HKRG colleagues had feelings similar to mine during their fieldwork. We all felt that somehow we must try to equalize our exchanges with the Ju/'hoansi, that somehow we must give back some compensation for the knowledge of their culture they had so freely given us.

In 1973, an opportunity presented itself to discuss this sense of responsibility that many of us shared. Lee and DeVore were at that time finalizing the manuscript of an anthology of HKRG work to be published by Harvard University Press (*Kalahari Hunter-Gatherers*, 1976). At the suggestion of Lorna Marshall, we decided to hold a book workshop at an inn near Peterborough, New Hampshire, and to use the workshop additionally as a retreat to discuss how our research group might redefine its role to address current Ju/'hoan issues. Out of these discussions came the idea of the Kalahari Peoples Fund, which was subsequently described in *Newsweek* magazine as one of the first people's advocacy organizations in the United States with professional anthropological expertise behind it. The attendees of the 1973 meeting at which the Kalahari Peoples Fund was formed were, besides myself and Lee, Irven and Nancy DeVore, Richard Katz, Marjorie Shostak, Melvin Konner, John Yellen, Patricia Draper, Henry Harpending, and John Marshall. Other supporters and colleagues included Jiro Tanaka, Mathias Guenther, Stewart Truswell, John Hansen, and Nicholas Blurton-Jones, all of whom contributed to the *Kalahari Hunter-Gatherers* book. Royalties from this book have been a small but steady mainstay for the Kalahari Peoples Fund for over twenty-five years and continue today, with the book now available only in electronic form.

The Kalahari Peoples Fund also received early funding from Lorna Marshall, through whose help it was established in 1978 as a non-profit organization. The late 1970s saw the beginning of a long series of KPF activities carried out jointly with the Ju/'hoansi, at first with those on the Botswana side of the international border with Namibia. From the beginning, KPF policy emphasized (1) carrying out only locally-initiated (rather than top-down) projects; (2) being available when needed rather than creating "make-work" activities; and (3) using all volunteer labor, so that every penny of earmarked funds went directly to projects in the Kalahari.

Most important in KPF's operations has been the continuous input of professional anthropologists in all phases of its activities. In recent years, as well, younger anthropologists have volunteered time to KPF, valuing the experience as part of their own training.

The Kalahari Peoples Fund and Collaborating Organizations

There has been close KPF participation through the years with local organizations such as the Nyae Nyae Farmers Cooperative/Nyae Nyae Conservancy; First Peoples of the Kalahari; and Ditshwanelo (the Botswana Centre for Human Rights); as well as with sister non-governmental organizations (NGOs) such as the Nyae Nyae Development Foundation of Namibia; the Kuru Development Trust; the Trust for Okavango Cultural and Development Initiatives (TOCADI) in Botswana; the Working Group of Indigenous Minorities in Southern Africa (Namibia and Botswana); and the South African San Institute.[1]

Since the 1990s, a series of papers (Biesele, 1992; 1993; 1994a; 1995; 2001a; Biesele and Hitchcock, 1996) given at the annual meetings of the American Anthropological Association detailed, along with the activities of collaborating organizations, the following themes in the Ju/'hoan and general San struggle to establish rights:

- Use of governmental land allocation processes to secure land, water and resource rights
- Defeat of "coercive conservation" projects such as game reserves that excluded people
- "Back to the land" movements by people who had been removed from their traditional areas
- Establishment of water infrastructure, cattle, and agricultural projects to secure land tenure
- Integrated rural development projects, including ecotourism, crafts projects, and other income-generation
- Promotion of community education projects in, and national policies favoring, the use of San languages
- Development of sophistication in the use of media and the establishment of a political voice in the national context

These themes have been closely linked in the histories of both Nyae Nyae in Namibia and the Dobe area of Botswana, as detailed in the following discussion.

Ju/'hoan Rights to Land, Language, and Political Representation

Like other indigenous peoples in the late twentieth century, the Ju/'hoan and other San have been gaining new ground in terms of land, language preservation, and political representation in the nation-states in which they live. In Namibia and Botswana, the Ju/'hoan San (also known as Bushmen, Basarwa) have been able to establish tenure rights in fairly sizeable blocks of land and to manage these areas themselves through government-recognized, community-based organizations. They have also been able to promote the teaching of San languages in village schools and to obtain political representation and have their political leaders recognized at both the national and the international levels. These gains have not been easy, but they do suggest that there is optimism for the Ju/'hoan and other San in the new millennium.

The Ju/'hoan (!Kung) San of northern Namibia and Botswana are some of the best-known indigenous peoples in the world. They have been the subject of numerous anthropological studies, films (e.g., John Marshall's *The Hunters* and *N!ai: The Story of a !Kung Woman*), popular books (e.g., *The Bushmen* by Anthony Bannister and Peter Johnson), development-oriented studies (such as John Marshall and Claire Ritchie's book *Where Are the Ju/wasi of Nyae Nyae?*), and children's books (such as *San*, a book I wrote with Kxao Royal /O/oo for US sixth-graders).

The Ju/'hoansi, who number some 15,000 in Namibia and 2,000 in northern Botswana, have undergone substantial social, economic, and political changes over the generations. One of the most important of these changes is the establishment of locally owned and managed community organizations that promote the interests of the Ju/'hoansi and other San.

In Namibia

The Nyae Nyae San development program in northeastern Namibia is an integrated rural development effort that began in 1981. Initiated originally as a "cattle fund" to provide Ju/'hoan San groups with livestock, tools, and seeds, it has grown into a multifaceted development program that is characterized by close cooperation between an NGO, the Nyae Nyae Development Foundation, and a community-based organization, the Nyae Nyae Farmers Cooperative, now called the Nyae Nyae Conservancy. A key feature of the program is the empowerment of Ju/'hoan communities through a bottom-up, participatory development approach.

In the early 1980s, Ju/'hoansi began to move out of a government-sponsored settlement at Tjum!kui in Eastern Bushmanland in order to reestablish themselves as independent units that supported themselves through a mixed production system of foraging, pastoralism-based agriculture, and small-scale rural entrepreneurial activities. The local organization also represented Ju/'hoan interests at the local and national levels. In 1983/84, the Ju/'hoansi and their supporters, including organizations such as the Kalahari Peoples Fund, were instrumental in lobbying against the establishment of a nature reserve in Eastern Bushmanland.

In 1986, the Ju/'hoansi of Eastern Bushmanland (now called Eastern Otjozondjupa) formed the Ju/Wa Farmers Union, an organization that assisted local people in raising livestock and conducting other development activities. The cooperative sought to protect Ju/'hoan land through lobbying at the local, regional, and national levels for their land and political rights. The cooperative later played a major role in the deliberations at the Namibian Conference on Land Reform and the Land Question held in Windhoek in June–July, 1991.

With assistance from a local NGO, the Ju/Wa Bushman Development Foundation (now known as the Nyae Nyae Development Foundation of Namibia), the Ju/'hoansi were able to set up new communities based on traditional kinship arrangements. By the time of the new millennium, thirty-seven such communities existed, many of them with their own herds and agricultural fields. The Ju/'hoansi have worked closely with the representatives of the Nyae Nyae Development Foundation and various aid agencies in locating and mapping the boundaries of their territories and in coming up with rules for how the land and its resources should be managed within these areas. They have also worked out methods for discussing issues facing local communities such as agricultural labor allocation, distribution of livestock, and maintenance of physical infrastructure.

The formation of the cooperative was the result of close consultation among local Ju/'hoansi, few of whom had much experience with setting up and running representational bodies. Initially, the Ju/'hoansi had open meetings in which literally hundreds of people participated in the traditional style of consensus-based decision making. Later on, the communities began to delegate some of the responsibility for attending meetings to specific individuals. Elections were held, and two representatives, known as "Rada," were chosen from each of the communities to take part in the co-operative meetings. Women's participation in the NFC leadership was encouraged actively by the Ju/'hoansi, and it was decided in the early 1990s that at least one of the Rada members from each community should be female. Ju/'hoan women and men alike have stressed the importance of maintaining "the health of the land" in northeastern Namibia. A potential environmental problem predicted by Namibian government planners was that the livestock owned by Ju/'hoansi would begin to have negative effects on the range in Eastern Otjozondjupa. Thus far, this has not happened, as herd sizes have been kept small through the Ju/'hoan recognition of range capacity.

The Ju/'hoansi have received assistance from various quarters, including donors in southern Africa, Europe, and North America. In the mid-1990s, the Living in a Finite Environment Project, a joint effort of the US Agency for International Development and the Government of the Republic of Namibia, began providing funds and technical assistance to the Nyae Nyae Farmers Cooperative to enable them to become self-sufficient. Emphasis was placed on social and economic development, as well as human resource development involving formal and informal education and training. The development workers used a variety of participatory development strategies, and the approaches employed have stressed communication and self-determination all levels.

The Kalahari Peoples Fund

137

Some of the activities of the Nyae Nyae Farmers Cooperative include seeking control over the land and resources of Eastern Otjozondjupa, promoting development activities, and taking part in land use and environmental planning with government agencies, nongovernmental organizations, and people in the private sector. The Nyae Nyae Farmers Cooperative acted as a corporate body in seeking to convince outsiders who have moved into the area with their cattle to move elsewhere. The Farmers Cooperative also collaborated with the foundation in seeking ways to promote better management of finances, fiscal policy, and human resources. Members of the Farmers Cooperative participated in studies and land use planning exercises (e.g., a conservation and development planning exercise conducted in early 1991 with the Directorate of Nature Conservation, an office now known as the Ministry of Environment and Tourism) that led to the formulation and implementation of recommendations on development and conservation.

The Farmers Cooperative was relatively successful in establishing a set of rules aimed at promoting conservation and sustainable development internally and preventing the overexploitation of local resources by outsiders. Its members sought to draw attention to issues relating to land tenure and resource rights at national and regional conferences (e.g., the Regional San Conference held in Windhoek in June 1992 and the meetings of the Working Group of Indigenous Minorities in Southern Africa, which was founded in 1996).

The Farmers Cooperative, now the Nyae Nyae Conservancy, operates as an independent body to consider public policy matters at its meetings. It undertakes trips to all the communities in the region in order to listen to the concerns of local people, and it provides them with information. It has raised awareness of political, economic, and environmental issues. It has its own bank account and runs its own shop and handicraft purchasing operation. Over the decade and a half of its existence, the Nyae Nyae Conservancy has evolved into a flexible, generally participatory organization for internal communication and external representation. No decisions are to be made without first seeking to gauge the opinions of the entire population. In some cases, this has meant that new projects have been held in abeyance until all communities could be contacted, a process that is by no means easy in a setting with thirty-seven different villages, dispersed across a 6,300-square-kilometer area of African savanna, with only sandy tracks connecting them. The advantage of this approach is that once initiatives are agreed upon, they have the full support of the Ju/'hoansi, who then play key roles in the projects' implementation, such as taking part in the construction of village schools and assisting in the formulation of curricula for those schools.

The Nyae Nyae Development Foundation has had an important impact in northeastern Namibia in terms of employment creation. Some of this employment was related to operating the Nyae Nyae Conservancy itself, which employs a number of individuals in leadership and administrative positions. Other than this organization, there are few opportunities in Namibia where San could play important roles in decision making and management. This has been particularly important for the status of traditional Ju/'hoan leaders. Formerly, the Ju/'hoan *n!ore kxaosi*, oldest men or women core-group siblings in whom stewardship of resource and habitation areas were vested, maintained coordinating relationships with other *n!ore kxaosi*, which involved balancing giving—and strategically withholding—key environmental accesses. With the independence of Namibia, both national and developmental expectations were that these leadership and resource management attitudes would vanish overnight and give way to smoothly functioning "democratic" structures and attitudes of commitment to the health of the region as a whole.

It was somewhat unrealistic, perhaps, to expect that Ju/'hoan leadership would rally without conflict to a regional or even ethnic cause. New Ju/'hoan leaders have been expected to transcend both the long-tenured social attitudes of their relatives toward non–self-aggrandizement and their own traditional altruism patterns as they have forged new public selves and organizational functions. Individuals have suffered mightily in this process, and communities' early faith in the new leaders was steadily eroded by seeing the widening gap between old and new social values.

Fortunately, this situation is changing. Part of the reason for this change is that the Ju/'hoansi have collaborated with the government of Namibia and various NGOs (e.g., World Wildlife Fund and Integrated Rural Development and Nature Conservation) in efforts to establish a conservancy, or an area of communal land where communities have control over natural resource management and utilization through a statutory body recognized officially by the government of Namibia. This conservancy, which was established in November 1997, was the first one established in Namibia, and has enabled the people to have greater control of what happens in their area. It has also served to instill new confidence and encourage new investment and entrepreneurial activities on the part of the Ju/'hoansi.

In Botswana

Similar changes are occurring on the Botswana side of the international border. The Ju/'hoansi of western Ngamiland realized that they needed to gain greater control over their areas in order to ensure long-term occupancy and use of the region. They chose to pursue this by participating in the Botswana government's Community-Based Natural Resource Management Program and by applying for rights over Community-Controlled Hunting Areas. In the mid-1990s, the people of the community of /Kae/kae, the largest predominantly Ju/'hoan community in Botswana, formed a Quota Management Committee as part of their efforts to gain access to the wildlife quota for NG 4,[2] a government-designated development area encompassing an area of 7,148 square kilometers. In October 1997, the people of /Kae/kae formed the Tlhabololo Trust, which applied for and received the rights to the wildlife in the NG 4 area. This trust engaged in a variety of activities, ranging from craft production to ecotourism. It has auctioned off a portion of its wildlife quota to a safari operator, who by the end of 2002 should have paid an estimated 2,500,000 Pula (about US $500,000) to the trust for the opportunity to bring safari clients to the /Kae/kae area. According to Charlie Motshubi, a representative of SNV Botswana (the Dutch NGO providing assistance to the Tlhabololo Trust), the people of /Kae/kae raised 40,000 Pula from hunting, 20,000 Pula from phototourism, and 20,000 Pula from craft production in the first year of operation.

Progress is clearly being made by the Ju/'hoansi as the new millennium starts, particularly in the areas of land rights, political representation, and cultural promotion. This progress can perhaps best be seen in the fact that today there are hundreds of Ju/'hoan children attending village schools, learning their own language, and hearing about Ju/'hoan customs and traditions from Ju/'hoan teachers. These activities, which were pioneered with Kalahari Peoples Fund input in the Nyae Nyae region of Namibia, are now influencing the ways in which rural development strategies are being implemented in Botswana, where the Kuru Development Trust and its offshoot, Trust for Okavango Cultural and Development Initiatives, both San-controlled non-government organizations, have been working with the Ju/'hoansi since 1998. Kuru, with KPF funding support, has assisted the Ju/'hoansi and their neighbors in Botswana in mapping their traditional areas and applying to the North West District Land Board for occupancy rights to blocks of land in western Ngamiland. Kuru has also assisted the Ju/'hoansi and other groups in institutional capacity building and economic development. The collaboration among the Ju/'hoansi, NGOs, and the international community will hopefully continue to benefit all concerned.

Namibian Ju/'hoan Land Tenure and the KPF

In Namibia around Independence, what proved decisive in the Ju/'hoans' process of establishing a national political voice was the excellent contact made between their organization, the Nyae Nyae Farmers Cooperative, and the South West African Peoples Organization (which eventually became the national ruling party). Relationships promoted by KPF and other advisers with party leaders who had returned from exile were key in allowing their participation in national life. Particularly important was Ju/'hoan participation in the 1991 Namibian Conference on Land Rights and the Land Question. As never before, the land needs and abrogated land rights of the Ju/'hoan and other San were brought before the eyes of a government in formation—one that itself was under international scrutiny. Gains made by the Ju/'hoan at that time laid the groundwork for the conservancy established in 1998. It also made provision for the safety of their range when, early in the life of the new nation, Herero pastoralists and their herds were repatriated into Namibia via Nyae Nyae. Today there are over thirty-seven re-formed and re-organized communities in Nyae Nyae, much like Australian Aboriginal "outstations," that form the basis for local governance via the Nyae Nyae Conservancy. Presidential and parliamentary awareness and respect of San land rights all over Namibia were given a great boost by the efforts of the Nyae Nyae Ju/'hoan. This entire process, in the decade following 1988, was perhaps the single most important contribution of the Kalahari Peoples Fund in Namibia.

Botswana Ju/'hoan Land Tenure and the KPF

In both Botswana and Namibia, conservancy-like bodies have been established and are acting as models for further community bodies. At /Kae/kae, Botswana, the Tlhabololo Development Trust was established, and the success of this comprehensive community project has been an inspiration for similar efforts at Dobe, some twenty miles to the north.

Dobe, of course, is the area so well studied by Lee and his students and colleagues. The KPF has been deeply involved in land-securing activities in Dobe since the mid-1970s, when KPF supporters and activists, including Lee, Polly Wiessner, Carl and Dr. Kathleen O. Brown, and myself, gave strategic help to the Dobe community to develop water infrastructure. The Botswana government's Basarwa Development Office, in its Ministry of Local Government and Lands, provided funds and hands-on assistance for excavating the hand-dug well that was to help the Dobe people establish security of tenure in the area. More recently, due to a "window of opportunity" in Botswana land allocation, as well as to unprecedented, generous international donations, KPF has been able to collaborate with the Kuru Development Trust and the Trust for Okavango Cultural and Development Initiatives to advance the land and resource control of the Dobe community as never before.

The project at Dobe today involves land use documentation, genealogical work and *n!ore* (resource territory) mapping, and makes direct use of several decades of anthropological research stemming from the original Lee and DeVore team in the area. It also uses the successful Nyae Nyae, Namibia example from the Nyae Nyae Development Foundation originally set up by John Marshall and Claire Ritchie as a "sister project" to the KPF. The success of Nyae Nyae in holding land was based on establishing water infrastructure as evidence of active land use and occupancy. As of April 2001, two successful boreholes had been drilled, and two more were in planning phases. In October 2001, Kabo Mosweu, Kuru's Team Leader in NG 3 (the Dobe area, Ngamiland), reported that consultations, permissions, and plans had been completed for deepening two more boreholes during 2002 and for beginning the same process for three more boreholes in the G!oci (Qoshe) area. Finally, community authority will eventually be established over NG 3. A large part of the support for this ambitious, but critical and timely, project came from the Kalahari Peoples Fund, with major funding provided by a consortium of information technology companies in Austin, TX. In December 2002, a well at Shaikarawe, Ngamiland, one critical to land-rights efforts in the surrounding area, was successfully dug by the Trust for Okavango Cultural and Development Initiatives thanks to KPF support.

KPF Activities

Mentoring and Publications

Best of all the news on this water-and-tenure project, perhaps, is that the two technical reports it has produced were written by local staff. In fact, a number of reports and papers by Ju/'hoan and other San individuals have emerged from the development mentoring and training supported by KPF and its sister organizations. KPF considers that publicizing these written resources and spreading knowledge of the conferences and other international venues at which San people have presented them is an important part of its work.[3]

A growing number of publications have been coauthored by San with academic colleagues (e.g., Biesele and /O/oo, 1996; Lee and Daly, 1999). Again, the KPF has taken a lead role in this desirable development, as well as in encouraging colleagues to designate San people or organizations as beneficiaries of publication royalties (e.g., Katz, Biesele, and St. Denis, 1991; Lee and DeVore, 1976; Schweitzer, Biesele, and Hitchcock, 1999; Beake and Biesele, 2002; Smith, Malherbe, Guenther, and Berens, 2000).

142   *The Politics of Egalitarianism*

Projects and Consultancies

Many of the Ju/'hoan efforts to establish rights and control resources were supported partially by Kalahari Peoples Fund contributions and volunteer efforts. Further, KPF's Ju/'hoan projects have successfully inspired neighboring communities in both Namibia and Botswana to start similar projects, and to apply to KPF for funding and advice. A list of KPF projects and consultancies related to land and community development follows.

Highlights of KPF Projects, 1975 to Present:

- Support of Ngamiland Research-Liaison Officer for Basarwa Development, Botswana
- Support of Ngamiland Agricultural Extension Officer, Botswana
- Brukaros Irrigated Gardening Project, Berseba, Namibia
- Rural Development Project, Manxotai, Botswana
- Women's Handicraft Grants, Central District, Botswana
- Community-based Educational Projects, such as Epako San Pre-School, Gobabis, Namibia; =Oenie School, !Xoo Community Marienthal, Namibia; Namibian College of Education Secondary Extension For Ju/'hoan San of Nyae Nyae, Namibia; Gqaina School, Omaheke Region of Namibia, San Language Curriculum Development; Moremogolo Trust, Bana ba Metsi School, Maun, Botswana
- Equipment and Uniforms for Nyae Nyae Soccer Team (Gift of Yo-yo E. Ma)
- Training for /Ui =Oma, Archaeology Laboratory, National Museum of Namibia
- Dobe Land-Mapping Project, Ngamiland, Botswana
- Okavango Sub-District Council, Community Action Planning, Dobe, Botswana
- Digital Photography of Lawrence Northam San Artifact Collection, College Station, Texas
- Shipping costs for vehicle for Regional Education Coordinator, Windhoek, Namibia

Highlights of KPF Personnel Research and Consultation:

- Impacts of the Tribal Grazing Land Policy on Peoples of the Kalahari
- Impacts of the Special Game License System on San Peoples, Botswana
- Provision of Technical Assistance and Information to Local-Level Resource Management Projects, Namibia and Botswana
- Documentation of the Formative Years of the Nyae Nyae Conservancy, Namibia
- Village Schools Project, Ju/'hoan Orthography, Curriculum Development, Nyae Nyae, Namibia

The Kalahari Peoples Fund

Current Activities of KPF

The current mission of the Kalahari Peoples Fund, stated broadly, is to benefit the San and other peoples of the Kalahari region. It works through local NGOs in Botswana, Namibia, and the semi-arid regions of surrounding countries, responding to locally initiated requests for development aid. KPF raises funds and provides technical and advisory assistance, principally in the areas of community-based education and land and resource rights. Most critical in its mission are progress in education, human rights, development, land-use planning, and institution building, all with professional anthropological input, on the local, national, and international levels.

One current project, promotion of community-based, San-language education initiatives, is rooted in work begun by KPF anthropologists and linguists over fifteen years ago. KPF is currently developing and helping to implement an interlocking set of proposals for comprehensive coverage of projects requested by San communities, ranging from preschools to help develop a culture of literacy to collaborative development of appropriate and effective curriculum materials in San languages. Both preschool and literacy materials development in the Ju/'hoan-speaking areas of Nyae Nyae, Namibia, and Omaheke are proceeding with the close cooperation of the Namibian National Institute for Educational Development.

Since 1999, KPF's website (http://www.kalaharipeoples.org) has served as a channel of communication between rural southern African peoples and the wider world, bringing information about their cultures and their needs to interested individuals, groups, and agencies who are able to help them. It also acts as an online resource for students, researchers, and the general public who wish to learn more about the San and their neighbors. It contains an extensive outline of scholarly articles, maps, and recent updates about the people, along with information about current projects, needs, and volunteer opportunities.

Since 2001 KPF has published a newsletter that features headline sections of late-breaking news on the situations of indigenous peoples in the several countries of the Kalahari, information about progress and needs for KPF projects, updates on regional organizations and listings of books and films.

KPF Sponsorship

In 2001, KPF gained two corporate sponsors, each manufacturing and distributing a Kalahari-related product. The first, the London-based Redbush Tea Company, agreed to dedicate a portion of the income from its organic herbal tea, which is native to southern Africa, to KPF. The second is Kalahari Limited in Atlanta, GA, which makes a number of flavors of rusks, which are familiar to all who have spent time in the Kalahari as a durable and delicious form of desert bread, as well as the rooibos tea now being successfully marketed as "Red Tea" in the United States.

Through the years, the KPF has been sustained financially by a few grants and many donations from individuals. Several individual donors must be recognized for their outstanding generosity, some contributing over US $50,000. They include Lorna J. Marshall, Carl and Dr. Kathleen O. Brown, Lawrence W. Northam, and Steve Smaha and Jessica Winslow. Such donations have enabled the KPF to invest a portion of its funds to ensure ongoing support for Kalahari projects, which is particularly important in the case of community education initiatives. In 2005, an anonymous US foundation gave KPF a matching grant, its first grant dedicated solely to operations, so that KPF's ongoing projects can function more effectively.

KPF volunteers have centered their activities in recent years on the day-to-day work at the organization's current US base in Austin, Texas. Volunteers have included anthropology students, electronic engineers, teachers, freelance editors, human rights activists, a nurse, and an accountant.

Affiliated projects include The University Centre for Studies in Namibia; Monday's Child Productions (promoting international storytelling); the Pilgrim Society (development projects in Nyae Nyae); and Deep Roots (local language survival and literacy).

New KPF projects, and those with ongoing needs, include the following:

- Epako San Pre-School and Hospital Playgroup, Gobabis, Namibia
- Gqaina School, San Language Curriculum Development, Omaheke Region of Namibia
- Strategic Support and Infrastructure for Land Claims, NG3 (Dobe Area, Botswana)
- Development of Elementary Ju/'hoan Readers for Tjum!kui School, Otjozondjupa, Namibia
- Provision of Computers for Tjum!kui School, Otjozondjupa, Namibia
- Addressing Problems of San in Formal Education Systems (Conferencing and Publications)
- Youth Community Theater Project in Nyae Nyae

Conclusion: An Activist Legacy

Throughout the 1950s and 1960s, the Marshall family and the Harvard Kalahari Research Group carried out research with San peoples that has become part of the ethnographic canon. These scholars joined the mass media in documenting what in those decades seemed a remote, exotic way of life. Today, the indigenous peoples of the Kalahari are remote and untouched only in our dreams (and in bad books and films). The achievement of organizations like the Kalahari Peoples Fund has been to bridge two worlds that a quarter of a century ago seemed impossibly distant from each other: the world of representation "about" these anthropological "others" and the world of hands-on involvement in their own bid for autonomy and human rights. The challenge in making this bridge has been to bring the two halves of the San image together, the "romantic" with the "revisionist," for a centered, contemporary picture of real people "just living their lives."

The Kalahari Peoples Fund has found that the best way for anthropologists to help center the image is to find ways for Ju/'hoan voices themselves to speak to the public. KPF's long-term work, based in its professional beginnings as a research group, has demonstrated the ability to contextualize San voices for public comprehension—to give faces and nuanced descriptions to the attempt to communicate contemporary San issues. As the Ju/'hoan and other San have come to political consciousness, groups like the KPF have been able to observe and document their emerging determination to take hold of their destiny. It has been possible to see, from HKRG and KPF work, how the imperatives and assumptions of their earlier lifeways have shaped both their assertion of rights and some of the problems they have experienced in assuming them.

Most recently, KPF members, like other activists the world over, have been met with the challenge of letting go of helping roles once they are no longer necessary. In this, the anthropologists can take precious pages from the notebooks of development workers, many of whom faced this challenge earlier. Believing that "letting go" does not mean ceasing to pay attention, KPF's activism strives to create a more centered image for anthropologists as well, one in which they themselves are people "just living their lives," collaborating now for global understanding with the San people they have come to know through joint endeavors as well as through study.

Notes

1. Documentation of the interactions among these organizations has been carried out by Robert K. Hitchcock and several coauthors (1997; 1999; 2000; 2001; Hitchcock and Murphree, 1998) and in publications coauthored by Lee and myself (2001), and by Richard Katz, Verna St. Denis, and myself (1997).

146   *The Politics of Egalitarianism*

2. NG 4 stands for the 4th Community Controlled Hunting Area in Ngamiland, North West District, Botswana. Each district in Botswana is divided into zones for planning and wildlife utilization and conservation purposes. NG 4 has been designated as being community-controlled, one of seven such Controlled Hunting Areas. Other such areas are designated for purposes of (1) safari hunting, (2) photographic safaris, (3) citizen hunting, (4) multipurpose, (5) conservation (e.g., the Tsodilo Hills, which has been proposed as a World Heritage Site and which is a national monument under the National Monuments and Relics Act). NG 5, to the south of NG 4, does not have a village. The community of /Kae/kae has rights to make decisions in both areas, although there is pressure to turn NG 5 into a multipurpose area that will allow the expansion of livestock (and ranches) into the area.
3. See Arnold, 1998; Gaeses, 1998; Naude, 2001; /Useb, 2000, 2001; =Oma and Broermann, 1998; and =Oma and Thoma, 1998.

References

=Oma, Kxao Moses, and Magdalena Broermann. 1998. "Do the San of Southern Africa Have a Say on Education?" Paper presented at the 16th Session of the United Nations Working Group on Indigenous Peoples, Geneva, 27–31 July.

=Oma, Kxao Moses, and Axel Thoma. 1998. "Does Tourism Support or Destroy the Indigenous Cultures of the San?" Paper presented at the Workshop on Tourism and Indigenous Peoples, Geneva, 28 July.

/Useb, Joram. 2000. "'One Chief is Enough!' Understanding San Traditional Authorities in the Namibian Context." Paper presented at the conference Africa's Indigenous People: "First People" or "Marginalised Minorities?" Center for African Studies, University of Edinburgh, 24–25 May.

———. 2001. "Indigenous People and Development." Address to the 19th Session of the United Nations Working Group of Indigenous Peoples, Geneva, 23–27 July.

Arnold, John. 1998. *A San Development Initiative: The Omatako Valley Rest Camp.* Windhoek, Namibia: Working Group of Indigenous Minorities in Southern Africa.

Bannister, Anthony, and Peter Johnson. 1980. *The Bushmen.* London: Chartwell Books.

Beake, Lesley and Megan Biesele. 2002. *Waiting for Rain: The Story of a Kalahari Village.* Stars of Africa Series. Cape Town: Maskew Miller Longmans.

Biesele, Megan. 1990. *Shaken Roots: Bushmen of Namibia Today.* With photographs by Paul Weinberg. Johannesburg: Environmental Development Agency.

———. 1992. "Integrated Environmental Development in Namibia: The Case of the Ju/'hoan Bushmen." Paper presented at the 91st Annual Meeting of the American Anthropological Association, San Francisco.

———. 1993. "Eating Crow in the Kalahari: Leveling Lessons Taught by the Ju/'hoan Bushmen to their NGO." Paper presented at the 92nd Annual Meeting of the American Anthropological Association, Washington D.C.

———. 1994a. "Human Rights and Democratization in Namibia: Some Grassroots Political Perspectives." African Rural and Urban Studies, 1(2): 49–72.

————. 1994b. "The Ju/'hoan Bushmen Under Two States: Impacts of the South West African Administration and the Government of the Republic of Namibia." Proceedings of the Seventh International Conference on Hunting and Gathering Societies, Moscow, Russia, August 1993.

————. 1995. "Governmental and Non-Governmental Development Policies in Namibia and Their Impact on the Reproduction of Ju/'hoan Social Equity." Paper presented at the 94th Annual Meeting of the American Anthropological Association, Washington, D.C.

————. 1997. "Idioms of Identity: Ju/'hoan-Language Political Rhetoric 1987–1993." Paper prepared for the conference Hunter-Gatherers in Transition: Language, Identity, and Conceptualization among the Khoisan, St. Augustin, Germany (Institut fuer Afrikanistik, University of Cologne, Germany), 5–8 January.

————. 2001a. "Ju/'hoan San Language Rights and Minority Education in Southern Africa." Paper presented at the 100th Annual Meeting of the American Anthropological Association, Washington D. C.

————. 2001b. "Establishing Rights to Land, Language and Political Representation: The Ju/'hoansi San at the Millennium." In *Spuren des Regenbogens/ Tracing the Rainbow: Art and Life in Southern Africa.* Oberoesterreichisches Landesmuseum, Linz, Austria: Arnoldsche.

Biesele, Megan, and Kxao Royal /O/oo. 1996. *San.* Heritage Library of African Peoples, ed. George Bond. New York: Rosen.

Biesele, Megan, and Robert K. Hitchcock. 1996. "Two Kinds of Bioscope: Practical Community Concerns and Ethnographic Film in Namibia." Paper presented at 95th Annual Meeting of the American Anthropological Association. San Francisco.

Biesele, Megan, Robert K. Hitchcock, and Richard B. Lee. 1996. "Thirty Years of Ethnographic Research among the Ju/'hoansi of Northwestern Botswana: 1963–1993." In *Botswana Notes and Records,* 28. Gaborone, Botswana.

Gaeses, Elfriede. 1998. "Violence against San Women." Paper prepared for the First African Indigenous Women's Conference. Agadir, Morocco. 20–24 April.

Hitchcock, Robert K. 1997. "Cultural, Environmental, and Economic Impacts of Tourism among Kalahari Bushmen." In *Tourism and Culture: An Applied Perspective,* ed. Erve Chambers. Albany: State University of New York Press.

————. 1999. "Organizations Devoted to Assisting Southern African San." In *Indigenous Peoples' Consultation: Report on an Indigenous Peoples' Consultation on Empowerment, Culture, and Spirituality in Community Development,* ed. Ruud van Trijp and Otto Oussoren. Ghanzi, Botswana: Kuru Development Trust and Working Group of Indigenous Minorities in Southern Africa.

————. 2000. "People of the Two-Way River: Socioeconomic Change and Natural Resource Management in the Nata River Region of Southern Africa." *Botswana Notes and Records,* 32. Gaborone, Botswana.

————. 2001. "Decentralization, Development, and Natural Resource Management in the Northwestern Kalahari Desert, Botswana." In *Shifting the*

Power: Decentralization and Biodiversity Conservation, ed. Barbara Wyckoff-Baird et al. Washington, D.C.: Biodiversity Support Program.

Hitchcock, Robert K., and Marshall W. Murphree. 1998. "The Kxoe of West Caprivi, Namibia: Conflicts over Land, Resource Rights, and Development." *Indigenous Affairs* 4.

Katz, Richard, Megan Biesele, and Verna St. Denis. 1991. *Healing Makes Our Hearts Happy: Spirituality and Transformation among the Ju/'hoansi of the Kalahari.* Rochester, VT: Inner Traditions International.

Lee, Richard B. 1984. *The Dobe !Kung.* 1st ed. Fort Worth: Harcourt Brace.

———. 1993. *The Dobe Ju/'hoansi,* 2d ed. Fort Worth: Harcourt Brace.

Lee, Richard B., and Megan Biesele. 2002. "Local Cultures and Global Systems: The Ju/'hoansi-!Kung and their Ethnographers Fifty Years On." In *Chronicling Cultures: Long-Term Field Research in Anthropology,* ed. Robert V. Kemper and Anya P. Royce. Walnut Creek, Calif.: Altamira Press.

Lee, Richard B., and Richard Daly, ed. 1999. *The Cambridge Encyclopedia of Hunters and Gatherers.* Cambridge: Cambridge University Press.

Lee, Richard B., and Irven DeVore, ed. 1976. *Kalahari Hunter-Gatherers: Studies of the !Kung San and Their Neighbors.* Cambridge: Harvard University Press.

Marshall, John, and Claire Ritchie. 1984. *Where are the Ju/wasi of Nyae Nyae? Changes in a Bushman Society, 1958–1981.* Cape Town: Centre for African Studies.

Naude, David. 2001. Address to delegates at the Regional San Education Conference, Okahandja, Namibia, 7–11 May.

Schweitzer, Peter P., Megan Biesele, and Robert K. Hitchcock, ed. 1999. *Hunters and Gatherers in the Modern World: Conflict, Resistance, and Self-Determination.* New York: Berghahn Press.

Smith, Andy, Candy Malherbe, Matt Guenther, and Penny Berens. 2000. *The Bushmen of Southern Africa: A Foraging Society in Transition.* Cape Town: David Philip/Athens, Ohio: Ohio University Press.

Thoma, Axel. 1998. "The San's Struggle to Participate in Directing Tourism Development." *Contours* 8 (3–4): November.

Chapter 9

LAND, LIVESTOCK, AND LEADERSHIP AMONG THE JU/'HOANSI SAN OF NORTH-WESTERN BOTSWANA

Robert K. Hitchcock

Many of the problems facing indigenous peoples today are the result of global processes, especially the expansion of economic development and the international trade of goods and services (Bodley, 1999; Gedicks, 2001; Maybury Lewis, 1997). In the face of competition for land and resources, and, in some cases, lack of recognition by nation-states of minority peoples' rights, indigenous peoples in various parts of the world have sought to claim ancestral territories and assert what they see as their basic human rights (Anaya, 1996; Durning, 1992; Hitchcock, 1994; Hodgson, 2002). In some parts of the world, such as Australia, New Zealand, and Canada, indigenous peoples have made some progress in recent years in obtaining land and resource rights (Fleras and Elliott, 1992; Young, 1995).

In Africa, peoples who define themselves as indigenous, such as the San of southern Africa and the Pygmies (Batwa) of central Africa, have generally had difficulties in obtaining legal rights to land and resources (Barnard and Kenrick, 2001; Veber, Dahl, Wilson and Waehle, 1993).

The indigenous peoples of southern Africa have utilized a variety of means to obtain land and resource rights, including lobbying government officials, often to little avail, and engaging in direct action. Their

Note for this section can be found on page 157.

efforts to lay claim to ancestral territories on the basis of "indigenous-ness," the notion that San peoples were "first comers" or were "native to the areas where they lived," have often received negative responses from the governments of African nation-states (Barnard and Kenrick, 2001; Saugestad, 2001). In 1997, the Hai//om San of Namibia block-aded the entrance into Etosha National Park in Namibia in order to bring national and international attention to their desire to reclaim their ancestral lands, which they had lost in the late nineteenth and early twentieth centuries (Dieckmann, 2001: 142). The only indige-nous peoples in Namibia who have been able to obtain some degree of control over a portion of their ancestral lands are the Ju/'hoansi, who in 1998 were able to establish what in Namibia is known as a conser-vancy, an area of communal land within which residents have the rights to resources and the economic benefits that derive from those resources (Biesele and Hitchcock, 2000; Hitchcock, Yellen, Gelburd, Osborn and Crowell, 1996). The approximately 1,800 Ju/'hoansi San of Botswana, on the other hand, have not been able to obtain secure land and re-source tenure rights. The reasons for this situation are complex, but they are due in part to the fact that the Botswana government (Africa's old-est democracy and the home to some 47,675 people who define them-selves as San or Barsarwa [Suzman, 2001]) has been unwilling to grant land rights to groups who make claims on the basis of custom-ary rights and traditional livelihoods (Hitchcock, 2002a; Wily, 1979).

This article examines the recent and contemporary ethnographic and political situations of the Ju/'hoansi San of Botswana, and it ad-dresses the complex issues surrounding land and resource rights. It draws upon the detailed work of Richard Lee and the Harvard Kala-hari Research Group and other social and natural scientists and devel-opment personnel who have worked with the Ju/'hoansi in north-western Botswana (Hitchcock et al., 1996; Lee, 1979; 2003; Lee and DeVore, 1976; Wilmsen, 1989). I pay particular attention to the Ju/'hoansi residing in two communities in the North West District (Ngamiland) of Botswana, XaiXai (/Ai/Ai), and Dobe. The article concludes that, al-though the Ju/'hoansi of Botswana have yet to obtain secure de jure legal rights to land and resources, they have made some progress toward gain-ing de facto control over the areas in which they reside. The Ju/'hoansi have been able to do this through the use of some innovative strategies and through building coalitions with other groups and organizations.

The Ju/'hoansi San of North-Western Botswana

The Ju/'hoansi (San) have been described in the past as hunters and gatherers. Today, they live settled lives usually near water points and

Land, Livestock, and Leadership 151

have diversified economic systems that combine some foraging with food production, cash earned through jobs and the sales of crafts and other goods, and, in some cases, dependence on food relief and cash provided by the nation-states in which they reside. While some Ju/'hoansi reside on freehold (private) farms belonging to other people, others live in villages and in small decentralized communities spread across portions of the northern Kalahari savanna (Biesele and Hitchcock, 2000; Lee, 2003). In Botswana, virtually all of the Ju/'hoansi reside in communities that include people from other groups, notably Herero (Mbanderu), Tawana,[1] and Hambukushu, all of whom are agropastoralists who speak Bantu languages. These communities range in size from several families to several hundred people. The Ju/'hoansi spend the majority of the year in these settlements, ranging out for brief periods in the rainy season to stay at places where water has accumulated so that they can collect wild foods and, as they put it, "get away from all the noise of the settlements." Some of this noise, they note, derives from the lowing of cattle and the sounds of goats, donkeys, and chickens that people keep near their homes.

In the past, the Ju/'hoansi lived in bands—groups of people who were tied together through kinship, marriage, friendship, and reciprocal economic exchange systems—that numbered between twenty-five and fifty people (Lee, 1979; 2003; Marshall, 1976). Leadership of these bands was relatively diffuse, and decision making was based on consensus. In recent years, Ju/'hoan headmen have begun to be recognized in Botswana, and Ju/'hoansi have become part of village development committees and other local institutions.

A relatively small proportion of the Ju/'hoansi in north-western Botswana have been able to build up sufficient livestock numbers to be self-sufficient. And even these people have faced major constraints, one example being outbreaks of livestock diseases, the worst being the spread of Contagious Bovine Pleuropneumonia (Hitchcock, 2002b; Hitchcock et al., 1996) that led the government to slaughter all cattle in the North West District in 1996. Since that time, the Ju/'hoansi and their neighbors have attempted to reestablish their herds, but most of them have yet to reach the numbers that they had prior to the government's action. Today, the Ju/'hoansi have relatively high rates of unemployment, and those that do have jobs generally receive relatively low wages, such as those males who herd cattle on the cattle posts of other people (Hitchcock et al., 1996; Suzman, 2001).

One of the problems faced by the Ju/'hoansi and other San is that the land boards of Botswana, established in the 1970s as a replacement for traditional authorities (chiefs), have generally been reluctant to grant rights over blocks of land for grazing to San, arguing that they have no need for such land since they are, in their view, "mobile

152   *The Politics of Egalitarianism*

hunters and gatherers" (Tawana Land Board members, personal communication, Maun, Botswana, 1995; see also Wily, 1979). The land boards sometimes grant rights to residences (homesteads) and to arable land, but thus far in the North West District, the land board has been unwilling to grant grazing and water rights to San communities.

Since the 1970s, some Ju/'hoansi have sought to obtain de facto control over land and resources through the establishment of wells, which, under Tswana customary law, are considered improvements on the landscape and thus deserving of recognition as investments. It was not until the early part of the new millennium, however, that the Ju/'hoansi were able to obtain a formal water right from the land board. This achievement would not have been possible were it not for the efforts of many Ju/'hoansi and the assistance of San support groups such as the Kalahari Peoples Fund and other nongovernmental organizations, notably the Trust for Okavango Cultural and Development Initiatives (TOCADI) (see Biesele, this volume).

Land and Resource Tenure Systems of the Ju/'hoansi San

In the past, Ju/'hoansi sometimes gained access to land through approaching individuals in their own communities who had stewardship over that land. These people were often elderly Ju/'hoansi, both males and females, who were recognized as having long-standing rights to an area and who were considered land managers. Known among the Ju/'hoansi as *kxai kxausi* or *n!ore kxausi* (Marshall, 1976: 184–95), the territory "owner" is responsible for organizing and managing natural resources. The *n!ore kxausi* made their decisions on the basis of whether or not the community deemed that there were sufficient resources and land available to sustain additional people. Such decisions were usually taken on the basis of public consensus, or, as one Ju/'hoan man put it, a "big talk."

The land use system of the Ju/'hoansi was seen by them and by outsiders as flexible and adaptable to change. The problem that arose, however, was that Ju/'hoan land authorities were not recognized as such by other peoples who moved into their areas and established occupancy rights. Over time, therefore, the authority of the Ju/'hoan *n!ore kxausi* eroded, leaving many Ju/'hoansi in the position of needing to seek help from non-Ju/'hoan leaders, some of whom tended to give preferential treatment to members of their own groups.

At XaiXai in 1973/74 and in Dobe in 1975, some Ju/'hoansi dug wells and attempted to apply for water rights from the Tawana Land Board. They were unsuccessful, however, and the water points were eventually taken over by other people along with their livestock. By the 1980s, the Ju/'hoansi had grown frustrated and angry, feeling that they were being discriminated against on the basis of their ethnicity. The Botswana government, for its part, took a position that allocations of land and development assistance should not be based on ethnicity but rather on need (Hitchcock, 1980; 2002a; Wily, 1979). As one Botswana government official said to me in 1988, "We give land and development assistance to people regardless of their ethnic background; we help all people as citizens of the nation-state of Botswana."

The problem faced by the Ju/'hoansi and their neighbors was that most of them lived in remote communities that did not contain sufficient numbers of people as to be considered above the threshold (500 people) where development assistance was provided by the North West District Council and the government of Botswana.

The Ju/'hoansi of XaiXai and Dobe decided to take matters into their own hands and lobbied the Botswana government for recognition of their rights. They attended district-level and national meetings; some Ju/'hoan leaders visited Namibia; and one Ju/'hoan representative attended a meeting of the United Nations' Working Group on Indigenous Populations in Geneva, Switzerland. The Ju/'hoansi built coalitions with San from other parts of Botswana, and in 1996 they joined with San in neighboring countries to establish the Working Group of Indigenous Minorities in Southern Africa, a regional San networking and advocacy organization.

In the 1970s, the Ju/'hoansi, with the aid of anthropologists and wildlife biologists, obtained a special game license for subsistence hunting (Hitchcock et al., 1996). Individual Ju/'hoansi also wrote letters to the president of the country and members of parliament, seeking recognition of their rights as citizens of Botswana to land and resources (Megan Biesele, Axel Thoma, personal communications, 1992, 1995, 2001).

In the 1990s the people of XaiXai, both Ju/'hoansi and Herero, were assisted through a program involving community-based natural resource management and institutional capacity-building funded by the Netherlands Development Organization (SNV). They established and began to operate a community-based organization that became known as the XaiXai Tlhabololo Trust. In 1995/96 the XaiXai people established a governing body and wrote a constitution for the trust. Once the constitution was agreed upon, the XaiXai Trust applied to the Botswana government for permission to receive the wildlife quota for the area from the Department of Wildlife and National Parks. The trust council then decided how they wished to allocate that quota, giving some of it to community members who were allowed to hunt for purposes of subsistence, and setting aside some of the quota for lease to safari companies that placed bids to oversee hunting and photographic safaris at XaiXai.

At Dobe, the Trust for Okavango Cultural and Development Initiatives, which was founded in 1999, began to assist the 100 or so Ju/'hoansi and Herero residents in digging wells and seeking water rights for those wells (see Biesele, this volume, for a discussion of the KPF). In so doing, the Ju/'hoansi were hoping that they could win rights not only to the water but also to the surrounding grazing area for their livestock, which were beginning to increase in number after having been decimated in 1996.

TOCADI conducted participatory rural appraisals and community-based needs assessments at Dobe, and worked with community members in establishing and enhancing their institutions. Local people from Dobe and other Ngamiland communities were employed by TOCADI to work at the grassroots level. At the same time, TOCADI and the Ju/'hoansi worked with district authorities and other nongovernmental organizations in designing strategies for establishing community organizations and winning land and water rights.

An objective of the Ju/'hoansi in Dobe was to achieve the same degree of control over their area as had the people of XaiXai. They approached this problem by digging wells in the areas surrounding Dobe where Ju/'hoan families visited during the wet season. Without rights over the area surrounding Dobe, which are granted with the designation of a community-controlled hunting area, the community could not legally charge fees to tourists for camping there. As one Dobe Ju/'hoan woman put it, "We want to *own* the land around Dobe, not just have access to it." By 2002, water had been struck in boreholes in several of the areas near Dobe, and Ju/'hoansi had filed requests with the Tawana Land Board for allocation of water rights. Progress was being made in the establishment of community trusts at Dobe and in some of the areas nearby.

There were efforts in the late 1990s to map the *n!oresi* in the Dobe area using local Ju/'hoan informants working in conjunction with personnel trained in the use of geographic positioning systems instruments. The maps created from this work were used in land board and other district-level meetings in order to argue for the efficacy of the traditional Ju/'hoan land use and tenure system as the foundation for an innovative decentralized system of resource control and management.

The impacts of the community mapping efforts in the Dobe area have been profound. They helped to awaken a sense of collective identity among the Ju/'hoansi and to instill in local community members the desire to learn more about past land use and resource management patterns. The Ju/'hoansi understand very well the fact that maps are far more than flat representations of landscapes that enable people to orient themselves on the ground; instead, as they put it, "Maps are power." They can be used in a variety of ways, not least of which is to legitimize claims over land and resources. They have been useful in generating donor interest and obtaining support in the international arena.

In December 2002, a water festival was held at Shaikarawe, another community in which San predominate in northern Botswana. In this community only a few years before, the Tawana Land Board and the North West District Council had ruled that the land on which the San lived was no longer theirs but rather belonged to a non-San man who had taken over the water point there. The San appealed the case. With the help of Ditshwanelo, the Botswana Center for Human Rights, they were granted the right to return to Shaikarawe, where they immediately began to dig a well. Eventually, with the support of San community-based development organizations, Ditshwanelo, and outside donors, the San of Shaikarawe prevailed, and today they have de jure rights over the water point and surrounding grazing. They are now in a position where they can control their own lives. As one man put it, "Without land, livestock, and leadership, we would still be living on the fringes of someone else's cattle post."

Conclusions

In the latter part of the twentieth century, the Ju/'hoansi of north-western Botswana employed a multipronged set of strategies in their efforts to gain control over land and natural resource rights. They have used their traditional system of land use and management, the *n!ore* system, as a foundation for managing their resources. At the same time, they have been quick to seize on opportunities offered by new Botswana government policies involving land and natural resource management, engaging in well-digging efforts and making formal claims to government land management institutions for land and water allocations. Unlike some other San groups in Botswana, they have not tied their claims to indigenous identity but rather have cooperated closely with non-San groups in seeking land and resource rights. They have built coalitions and formed alliances with Ju/'hoan groups and other San groups in neighboring countries.

The Ju/'hoansi of north-western Botswana have been careful about the ways in which they have asserted their collective identity. On the one hand, they have proclaimed their identity as Ju/'hoansi in struggles for recognition and rights at the community level. However, they have been careful not to make such claims at the national level in Botswana, realizing that the idea of indigenousness does not sit well with the country's government officials (Hitchcock, 2002a; Saugestad,

2001; Sylvain, 2002). The Ju/'hoansi have accepted the government's classification of them as Remote Area Dwellers in order to access government programs. Moreover, they have utilized other government programs to their advantage, such as those aimed at providing livestock and agricultural inputs. As one Ju/'hoan woman at Dobe put it, "We know that the government wants us to have livestock and crops and to live like other people, so that is why we get these things whenever the Ministry of Agriculture offers them."

The Ju/'hoansi of Botswana have learned a great deal from their interactions with other groups involved in the global indigenous rights movement. They have learned new ways to negotiate with nation-states, and they have put this knowledge to use at the local, national, and international levels. They have also benefited from collaboration with international NGOs, donors, and researchers.

Finally, the Ju/'hoansi and their neighbors in north-western Botswana have purposely linked their systems of governance with conservation and development efforts. They have established multi-ethnic, community-based institutions that have sought and received government recognition. These community-based bodies have generated income for their members, sometimes in substantial amounts, as was the case with the XaiXai Tlhabololo Trust, which in 2001/02 raised $200,000 and generated over a dozen jobs for local people (Bernard Horton, Charlie Motshubi, personal communications, 2002). Without having participated in Botswana's community-based natural resource management program and the work of the various non-governmental organizations engaged in integrated conservation and development programs, the Ju/'hoansi would not have been able to obtain the rights to land and resources around communities in north-western Botswana, and they would still be marginalized minorities, living in, as one Ju/'hoan woman put it, "a sea of poverty."

Acknowledgments

An earlier version of this paper was presented at the symposium entitled "The Art and Politics of Egalitarianism: The Legacy of Richard Lee's Kalahari Research," organized and chaired by Jackie Solway and Christine Gailey, held at the Canadian Anthropology Society meetings in Montreal, 2–6 May 2001. I wish to thank Jackie Solway, the editor of *Anthropologica*, Winnie Lem, and several anonymous reviewers for their useful comments and advice on this article. I also wish to thank

Megan Biesele, Axel Thoma, Joram /Useb, and the staff of the Trust for Okavango and Cultural and Development Initiatives for the information and assistance they so willingly provided. Funding for some of the research upon which this paper is based was provided by the Natural Resources Management Project of the Government of Botswana, the US Agency for International Development, and by the Hivos Foundation of the Netherlands.

Note

1. The Tawana predominate politically but not numerically in the North West District of Botswana. They are a Setswana-speaking group for whom the district land board is named.

References

Anaya, S. James. 1996. *Indigenous Peoples in International Law*, New York and Oxford: Oxford University Press.

Barnard, Alan, and Justin Kenrick, ed. 2001. *Africa's Indigenous Peoples: "First Peoples" or Marginalized Minorities?* Edinburgh: Center of African Studies, University of Edinburgh.

Biesele, Megan, 1992, personal communication, interview by author, Nyae Nyae, Namibia.

Biesele, Megan, 1995, personal communication, interview by author, Tsumkwe, Namibia.

Biesele, Megan, 2001, personal communication, email to author.

Biesele, Megan, and Robert K. Hitchcock. 2000. "The Ju/'hoansi San Under Two States: Impacts of the South West African Administration and the Government of the Republic of Namibia." In *Hunters and Gatherers in the Modern World: Conflict, Resistance, and Self-Determination*, Peter Schweitzer, Megan Biesele, and Robert Hitchcock, ed. Oxford and New York: Berghahn Books.

Bodley, John H. 1999. *Victims of Progress*. 4th ed., Mountain View, Calif.: Mayfield.

Dieckmann, Ute. 2001. "'The Vast White Place': A History of the Etosha National Park in Namibia and the Hai//om." *Nomadic Peoples* 5(2): 125–53.

Durning, Alan. 1992. *Guardians of the Land: Indigenous Peoples and the Health of the Earth*. WorldWatch Paper 112. Washington, D.C.: WorldWatch Institute.

Fleras, Augie, and Jean Leonard Elliott. 1992. *The Nations Within: Aboriginal-State Relations in Canada, the United States, and New Zealand*. Toronto: Oxford University Press.

Gedicks, Al. 2001. *Resource Rebels: Native Challenges to Mining and Oil Corporations*. Cambridge: South End Press.

Hitchcock, Robert K. 1980. "Tradition, Social Justice, and Land Reform in Central Botswana." *Journal of African Law* 24(1): 1–34.

———. 1994. "International Human Rights, the Environment, and Indigenous Peoples." *Colorado Journal of International Environmental Law and Policy* 5(1): 1–22.

———. 2002a. "'We Are the First People': Land, Natural Resources, and Identity in the Central Kalahari, Botswana." *Journal of Southern African Studies* 28(4): 797–824.

———. 2002b. "Coping with Uncertainty: Adaptive Responses to Drought and Livestock Disease in the Northern Kalahari." In *Sustainable Livelihoods in Kalahari Environments: A Contribution to Global Debates*, ed. Deborah Sporton and David S.G.H. Thomas. Oxford: Oxford University Press.

Hitchcock, Robert K., John E. Yellen, Diane J. Gelburd, Alan J. Osborn, and Aron L. Crowell. 1996. "Subsistence Hunting and Resource Management among the Ju/'hoansi of Northwestern Botswana." *African Study Monographs* 17(4): 153–220.

Hodgson, Dorothy L. 2002. "Introduction: Comparative Perspectives on the Indigenous Rights Movement in Africa and the Americas." *American Anthropologist* 104(4): 1037–49.

Horton, Bernard, 2002. letter to author.

Lee, Richard B. 1979. *The !Kung San: Men, Women, and Work in a Foraging Society*. Cambridge: Cambridge University Press.

———. 2003. *The Dobe Ju/'hoansi*. 3rd ed. Toronto and South Melbourne: Thomson Learning.

Lee, Richard B., and Irven DeVore, ed. 1976. *Kalahari Hunter-Gatherers: Studies of the !Kung San and Their Neighbors*. Cambridge: Harvard University Press.

Marshall, Lorna. 1976. *The !Kung of Nyae Nyae*. Cambridge: Harvard University Press.

Maybury-Lewis, David. 1997. *Indigenous Peoples, Ethnic Groups, and the State*. Boston, Mass.: Allyn and Bacon.

Motshubi, Charlie, 2002, interview by author, Gaborone, Botswana.

Saugestad, Sidsel. 2001. *The Inconvenient Indigenous: Remote Area Development in Botswana, Donor Assistance, and the First Peoples of the Kalahari*. Uppsala, Sweden: Nordic Africa Institute.

Suzman, James. 2001. *An Introduction to the Regional Assessment of the Status of the San in Southern Africa*. Windhoek, Namibia: Legal Assistance Center.

Sylvain, Renee. 2002. "'Land, Water, and Truth': San Identity and Global Indigenism." *American Anthropologist* 104(4): 1074–85.

Tawana Land Board Members, 1995, Interviews by author in Maun, Botswana, October, 1995.

Thoma, Axel, 1992, interview by author, Nyae Nyae, Namibia.

Thoma, Axel, 1995, interview by author, Windhoek, Namibia.

Thoma, Axel, 2001, email to author.

Veber, Hanne, Jens Dahl, Fiona Wilson, and Espen Waehle, ed. 1994. *"Never Drink from the Same Cup"* Proceedings of the Conference on Indigenous Peoples in Africa, Tune, Denmark, 1993. Copenhagen: International Work Group for Indigenous Affairs and Centre for Development Research.

Wilmsen, Edwin N. 1989. *Land Filled with Flies: A Political Economy of the Kalahari*. Chicago: University of Chicago Press.

Wily, Elizabeth. 1979. *Official Policy Towards San (Bushmen) Hunter-Gatherers in Modern Botswana: 1966–1978*. Gaborone, Botswana: National Institute of Research.

Young, Elspeth. 1995. *Third World in the First: Indigenous Peoples and Development*. London: Routledge.

Chapter 10

CONTEMPORARY BUSHMAN ART, IDENTITY POLITICS, AND THE PRIMITIVISM DISCOURSE

Mathias Guenther

> I like to paint because I like to show other people the customs and the
> manners of life of my own people. I like to go forward and to show other
> people that they [the San] might do something on their own.
> —Thamae Setshogo, D'Kar, June 15, 1995

> The San believe that their cultural practices form the backbone of a
> healthy and socially intact community. Injustices such as land and re-
> source dispossession are so disruptive that affected communities are often
> unable to uphold their traditional consensual decision-making processes.
> But the memory of once-strong and unified communities keeps alive the
> longing for the revival and reconstruction of culture and identity.
> —Kxao Moses =Oma and Axel Thoma, 2002

An exciting development on the cultural front of contemporary San[1]
has been the production of a body of easel art and prints, by over a
dozen artists at two centers in southern Africa. The art is of the type of
non-Western, Fourth World, "tribal" art that Nelson Graburn would
call "assimilated fine art"[2]—that is, its aesthetic sources, its epistemol-
ogy, materials and techniques, and its intended audience are all external to the culture and community of the artists (Graburn, 1976: 8).

Contemporary San art also has no connection to the rock art San in
other parts of the subcontinent and from other linguistic groupings

Notes for this section can be found on page 181.

produced in the recent and remote past (from as early as 30,000 years ago, until the turn of the last century, when the art and its creators disappeared altogether). While loosely connected to such other traditional forms of decorative art as bead work and the etched or burnt patterns on ostrich eggshells and wooden objects, the new art is sufficiently different in form and content to be considered an altogether new art form. Being essentially free of cultural precedents, the art is immensely innovative in style and content, both from artist to artist and, to varying degrees, within the oeuvre of each individual artist. It has found much favor with Western collectors, who cherish it for its alleged primitivism and its "eerie echoes" with rock art of yore. The art has become an important source of income to the artists and their families and has provided revenue for projects operated by nongovernmental organizations (NGOs) at their respective villages.

Concurrent with the appearance of the art, in 1990, was the political awakening of the San, who until very recently had been a politically passive and oppressed minority group. They are that no longer; having become embroiled in the cultural politics of the southern African region that were generated by the dismantling of Apartheid, the San, along with the other hitherto disenfranchised, disadvantaged, and dispossessed nonwhite ethnic groups, are staking out long-denied political, civic, and territorial rights and claims. The issues and buzzwords of the day, or the decade, are "ethnicity," "identity," "authenticity," "heritage" (Barnard, 1998), and it is to these issues that the images produced by the San men and women today are especially relevant.

The connection between these two recent developments in the lives of the San, politics and art, is the principal concern of this paper. A second concern is to examine the effect on this connection of the primitivism discourse that surrounds the art, from the perspective of its non-San consumers. It is a perspective that is at variance with that of the San producers and San viewers as it takes the art into primordialist channels that are detrimental to the ethnic and political goals of contemporary San.

The Setting

There are two centers in southern Africa where the San produce paintings and prints, for sale to outsiders, galleries, and a growing number of individual collectors. They are at the village of D'Kar, in the Ghanzi District of western Botswana, and the tent city of Schmidtsdrift, near Kimberley, in Northern Cape Province. In this paper I deal primarily with the D'Kar project, the site of my fieldwork. D'Kar is a village of approximately 1,000 people, two-thirds of whom are fourth- or fifth-

Contemporary Bushman Art, Identity Politics, and the Primitivism Discourse   161

generation farm Bushmen, primarily belonging to the Naro linguistic grouping. D'Kar is also the site of a large San development agency, the Kuru Development Trust,[3] as well as of a Dutch Reformed church congregation engaged in mission work among the region's San. Schmidtsdrift consists of two communities of !Xun and Khwe Bushmen from northern Namibia, the former group having fled there from Angola in the 1970s. They had been drafted into the South African army during the antiguerilla wars against the South West African Peoples Organization in the 1970s and 1980s, when South Africa was the immoral (and arguably illegal) occupant of Namibia. When Namibia gained her independence in 1990, more than 4,000 San people, soldiers along with their dependants, received the offer from the South African military to go back "home" with them to South Africa, along with the assurances that the military "would look after them." To this day, they are living in a sprawling settlement of close to 2,000 large military tents, waiting for the government to place them in jobs and on land, or to clear the way for them to return to Namibia.[4]

These two San communities, like many others across southern Africa, have recently begun to establish local, regional, and interregional community organizations or advocacy groups, usually with expatriate involvement, through the agency of such NGOs as the Kuru Development Trust or the !Xu and Khwe Communal Property Association, at D'Kar and Schmidtsdrift respectively (Godwin, 2001: 112–17; Hitchcock, 1996: 81–82; Lee, Hitchcock, and Biesele, 2002; Robins, Madzudzo and Brenzinger, 2002: 13–25; Smith, Malherbe, Guenther and Berens, 2000: 88–89). An especially promising initiative is the Ghanzi-based Kgeikani Kweni group, or the First People of the Kalahari, which is run solely by San without any expatriate involvement (Gall, 2001: 171–235). In 1995 these diverse groups became consolidated, forming the well-organized, highly effective interregional organization Working Group of Indigenous Minorities in Southern Africa (WIMSA). WIMSA's well-trained expatriate and local staff are accountable to an all-San board composed of elected representatives from a number of San villages and regions. Its aims, as that of the regional organizations, are such things as community development, mobilization and leadership, the realization of the San's minority's political rights and their informed participation in the nation's political process, and their recognition as a distinctive ethnic group with rights, especially to land (Broermann, 2002). These political stirrings and initiatives began in the late 1980s and gained momentum in 1993 (the United Nations Year of Indigenous People, which, in 1995, was extended to the decade of Indigenous People). This momentum has been maintained to this day, all the more so as complex human rights and land issues emerged on numerous fronts during the century's last decade, which galvanized WIMSA and other groups into action (Gall, 2001; Godwin, 2001; Hitchcock, 1996; Lee et al., 2002: 34–55; Smith et al., 2000: chap. 9–10).

The two contemporary San art projects in southern Africa arose during the same period. Art exhibitions were a component of a number of conferences dealing with San identity and political rights; for instance, in 1993, the aforementioned Year of Indigenous People, the D'Kar artists held as many as thirteen exhibitions, most of them abroad, in England, Holland, Denmark, Finland, and Norway. The artists were part of a number of delegations of Ghanzi San who, along with their expatriate spokespersons, visited Europe that year on exhibition, fund-raising, and networking trips (the latter with indigenous Greenlanders and with Sami). In 1997, a delegation of artists and other Kuru people went to Australia on an exhibition and networking tour, where they met their Aboriginal counterparts and compared notes on political matters.

The Artists and their Art

A total of fifteen artists work, or worked at Kuru, nine of them men and six women.[5] The majority are Nharo San; one of them (Qãetcao Moses, or Olebogeng) is not a San, but a Nharo-speaking MoTswana. Prior to their careers as artists, the men and women had been farm laborers and domestics for white, largely Afrikaans-speaking Boer farmers; two of the older Kuru artists (one a man, the other a woman) were trance dancers in their younger years. The artists have been with the art project for varying lengths of time, since its inception in 1990. Six women and nine men are members of the art project at Schmidtsdrift,[6] which was founded two years after the Kuru project. The joint output of paintings and prints of these thirty San artists has been vast and its exposure to the world extensive, especially that of the Kuru artists, which has been shown on four continents. Their art provides the men and women with sorely needed income, which for some may be substantial[7] and which they keep in bank accounts at Kuru, enabling them to accumulate stock animals (or, the more likely scenario, to provide for unemployed and needy kin).

Two things should be noted about the artists, both of them observations that expose Western-held, erroneous, and hegemonic notions about "tribal artists" in general. One is that they are each highly individuated men and women, each with his or her own life history, temperament, artistic vision, and skill. I note this in order to counter the reprehensible Western tendency, when dealing with tribal art, of obliterating the artist and treating the work as deriving from an ethnic col-

Contemporary Bushman Art, Identity Politics, and the Primitivism Discourse   163

lectivity or tribal tradition, rather than from an individual artist with his or her own creative intentions and stylistic idiosyncrasies (which, in the case at hand, are exceptionally developed). The second point is that the artists are acculturated, Westernized, widely traveled, fourth-generation erstwhile farm laborers or domestics, some of whom have attended school, speak Afrikaans, and belong to the Dutch Reformed Church. About half of them are also politically alert and astute. They are decidedly modern people, as well as modern-looking ones, rather than leather loincloth-clad and seminaked, as some Western newspaper articles on exhibitions of their work may lead one to believe. Nor are they tribal rustics unversed in Western ways, as reported in another newspaper account of a 1993 exhibition in London. The journalist commented on how lost the Bushman artist and her San companion were in the big city and how cold the two African desert dwellers felt—notwithstanding London's early summer heat wave at the time—and how it amazed them "that there were no thorns on our pavements." The artist and her companion were said to miss their mealie porridge, yet "rather enjoyed the variety of berries at Kew Gardens" (*The Independent on Sunday*, May 1993: 23). The primordialist depiction of the artists in some of these Western newspaper reports is in line with the primitivist discourse that surrounds their art, to which I will turn below.

Of the two projects, the art at Schmidtsdrift is decidedly more political. The experience of some of the artists, as soldiers in the highly volatile region of northeastern Namibia during the preindependence guerilla war, has evidently left its mark on some of the pictures. Here, in a small proportion of pictures, one comes across such motifs as rifles and bayonets, army tents and trucks, and depictions of soldiers. A few pictures deal quite stridently with such political and military themes as soldiers recruiting or abducting San from their veld camp or of a soldiers' raid on a tent city. A number of the many pictures that are not explicitly political contain Western elements such as houses, kitchens, cups, bottles, chairs, jeans, radios, trucks, minibuses, numbers, and letters, as well as one of a soldier's identification card, a rickshaw man, and a dinosaur (a picture of which the artist had on the back of a telephone book on a visit to Durban). These new, "foraged" motifs are juxtaposed with old ones, antelopes, veld plants, vines, and trees, in compositions that balance the world of the present with that of the past.

Returning to the Kuru art, we find very few pieces that are explicitly political—that is, that deal head-on, as do the Schmidtsdrift pictures, with social and political issues faced by the San today. What their art depicts primarily are nostalgic veld scenes from the past, which the older artists—such as Dada and the late Qwaa and Qgoma Ncokg'o—remember from their childhood and the middle-aged and younger artists from the stories their parents or grandparents told them. The men's favorite topic is large veld animals, especially antelopes, as well as the large mammals that once roamed the Ghanzi veld, elephants, rhinos, giraffes, eland, as well as lions and herds of wild dogs. (Fig. 1 provides an example.[8]) These have now all disappeared from land that has become grazing ranges for cattle. The men also like to paint mythological themes, especially Qwaa, who, as a one-time trance dancer, has had the mystical experiences of altered states of consciousness, outer body travel, and encounters with spirits. These themes inform some of his art. He was wary about depicting some of them on his pictures and did so cryptically; for instance, by using the concealment technique[9] of

Figure 1: Untitled, oil on canvas, Qāetcao Moses, ca. 1995

tucking the supernatural element away in one of the nooks and crannies of busy scenes showing things that were uncharged mythologically (and had "no *huwa* [story] in them," as he pointed out to me). Another mythic theme, also of Qwaa's nephew Thamae Setshogo as well as of the late Qgoma, are were-animals that conflate animal with human features, or those from other species or phyla, creating bird- or insect-headed humanoids, bird-antelopes, crocodile-hippos and similar combinations. These figures may be depictions of transformation, a mystical process of trance ritual, which appears as a motif on a few of the men's pictures.

Women's pictures, too, deal with *veld* scenes or with everyday domestic or ritual events. They are frequently also pictures that have explicit narrative content. The artist may reveal the latter to her children, using her picture as a visual aid to accompany a story or remembered events, perhaps about a woman and a man out gathering in the veld who happen on a leopard that chases them, or a circle of women chanting the trance dance for the dancer-men, the event interrupted by two white farmers who appear on the scene. By so drawing a picture into the expressive form of story telling, which in San culture is highly individuated (Biesele, 1993; Guenther, 1999: 126–45), the art's element of individual creativity becomes more enhanced.

Rather than mammals, the women's favorite motif tends to be plants, especially veld foods, each of which the artist will identify by name, as well as flowers, vines, and trees. (See Fig. 2 for an example.) Birds, along with insects—Ncg'abe Eland's favorite motif—and butterflies, worms and caterpillars, scorpions, spiders and snakes, tortoises, lizards and frogs, all of them part of a traditional San woman's store of gatherable foods, also appear on the woman artists' canvases. So do the bags they used and still use for foraging, as all of the woman artists still gather plants, whenever they are in season and their busy artists' schedules allow it. Other such feminine motifs are aprons, skirts, and headdresses, all decorated with glass beads. Cg'oise Ntcox'o and Coex'ae Bob are especially fond of this set of female motifs (see Fig. 3). Another gendered aspect of the art pertains to style: the women's art tends to be more abstract than the men's, and may be altogether non-representational, depicting geometric or fluid patterns.

It should be noted that this stylistic feature and the substantive element—birds, as well as bugs and reptiles—are not the exclusive domain of the women. Very little is in San society, in which gender roles have always overlapped and gender equality prevailed (Biesele, 1993; Guenther, 1999: 146–63). Some of the men (especially Qwaa and Thamae Setshogo, as well as Qãetcao Moses) make use of these motifs. Here, one bird, the Kori Bustard, particularly stands out, perhaps because of its prominent role in San mythology (Biesele, 1983: 124–33,

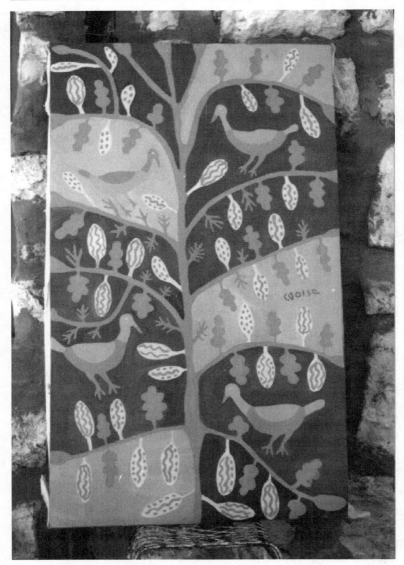

Figure 2: "Veld Birds and Plants," oil on canvas, Cg'ose Ntcox'o, 1995

passim). Likewise, women will paint antelopes and other game animals, including domesticated ones—goats, cattle, hens—which appear on the women's canvases with somewhat greater frequency than on the men's.

The last motif brings up a significant feature of the art: while the majority of pictures depict such culturally idiosyncratic themes as veld

Figure 3: Untitled, oil on canvas, Coex'ae Bob, 1995

animals and old-time lifeway scenes, not all of the Kuru art bears the stamp of tradition. Some artists also depict the things that today surround and intrigue them and that are useful to them, that derive from the modern world: items of Western clothing, watches, radios, guitars, trucks, bicycles, helicopters, tables, chairs, pots and pans, cupboards and cups, Boers and Blacks, cattle and goats, horses and donkeys, mealie fields, and European houses (see Fig. 4). One can even come

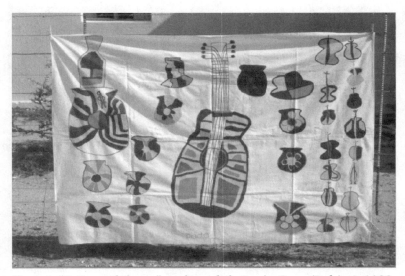

Figure 4: "Guitars and Shapes," acrylic on cloth, Coex'ae Qgam (Dada), ca. 1990.

across angels, which the artist Thamae Setshogo had heard about at a church service and which, unversed in Western sacred iconography, he depicted with insect-like wings, oval in shape and held at a stiff angle, like a mayfly at rest. Also in the unusual category, in content and presentation, is Dada's whimsical picture of a beauty contest. AIDS is another contemporary motif, which appears with disturbing poignancy on the canvases of several of the artists.

Some pictures are not just modern but postmodern, juxtaposing or conflating, sometimes with wry irony and droll or poignant incongruity, old motifs with new ones—such as pants and watches with the spirit being //Gāuwa, who points to the latter objects with insect claws and whose huge, baleful eyes recapitulate the watches' dials (see Fig. 5). The artist Qwaa was especially fond of this sort of picture, which, in addition to being humorous, at times had a political edge.

One is his self-portrait, which blends his modern and traditional occupational roles, of farm laborer and trance healer. We see him wearing European work boots, socks and a T-shirt, and standing in the posture of trance: erect stance, intent gaze, entoptics whirring about his head (which, he told me, enigmatically and wryly, were buttons!). As a commentary on a modern farm Bushman's experience with modernity, the picture seems to suggest that, while contradictory and disjunctive, the old and the new can also somehow be cobbled together and bridged.

Figure 5: Untitled, acrylic on paper, Xg'oa Mangana, ca. 1994.

Another politically cast picture is Qwaa's painting of a Boer elephant hunt (see Fig. 6). When he showed me the picture, he also offered a lengthy narrative that dwelt on the serious and hilarious elements of the portrayed scene. The first, the serious, was its depiction of a painful and signal event in the local history that forms part of people's oral tradition: the infamous slaughter, by Boer ivory hunters, of the elephants of the Ghanzi veld back in the nineteenth century, leading to their local extermination. The hilarious touch is that one of the three Boers is scared out of his wits, his legs are shaking, and he is squatting down, ready to loosen his bowels.

Figure 6: "Boers hunting Elephants," oil on canvas, Xg'oa Mangana (Qwaa), 1994

Qwaa was fond of lampooning the Boers, the farm San's paternalistic bosses, as in the picture of two Boers in a fist fight, with four birds looking on bemusedly. This sort of picture is an instance of the time honored technique in traditional San politics of bringing an uppity person in line through ridicule (Guenther, 1999: 34–37). In the context of the acculturated farm Bushmen, it may perhaps be regarded as an instance of passive resistance or subversion (or the deployment of one of the "weapons of the weak," à la James Scott).

Another example of the same is Qwaa's picture of the helicopter game warden, hovering above and in amongst an array of animal tracks (see Fig. 7). He pursues the mounted hunter, who has just demonstrated his outstanding skill by throwing a spear through the

Figure 7: Untitled, felt tip on paper, Xg'oa Mangana (Qwaa), ca. 1993

neck of a kori bustard. The hunter is equally adept at evading the warden (the bane of the contemporary San hunter, now that the government has criminalized hunting), whose helicopter, on the picture, becomes just another animal track, a thing the hunter is as eminently competent to evade as to pursue.

Finally, we get to the picture Qwaa regarded as his masterpiece (see Fig. 8): on a green veld laze and graze eight elands, the San's favorite meat (and spirit) animal (Lewis-Williams, 1981; Vinnicombe, 1976), because of its bulk and fat (and healing potency) and its tractability as a prey animal. Each bears the artist's "brand"; he has laid claim, by means of this Western device for ownership demarcation, to the eland; they are "Bushman cattle," as he put it to me.

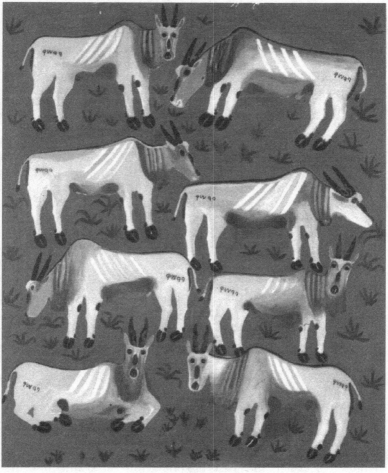

Figure 8: "Eland," oil on canvas, Xg'oa Mangana (Qwaa), 1995.

The Political Dimensions of the Kuru Art

While not as explicit as in some of the Schmidtsdrift pictures, there nevertheless is a political dimension to the Kuru art. It is subtle in almost all of the Kuru works. In fact, on the face of it, Kuru art does not generally strike one as being political. At least half of the artists are themselves not that aware of politics, or engaged politically. Additionally, the artists' preferred motifs—bucolic veld scenes—are also the motifs preferred by Western buyers. This sort of correspondence may lead a cynic to dismiss any contention that political, rather than market-driven economic, considerations are what lie behind the art.

However, the art is also decidedly political. Beyond an artist's personal intentions when he or she paints a picture, and transcending the same, are the group-wide issues of self-representation and self-identity. These envelop the lives of San today, including the artists and their art, both of which become drawn into a political trajectory. Pictures that seem devoid of any political subtext, that instead depict nostalgic veld-set scenes of a somewhat other-worldly past, become political in an environment that draws such scenes into an identity discourse. The politics of the San of South and southern Africa in the early twenty-first century give center stage to the issue of identity (sharing that spot with two other issues, political rights and land). Concern about identity is seen, for example, in the statement by the chairman of the Kuru Development Trust that "a nation without a culture is a lost nation" (the nation referred to here by the speaker, Robert Morris, is that of the *ncoa khoe*, the "red people," the Ghanzi Bushmen's term of self-designation). The motto of the Kuru Cultural Center, which operates a museum and library at D'Kar and to which the Art Project is linked, is "/au ba kg'oe dim dao me e" (which literally translated means "the people's lives' ways is the path"). This is also the message of the First People of the Kalahari, expressed in the group's slogan "survival through cultural revival" and of its logo, which shows a circle of dancers' feet surrounding the trance dance fire, flanked by a digging stick and an archery set.

The art and artists produce visually striking images that are displayed locally, nationally, and internationally (at over 60 exhibitions, between 1990 and 1999, in fourteen countries on four continents), as well as on the internet. At times artists may accompany an exhibition to field questions from outsiders about what the art means. Their answers are given significance by the outsiders. These may be members of the media, who report on the pictures, and the artists and their deportment and comments—in edited form, as we will see below—in the next day's newspaper or the cultural supplement of the weekend edition. In this fashion, the artists are drawn into the identity discourse

Contemporary Bushman Art, Identity Politics, and the Primitivism Discourse 173

and, irrespective of their own intentionality, they and their art become political.

The art constructs identity in three modes, each corresponding to one of the three sets of motifs described above. One is set in the past and in tradition, whereas the second and third engage the present, one by depicting elements from the new economic and political reality, the other by juxtaposing these with traditional motifs. Regarding the first mode, the self-identifying and self-representing functions of the pictures could be seen as instances of "autoethnographic expression" (à la Mary Louise Pratt, 1992: 7); another manifestation of the same process can be seen in the half-dozen "traditional villages" and cultural performances presented by the San to tourists at various places in the region (=Oma and Thoma, 2002; Guenther, 2002). What these "traditional" pictures depict are veld scenes, especially the large animals that have vanished from the Ghanzi veld and that were around, and hunted, at a time when Bushmen lived alone on the land. Veld plants are next, the kind that only San women know. Another highly idiosyncratic set of cultural traits that appears in a few of the pictures is drawn from the culture's inner core or sanctum: the myths and spirit beings, therianthropes and animal transformation, and the ritual of the trance curing dance. To this day, the latter is practiced and stands as the most salient feature of San ethnic identity (Katz, Biesele, and St. Denis, 1997), recognized and acknowledged as distinctive and significant by non-San (Lee, 2003: 201–205).

However, the pictures are not merely of an iconographic, static, "traditional," and increasingly irretrievable past. Quite a few also depict those elements of the new economic and social order that are useful and desirable to contemporary San—such as jeans, watches, radios, pots, tables, and stock animals. While some pictures depict just these new things—consumer or capital goods from the Western cash economy, of which the modern San have become a part—the pictures are more than just a shopping list of coveted goods (a San Sear's catalog, as it were). Most of the images depicting Western things or themes juxtapose the same to select elements from the past, in an exercise either of confrontation or negotiation. This enhances the artists' grasp of the modern world that has encapsulated them for over a century and that they now have begun to enter, on their own initiative. By blending, in their "hybrid"[10] pictures, old with new, the artists engage the new economic and social order while also keeping in check its hegemonic impact. By juxtaposing elements of modernity with those of tradition, they refer the former back to the latter, thereby embracing the new postforaging order on their own terms. Brakes are placed on too rapid a process of absorption of this ethnic minority of erstwhile hunter-gatherers into the economy, society, and polity of the nation–

174

state, which stands at the opposite end of the nomadic, loose, and egalitarian lifeways they followed until recently. The art acts as a counterhegemonic force for the contemporary San.

These processes, of self-identification and self-representation, confrontation and negotiation, are happening not just at exhibitions in far-off places. They occur also within the San's own community. The production of art, in D'Kar's studio building or at home, in front of the artist's hut, or in his or her courtyard (on the door, wall, or fence of which may hang one of his canvases) occurs very much in the open, in public, and is noted and watched by all. Works selected for major exhibitions may be displayed in the village prior to being shipped off; thus they, too, gain local public exposure, before being lost to distant galleries. Some works may actually remain within the community, as are works acquired by Kuru for D'Kar's permanent collection, which are displayed in the museum of the village's cultural center. Copies of the annual Kuru art calendar hang on Kuru office walls, and one or another separated page may also hang on the inside wall of a D'Kar resident's hut. Another type of art exhibited in the community are the works of children who are encouraged to draw and paint at the Kururun preschool, which itself is a huge open-air canvas, with its four walls decorated with close to 400 images, with veld and farm motifs of every description. The decorated walls are the result of a day-long paint-in that involved all of the people of D'Kar, young and old, artist and nonartist. In such ways, art, even though destined for the outside world, also enters the artist's community and plays out within it identity-constructing, modernity-engaging effects.

San Art and the Primitivism Discourse

These effects are in danger of being undermined by the outside world, however. The galleries that exhibit the art, as well as the catalogs and media articles that report on the exhibits, appear to have their own distinctive vision about "Bushman art," which departs to a significant degree from that of the artists and their cultural community.[11] The outside exhibitors, buyers, and writers all form part of a distinctive and distinguished, urban and urbane "taste culture" (Lee, 1999) that has cultivated its own exclusive *connaissance* (Price, 1989: chapter 1) and rarified *amour de l'art* (Bourdieu, Darbel and Schnapper, 1969). This culture has its own "exchange sphere" and "discriminating classifications" on the value and worth of African art (Kopytoff, 1986: 78–79). It also has its own elitist notions and preferences on "the Primitive" as it manifests itself within the connoisseurs' guarded aesthetic domain, as "Primitive Art" or, with respect to the case at hand, a sample of "African art" (which, to some collectors and art critics is in fact synonymous with "primitive art" [Price, 1989: 54–55, 131]). These preferences are for the nostalgic, bucolic stuff: the veld scenes—of beads and bags, hunts and dances, trees and flowers, as well as for ritual and mythological scenes. More than anything, they are for the animals—to them the ideational and aesthetic core of San pictures—the bucks, as well as the birds and butterflies (but not the scorpions, spiders, and centipedes—"nobody wants to hang bugs on their walls," one commercial gallery owner told me). They also do not much care for the pictures that show modern scenes, and, true to the maxim that "the essentialist discourse hates a hybrid" (Phillips, 1999: 35), they care even less for the postmodern pictures that, in the spirit of pastiche, combine, conflate, and juxtapose old and new and negotiate the new in terms of the old. Yet, as I suggested above, it is these sorts of pictures that are especially meaningful for some of the artists and contemporary Bushmen. For the Western collectors, though, they are pieces that are largely "indigestible," "unnatural," and "inauthentic" (Clifford, 1985: 177).

What Western buyers seek are images of the Bushman of yore, and of the distant veld, which he—the Bushman, in the iconic, composite singular—shares with the animals. This was made clear to me when I went through my scrapbook of exhibition catalogs, press releases, and newspaper and magazine articles about exhibitions, with a deconstructionist eye. Of the thirty-three pieces of writing on exhibitions in southern Africa, Europe, and Australia from 1991 to 1998, over half reveled in primitivist, primordialist rhetoric (while the rest offered more or less sober, sensitive, and politically contextualized reportage). In addition to the rock art trope and its "eery echoes" discussed at the beginning, writers found resonances not only with hunter-gatherers, but also with Australian Aborigines (and generic "aboriginals" generally), with the Stone Age and other "distant ancestors." Others were struck by the art's connection to animals—the most common observation—and to nature and the earth. The last is evidenced by the artists' alleged special affinity for "earthen colors" (which is an inaccurate characterization, in view of the artists' general preference for primary colors). As common as the zoomorphic trope is the element of childlike, untutored simplicity, expressed in such *bon mots* as "lack of sophistication and appealing innocence," "clumsy yet magical," "primitive charm," "innocence of vision," "unselfconscious immediacy." In the same discursive vein, "uncanny similarities" to Western art are noted, to such unlikely figures as Miró, Chagall, and the surrealist Alan Davie, as well as Cézanne and Gaugin (a case, it would seem, of the Modern in the Tribal, or Fauvism in reverse). Yet others commented sententiously on the art's "ancient power" and "dark mystery"; indeed, two articles, to underscore the darkness trope, made allusions to the "Dark Continent," using this colonialist baggage-laden sub-trope unselfconsciously, devoid even of the conventional, if not obligatory, quotation marks.

Another way of placing the contemporary art into the primitivism trope is to link it, in terms of style, content, and aesthetic evocativeness, to San rock art of the past. Its echoes in the contemporary corpus are either hinted at by Western commentators, or they are explicitly drawn out by a curator, through side-by-side exhibitions of the two bodies of art. While a certain similarity in style and content can be noted in some of the paintings—in part, because some of the artists have taken Kuru-sponsored trips to far-away rock art sites that may have left an impression on some works[12]—for the most part these eerie echoes collectors and viewers detect in the contemporary art is just romantic ringing in their Western ears. They are transmitted through eyes that look at the pictures selectively and through glasses that have the tinge of primitivism. The rock art is altogether dissimilar: it is from a different time—centuries and millennia in the past—and a different place—the mountainous regions of southern Africa, the locale for most of the sites, thousands of kilometers from the Kalahari plains, a region devoid of boulders and shelters (and rock surfaces to paint on). It differs in style, content, and function, primarily in that rock art was for the most part ritual, mystical, and metaphorical, whereas the contemporary art is commercial and political, and largely perceptual. And such mystical and ritual motifs as we do find—the occasional portrayal of mythological beings and mythic or ritual events, such as human-animal transformations and depictions of trance dancing— are largely narrative and symbolic (of San identity). They are not, as in rock art, central themes of a body of "shamanic art" that arguably has trance and transformation as its principal concern (Lewis-Williams, 1981; Lewis-Williams and Dowson, 1988; 1989). The key difference is that rock art was embedded in the San's own expressive, cosmological and ritual culture, while the contemporary art has no roots within the San artists' culture, being externally derived, through the actions of Western, NGO-funded art instructors.

Tribal, feral, childlike, primal, ancient and archaic, dark, at one with nature and kindred to animals: here we have all of the ingredients of primitivism (Price, 1989; Torgovnick, 1990), which revitalized Western art at the turn of the twentieth century (Rubin, 1984) and which was held to be especially pure and vibrant in pieces of "African art," in which these traits are held to vouchsafe the authenticity of an African art piece (Bascom, 1976). They are looked for and found, in a body of art that patently transcends the primitivist slot, in creative and subtle ways to which so many of the Western commentators have evi-

Contemporary Bushman Art, Identity Politics, and the Primitivism Discourse 177

dently chosen to blind their art critics' eyes. It should be noted that of the exhibitions reported on in this manner about half of these actually did fall in line with the primitivist trope writers projected on them. It is in evidence in the bias—in favor of bucks, birds, and beads—that guided the selection of paintings to be exhibited, the florid and romantically tribal title or subtitle for the exhibition—"Return of the Moon," "Eland and Moon," "Rise with the Sun," "Mongongo," "!Kung"—and the tenor of the galleries' press releases and exhibition catalogues announcing and reporting on the exhibitions. The fact that in a number of cases rock art was actually exhibited alongside the contemporary corpus further underscored the exhibited art works' primitivist aura.

Why this almost compulsive penchant for Western collectors to place what is in many ways so patently modernist art into the primitivist slot? The reason can be found in the common tendency for non-Western, tribal, or "ethnic" art to be identified not with the individual artist, who works as a creative agent in tune with his or her own personal aesthetic vision, but with the artist's ethnic provenance (Graburn, 1976: 21–23)—which, deriving ideally from Africa or New Guinea, Australia, or the Canadian Arctic, bears the stamp of the tribal. The maxim at work here, as noted by Sally Price (1979: 100), is that "if the artist isn't anonymous, the art isn't primitive" (also see Berlo, 1999: 183, Steiner, 1994: 92–93). The art and artist are viewed not as individual and singularized, freely expressive, idiosyncratic but as collective, traditional, culturally uniform, tribally ethnic. Mediated through art, an expressive form of culture that conveys visual images and evokes an aesthetic response, that collectivity gains special salience and potency in the Western viewer. What (s)he will look for, and find, in a body of tribal or ethnic art—and, in the case of a curator, select for public display—are those features that define the art's collective or tribal/ethnic dimension, overriding and obliterating in the process the individually conceived, extra-ethnic, idiosyncratic, or modernist elements actually found in the art (and in the process also putting brakes on the artist's creative agency and integrity).

We see just that process at work to a significant extent in the body of art at hand: "Bushman art," along with its valorizing rock art cousin and alleged predecessor, is seen as an exemplar of Bushman culture and ethnic identity. And the qualities ascribed to the San ethnic minority—of timeless, history-less pristineness, and primordialism—are ascribed also to their art, all the more so in view of its visual salience and evocativeness. Bushman (rock) art becomes the embodiment of "Bushman-ness," as noted by the South African art historian Barbara Buntman (2002: 75–77), and it stands in a feed-back relationship to the essentialist, primordialist discourse that surrounds this ethnic minority in the countries of southern Africa, especially South

Africa, the country in which the art is most frequently exhibited. Of all such minorities, the San, notwithstanding their numerical minority, are the most visible, the most mythic and iconic, either within academe, where, at one time, they stood as the paradigmatic, anthropology textbook case of "the hunter-gatherer" (Wilmsen, 1989), or outside academe. There, in South—and southern—Africa, we find a bowdlerized variant of the academic alterity Bushman figure, in the form of a crassly, unselfconsciously profiled archaic hunter-gatherer of the distant veld, "digging roots in bleached landscapes" (Landau, 1996: 141).

This figure has been appropriated and manipulated by government and corporate agencies for various ends. One is to promote national unity, with reference to South Africa's "First People": so cast, as a "baseline monoculture" who precede and thus transcend all of the other divided groups of the land, the Bushmen are seen, by post-Apartheid intellectuals, as having the capacity to bridge the past and the future and to bring together divided communities by symbolically decentering competing nationalisms (Blundell, 1998: 155; Douglas, 1994: 73; Lewis-Williams, 2000: 41; Masilela, 1987; Tomaselli, 1993; 1995). This idealistic notion has also been adopted by the new nation builders, as evidenced in South Africa's Olympic flag design depicting rock art figures, and its new national crest, which bears a mirror-imaged human figure in the center that is based on a San rock art painting from South Africa's Eastern Cape province. The image is accompanied by the motto, in the extinct /Xam language, *!Ke e:/xarra //ke*, which means "people who are different join together" (Lewis-Williams, 2000; Lewis-Williams & Pearce 2005:233–38; Smith et al., 2001). Less loftily and commendably, the purpose of the coopting and manipulating San cultural elements may be to advertise a company or its products, by means of a salient, iconic image, for which the Bushmen, in their splendid Otherness, provide all of the right stuff. One finds them, or elements of their culture (especially rock art), on stamps, specially minted precious-metal coins and telephone cards, or as logos for museums or Cape wine labels. A new product for the jaded Western palate is the cordial "Kalahari Thirstland Liqueur," which invites the buyer to "experience the unique Kalahari" and underscores the point with advertisements that depict pristine loin clothed Bushman hunters and generic rock art figures (which are quite out of place in the Kalahari) (Buntman, 2002: 74). Crown and private corporations use rock art or other traditional Bushmen motifs for advertising; for instance, the South African Broadcasting Corporation and the South African Railways (Spoornet), or Mazda and Lemontwist, in television commercials (Blundell, 1998; Dowson, 1996). Instead of television commercials, there may be documentaries, such as Paul

Myburgh's "The People of the Great Sandface" dripping with primordialist primitivism (Gordon, 1990; Guenther, 1990; Wilmsen, 1992), or feature films, such as the bizarrely pristinist blockbuster "The Gods Must be Crazy," parts I and II, which has become famous—and infamous (Lee, 1985; Volkman, 1988)—internationally.

As the most photographed human subject since the 1880s, in the early travel and tourism literature on southern Africa and the genre's ultimate "coffee-table book people" (Landau, 1996: 141), the Bushmen are especially prominent within the tourism industry (which, like ethnotourism, has become one of the industry's most important branches during post-Apartheid times, as well as a significant element of the politics—and economics—of identity[13]). Souvenirs with San cultural and rock art motifs abound—coasters, beer mugs, T-shirts, place mats, fridge magnets, key rings, decks of playing cards (Buntman, 2002: 75–77). Such motifs appear on post and greeting cards and on tourist boutique signs. The British Airways' jumbo jets carrying the tourist to his South African destination may have a contemporary San art painting—which the corporation bought from one of the Kuru artists (Cg'oise)—gracing its tail, as well as the coasters, napkins, and sugar packets handed out to passengers. The tourist heading to the Sun City resort and casino near Johannesburg will come across rows of walking rock art women and men, some with antelope heads, heading purposefully towards the washroom, directing the visitor to his or her toilet facility (Dowson, 1996; Hall, 1995). The ultimate "Bushman experience" awaits the international tourist at one of the two "cultural villages," Kagga Kamma in South Africa and IntuAfrika in Namibia (Buntman, 1996; Crowe, 1996; Guenther, 2002: 47–51; Isaacson, 2002: 78–92; Whyte, 1995), where, in the context of an upscale and pricey safari-style lodge, with swimming pool and "sundowner cocktails," loin-clothed Bushmen take tourists on bush walks or perform dubious trance dance numbers; bare-breasted Bushwomen squat in front of grass huts drilling and stringing ostrich eggshell beads; and half-naked Bushchildren frolic about, offering to the tourist a highly photogenic *tableau vivant*.

A number of South African cultural critics (Blundell, 1998; Buntman, 1996; 2002; Dowson, 1996; Tomaselli, 1995) have decried this process of (mis)appropriation and manipulation of San cultural elements, which has deep roots in the country's history and collective consciousness (Skotnes, 1996). They see this process as a mechanism of increasing reification of the Bushmen ethnic minority as tribal stereotypes, as well as isolates and innocents, and as "marginalized others" excluded from "the political, economic and cultural centres" (Buntman, 1996: 279) of the modern society and nation-state. "Primordialism," notes the South African social anthropologist Stuart

Douglas, "lends itself to being a function of oppressive power relations" (1994: 10), indeed, to ideologies of ethnic cleansing, as ominously hinted at by Ed Wilmsen (1995: 19). Its attributes of cultural backwardness and stasis are counterproductive to the change and betterment for which contemporary Bushmen strive.

In sum, through a barrage of crass, commercial measures of this sort, the ethnic identity of the Bushmen gets distorted and essentialized into a primordial primitive, a hunter-gatherer par excellence, the agropastoral, urban-industrial world's quintessential tribal Other. That otherness is projected by the Western viewer also onto "Bushman art" (via rock art), which, through this projection, becomes replete with primitivism and primordialism. Inescapably, the latter becomes the aesthetic mystique of the art, through a process of stereotypical attribution of primordial ethnicity that is deeply rooted within the culture and collective mentality of the non-San consumers of the art, especially in southern and South Africa.[14]

Conclusion: Keeping Primitivism in Check

As yet, the Western aesthetic predilection for the "primitive" pieces in the contemporary San oeuvre—the bucks, birds, plants, and beads motifs—has not become a canon, however, as it has in other bodies of "ethnic art."[15] And as yet, it does not appear to have placed aesthetic fetters on the artists or subjected them to any form of aesthetic hegemony, as has happened elsewhere in the world.[16] At Kuru the artists are enjoined by the project supervisor to create pieces in accordance with their own creative dictates. The individual style, vision, and talent of each artist is recognized and fostered, and in marketing Kuru art, the fact that an individuated artist stands behind each painting and print is emphasized (for example, by applying prominent signatures to each picture and placing biographical sketches and photographs of the artists into the Kuru art brochure and annual art calendar). Presenting the art in this way to the outside world can be expected to counteract the tendency to place the art within a generic ethnic slot. Sometimes a theme might be set for the artists, such as a certain folktale or myth, or such modern issues as building a house, keeping cattle, or the problems of alcohol or AIDS. This encourages artists to turn their creative talents towards modern subjects and acts as a countermeasure to an externally derived and imposed aesthetic of primitivism. Some artists continue to produce primarily "traditional" motifs, in part because they are most adept at this sort of picture, enjoy doing such paintings or prints the most, and, in some instances, because these pieces are most likely to be sold. Thus, while some artists have become and are becoming attuned to market preferences, most of them paint what they like, including pictures of bugs, of modern and postmodern scenes.

If the latter pieces should turn out not to sell as readily and ultimately remain at D'Kar village, that is just as well. These pieces, with their wry commentary on the modern life of the postforaging Bushmen, their conflation—and at times deflation—of things old and new, engage modernity and try to work out its ambiguities and contradictions; they subtly subvert its economic and hegemonic hold through juxtapositioning, conflation, bemusement, irony. Such hybrid art is as meaningful to the San artists and their community as it is "indigestible" to the outside collector.

Acknowledgment

I gratefully acknowledge the feedback I received on this paper from two anonymous *Anthropologica* referees, which was exceptionally insightful, germane, and comprehensive.

Notes

This article is written to honor Richard Lee. It is on the contemporary San's struggle for recognition, rights and land, a topic I know to be close to his heart. Issues of social justice, of empowerment and advocacy, as they affect the San and other Fourth World minorities, have been preoccupations of Richard throughout his career, both scholarly and personal. I became aware of them thirty years ago, when Richard was working on *Kalahari Hunter-Gatherers*, the volume he edited with Irv DeVore. The volume bore the dedication "to future generations of San in a Free Africa" (I might add that, as well, it committed the book's royalties to the Kalahari People's Fund, a San advocacy group that is still around and that Richard and a number of other Kalahari researchers had previously founded). As one of the contributors to that volume I always felt good about that dedication, all the more so in that my contribution to the volume described San people—the farm Bushmen of Botswana's Ghanzi District—who were in the grips of *baaskap* oppression and exploitation. My paper today might well bear the same dedication, although with, perhaps, a touch more optimism as the San, a generation later, have moved a few steps closer to the freedom Richard had wished for them.

1. Breaking with previous practice (Guenther, 1986), I have in this paper adopted the term "San" as the overarching designation for the click-speaking, erstwhile hunting-gathering Khoisan people known also as "Bushmen" (along with a number of other designations; see Hitchcock and Biesele n.d.). The question—"San" or "Bushman?"—is still not entirely settled, however, neither amongst scholars, nor

the people themselves, amongst whom we can find members of the same family in disagreement over the matter, one brother opting for "Bushman," the other for "San" (as was the case at a 1991 community meeting in the Nyae Nyae region of north-eastern Namibia [Hitchcock and Biesele, *op. cit.*]). Yet, it seems that amongst the people themselves, including Khoisan and Coloured of the Cape in South Africa, who lay claim to a Khoisan heritage, San is becoming the preferred term of self-appellation. It was agreed upon in 1996 by delegates from various San groups at a meeting in Namibia as the designation for the people as a whole, vis-à-vis the outside world. Amongst themselves, the group also decided, specific groups should be referred to by their own specific designations, thereby maintaining regional cultural diversity (one of the hallmarks of San people and culture). At the 1997 Cape Town conference, "Khoisan Identities and Cultural Heritage," a landmark event in Khoisan identity politics (Bank, 1998), that position was reconfirmed. Possibly, the reason the San received an endorsement from this group is its gloss as "original people" (Gordon, 1992: 5–6). The term sits well with the current claim made by or for the San of South and southern Africa as the region's or country's "First People" (Masisela, 1987; Tomaselli, 1995). Deliberations of this sort—no longer by scholars, for reasons academic, but by the people themselves, out of political considerations—reveal just how important this issue is to them, as a symbolic acknowledgment not only of their identity but of their struggle for empowerment and land.

2. This "fine art" and its opposite, "applied art," have not appeared in San culture as a conceptual type and pair, let alone as one whose members are unequally valued, with the "applied art" (or its cognate forms, "crafts" or "artifacts"), generally associated with women, held as the inferior form (Faris, 1988; Phillips and Steiner, 1999: 5–7). In the San case, the fine art, the easel paintings and prints, receive some of their motifs from traditional ostrich eggshell and glass bead work and the decorations that are etched or burnt onto ostrich eggshell water containers or wooden vessels or pipes or spoons. Some of the print images appear, as new "applied art," on T-shirts and greeting cards sold to tourists at the Kuru craft shop. Half of the "fine" artists are women and a number of them also make "applied" crafts. Because of such overlap between the fine and the applied art forms, the questions and issues this conceptual pair elicits in the art complex of Western and other societies are largely irrelevant in the San case.

3. As a result of a massive restructuring of the Kuru organization, the Kuru Development Trust is now called the Kuru Family of Organizations (KFO), consisting of seven smaller organizations, one of which, the D'Kar-based D'Kar Kuru Trust, administers the art project, while another, the Ghanzi-based Kalahari Crafts, markets the art works (Kuru Staff Members, 2002). What I report in this paper describes the situation as it existed during the time of fieldwork (1994–97), before KDT's restructuring.

4. In 1999 the !Xu and Khwe at Schmidtsdrift were officially awarded title deeds to three farms the South African government had purchased, on which they are to be resettled, once housing has been built at the new sites (Robins et al., 2002: 13–14). Today, the process of resettlement is expected to be complete by the end of 2002, at which time the Schmidtsdrift tents will be dismantled.

5. Their names are, for the men, Xg'oa Mangana (Qwaa, deceased), Qgoma Ncokg'o (Qmao, deceased), Thamae Setshogo, Xgaoc'o X'are, Thama Kase (Thamae Kaashe), Sobe Sobe, Qãetcao Moses (Olebogeng), Gamnqoa Kukama and Xgaiga Qhomatca and, for the women, Nxaedom Qhomatca (Ankie, deceased), Coex'ae Qgam (Dada), Cg'ose Ntcox'o (Cgoise), Ncg'abe Taase (Nxabe Eland), Coex'ae Bob (Ennie), X'aga Tcuixgao. It should be noted that the artists' names are transcribed by means of the "official" Nharo orthography, as developed by the linguist by Hessel Visser at D'Kar. In lieu of click symbols it uses consonants, in the following

Contemporary Bushman Art, Identity Politics, and the Primitivism Discourse   183

manner: "c" for "/" (dental click), "tc" for = (alveolar click), "x" for "//" (lateral click) and "q" for "!" (alveo-palatal click).

6. In 1995, when I visited the community, their names were, for the men, Joao Wenne Dikuanga, Fulai (Flai) Shipipa, Carimbwe Katunga, Steffans Samcuia, Freciano Ndala, Alouis Sijaja, Monto Masako, Bernardo (Tahulu) Rumau, Manuel Masseka, and, for the women, Zurietta Dala, Madena Kasanga, Andry Kashivi, Bongi Kasiki, Donna Rumao, and Julietta Calimbwe.

7. For example, at D'Kar over 152,300 Pula (or $50 000) were earned by the artists from 1993–95. About 75% of the proceeds went to the Kuru artists, each getting different sums, proportionate to his or her sales. Incomes of this magnitude put most of the artists into the relatively affluent sector of the D'Kar village residents, the majority of whom are poor and unemployed and live in hovels (Guenther, forthcoming).

8. In its conference version (at the 2001 CASCA meetings in Montreal) this paper was a slide presentation (consisting of close to 30 pictures). Because of practical constraints, the printed version can only offer a few pictures, a regrettable circumstance, given the subject matter. Samples of the art, by artists from both communities, can be viewed on the internet (at such sites as http://www.kalaharicraft.com/cgoise_text.htm, http://www.sanart.com/editione.htm, and http://www.africaserver .nl/kuru/). The art of the !Xun and Khwe artists is showcased in a recent book by Marlene Sullivan Winberg (2001).

9. This technique is also used by Australian Aboriginal artists (Krempel 1993; Morphy, 1989).

10. Formally, these pictures very much fit Bakhtin's classic definition of hybridization: "... a mixture of two social languages within the limits of a single utterance, an encounter, within the arena of an utterance, between two different linguistic consciousnesses, separated from one another by an epoch, by social differentiation, or by some other factor" (1981: 358).

11. Valda Blundell (1989) has described the same process—of ethnic art primordialization through media reportage—for the Canadian Inuit art scene.

12. As noted by one of the anonymous reviewers of this paper, one of the N/u men at Kagga Kamma has recently started creating rock engravings "in the spirit and form of the original rock engraving tradition." The same was reported by Rupert Isaacson—two men painting small gemsboks and hunters onto smooth slabs of rock, with a pigment of powdered red rock and animal fat mixed in a tortoise shell, all for tourist consumption (2002: 84).

13. Ethnotourism draws in a number of the country's and region's other ethnic groups, especially such photogenic groups as the Zulu, Pedi, Sotho, Ndebele or Himba (Crowe, 1996).

14. One of the anonymous referees felt that my paper presents primitivism in an "overwhelmingly bad light." As mitigating factors s/he points to such positive aspects as the San finding gainful employment through their involvement in cultural performance schemes and using these as an advocacy base for reclaiming ancestral land (as exemplified by the celebrated, successful Khomani case in South Africa's Kalahari Gemsbok National Park). The point is also made that the San themselves (for instance at Kagga Kamma) are not dupes in such schemes, that display, market and exploit their heritage, but willing and astute participants. Another point made is that the San themselves are not infrequently "dominantly conservative," in contrast to the "people researching them [who] are often more left-leaning and tend to be made uncomfortable by things that do not always cause concern to the Indigenous people themselves." Finally, the referee points out that in South Africa the Primitivism movement "found root," amongst White artists (such as Walter Battiss, Pippa Skotnes and others) who found inspiration in San art, aspects of which

they incorporated into their own work. This is presented as a positive instance of cultural appropriation, because it raised the profile of the San and made Whites aware that "both 'they' and 'us' make 'art'." While I appreciate these points (to some of which I have addressed myself elsewhere [2002, forthcoming]), I remain troubled by what I see as the dark side in the primitivism trope, as applied to contemporary, "modern" San art: its penchant for reifying stereotypes and the damaging implications this has for the post-foraging San people's political struggle.

15. For instance Australia, where Judith Ryan (1993) has noted an "ochre canon" in modern Aboriginal bark paintings, which constrains the Aboriginal artists' range of artistic expression.

16. For instance, on artists amongst the Ainu (Low, 1976: 221), Australian Aboriginals (Lüthi, 1993: 26–29; Ryan, 1993: 61–63; Williams, 1976: 278), Baule (Steiner, 1994: 108) and Inuit (Berlo, 1999: 190–192; Mitchell, 1998; Seagrave, 1998).

References

=Oma, Kxao Moses, and Axel Thoma. 2002. "Will Tourism Destroy San Culture?" In *The Kalahari San Self-Determination in the Desert*, ed. Richard B. Lee, Robert Hitchcock, and Megan Biesele. Special issue of *Cultural Survival Quarterly* 26: 39–41.

Bakhtin, M.M. 1981. *The Dialogic Imagination.* Austin: University of Texas Press.

Bank, Andrew, ed. 1998. *The Proceedings of the Khoisan Identities and Cultural Heritage Conference.* Cape Town: The Institute for Historical Research, University of the Western Cape.

Barnard, Alan. 1998. "Problems in the Construction of Khoisan Ethnicities." In *The Proceedings of the Khoisan Identities and Cultural Heritage Conference*, Bank, 51–58.

Bascom, William. 1976. "Changing African Art." In *Ethnic and Tourist Art*, ed. Nelson Graburn. Berkeley: University of California Press, 303–19.

Berlo, Janet C. 1999. "Drawing (upon) the Past: Negotiating Identities in Inuit Graphic Arts Production." In *Unpacking Culture: Art and Commodity in Colonial and Postcolonial Worlds*, ed. Ruth Phillips and Christopher Steiner. Berkeley: University of California Press, 178–93.

Biesele, Megan. 1993. *Women Like Meat: The Folklore on Foraging Ideology of the Kalahari Ju/'hoan.* Johannesburg: Witwatersrand University Press.

Blundell, Geoffrey. 1998. "Some Aspects Concerning Rock Art and National Identity in South Africa." In *The Proceedings of the Khoisan Identities and Cultural Heritage Conference*, Bank, 153–57.

Blundell, Valda. 1989. "Speaking the Art of Canada's Native Peoples: Anthropological Discourses in the Media." In *Australian-Canadian Studies* 7: 23–42.

Bourdieu, Pierre, Alain Darbel, and Dominique Schnapper. 1969. *L'Amour de l'art: Les musées d'art européens et leur public.* 2d ed. Paris: Editions Minuit.

Broermann, Magdalena. 2002. "WIMSA." In *The Kalahari San Self-Determination in the Desert*, Lee, Hitchcock, and Biesele. *Cultural Survival Quarterly* 26: 45–47.

Buntman, Barbara. 1996. "Bushman Images in South African Tourist Advertising: The Case of Kagga Kamma." In *Miscast: Negotiating the Presence of the Bushmen,* ed. Pippa Skotnes. Cape Town: University of Cape Town Press, 257–70.

Buntman, Barbara. 2002. "Travels to Otherness: Whose Identity Do We Want to See?" In *Self- and Other-Images of Hunter-Gatherers,* Senri Ethnological Series No. 60, ed. Alan Barnard and Henry Stewart, 65–84.

Clifford, James. 1985. "Histories of the Tribal and the Modern." *Art in America* (April 1995): 164–77.

Crowe, Sarah. 1996. "African Pride Village Life." *Springbok* (June 1996): 69–76, 209.

Douglas, Stuart. 1994. "Images of Difference: The Textualization of the Schmidtsdrift Bushmen." Paper presented at the conference "People, Politics and Power: Representing the Bushmen People of Southern Africa." Johannesburg, 4–7 August 1994.

Dowson, Thomas. 1996. "Re-production and Consumption: The Use of Rock Art Imagery in Southern Africa Today." In *Miscast,* Skotnes, 315–22.

Faris, James C. 1988. "'ART/artifact': On the Museum of Anthropology." *Current Anthropology* 29: 775–79.

Gall, Sandy. 2001. *The Bushmen of Southern Africa Slaughter of the Innocent.* London: Chatto & Windus.

Godwin, Peter. 2001. "Bushmen Last Stand for Southern Africa's First People." *National Geographic* 199: 90–117.

Gordon, Robert. 1990. Review of *People of the Great Sandface,* by Paul Myburgh. *CVA Review* (Commission on Visual Anthropology) (fall): 30–34.

———. 1992. *The Bushman Myth: The Making of an Underclass.* Boulder: Westview Press.

Graburn, Nelson. 1976. *Ethnic and Tourist Art.* Berkeley: University of California Press.

———. 1999. "Epilogue: Ethnic and Tourist Arts Revisited." In *Unpacking Culture,* Phillips and Steiner, 335–54.

Guenther, Mathias. 1986. "San" or "Bushman?" In *The Past and Future of !Kung Ethnography: Critical Reflections and Symbolic Perspectives. Essays in Honour of Lorna Marshall,* ed. Megan Biesele, Robert Gordon, and Richard B. Lee. Hamburg: Helmut Buske Verlag, 347–73.

———. 1990. Review of *People of the Great Sandface,* by Paul Myburgh. *CVA Review* (Commission on Visual Anthropology) (fall): 44–45.

———. 1998. "Farm Labourer, Trance Dancer, Artist: The Life and Works of Qwaa Mangana." In *The Proceedings of the Khoisan Identities & Cultural Heritage Conference,* Bank, 212–34.

———. 1999. *Tricksters and Trancers Bushman Religion and Society.* Bloomington: Indiana University Press.

———. 2002. "Ethnotourism and the Bushmen." In *Self- and Other-Images of Hunter-Gatherers,* Barnard and Stewart, 47–64.

———. forthcoming. *The Kuru Art Project at D'Kar, Botswana Art and Identity among Contemporary San.* Forthcoming.

Hall, Martin. 1995. "The Legend of the Lost City: Or, the Man with the Golden Balls." *Journal of Southern African Studies* 21: 179–99.

Hitchcock, Robert. 1996. *Bushmen and the Politics of the Environment in Southern Africa*. IWGIA Document No. 79. Copenhagen: International Work Group for Indigenous Affairs.

Isaacson, Rupert. 2002. *The Healing Land: A Kalahari Journey*. London: Fourth Estate.

Katz, Richard, Megan Biesele, and Verna St. Denis. 1997. *Healing Makes our Hearts Happy: Spirituality and Cultural Transformation among the Kalahari Ju/'hoansi*. Rochester: Inner Traditions.

Kopytoff, Igor. 1986. "The Cultural Biography of Things: Commoditization as Process." In *The Social Life of Things: Commodities in Cultural Perspective*, ed. Arjun Appadurai. Cambridge: Cambridge University Press, 64–91.

Krempel, Ulrich. 1993. "Wie liest man fremde Bilder?" In *Aratjara Kunst der ersten Australier*, ed. Bernhard Lüthi. Cologne: DuMont Buchverlag, 37–40.

Kuru Staff Members. 2002. "The Kuru Family of Organizations." In *The Kalahari San Self-Determination in the Desert*, Lee, Hitchcock, and Biesele. *Cultural Survival Quarterly* 26: 48.

Landau, Paul. 1996. "With Camera and Gun in Southern Africa: Inventing the Image of the Bushmen c. 1880–1935." In *Miscast*, Skotnes, 129–42.

Lee, Molly. 1999. "Tourism and Taste Cultures: Collecting Native Art in Alaska at the Turn of the Twentieth Century." In *Unpacking Culture*, Phillips and Steiner, 267–81.

Lee, Richard B. 1985. "The Gods Must be Crazy but the Producers Know Exactly What They Are Doing." *Southern Africa Report* (June): 19–20.

———. 2003. *The Dobe Ju/'hoansi*. Belmont, Calif.: Wadsworth Thomson Learning.

Lee, Richard B., Robert Hitchcock, and Megan Biesele, ed. 2002. *The Kalahari San Self-Determination in the Desert*. Special issue of *Cultural Survival Quarterly* 26.

Lewis-Williams, David J. 1981. *Believing and Seeing: Symbolic Meanings in Southern San Rock Paintings*. New York: Academic Press.

———. 2000. *Stories That Float from Afar Ancestral Folklore of the San of Southern Africa*. Cape Town: David Philip.

Lewis-Williams, David J., and Thomas Dowson. 1988. "Sign of All Times: Entoptic Phenomena in Upper Paleolithic Art." *Current Anthropology* 29: 201–45.

———. 1989. *Images of Power: Understanding Bushman Rock Art*. Johannesburg: Southern.

Lewis-Williams, David J., and David G. Pearce. 2005. *San Spirituality: Roots, Expression and Social Consequences*. Walnut Creek, CA: Altamira.

Low, Setha M. 1976. "Contemporary Ainu Wood and Stone Carvings." In *Ethnic and Tourist Art*, ed. Nelson Graburn. Berkley: University of California Press, 211–25.

Lüthi, Bernhard. 1993. *Aratjara Kunst der ersten Australier*. Cologne: DuMont Buchverlag.

Masilela, Ntongela. 1987. "The White South African Writer in Our National Situation." *Matatu* 3/4: 48–75.

Mitchell, Marybell. 1998. "Constructing Cultural Forms of their Own Choosing." *Inuit Art* 13: 2–3.

Morphy, Howard. 1989. "From Dull to Brilliant: The Aesthetics of Spiritual Power." *Man* 24: 21–40.

Phillips, Ruth. 1999. "Nuns, Ladies and the 'Queen of the Huron': Appropriating the Savage in Nineteenth-Century Huron Tourist Art." In *Unpacking Culture*, Phillips and Steiner, eds. Berkeley: University of California Press, 33–50.

Phillips, Ruth, and Christopher Steiner. 1999. In *Unpacking Culture: Art and Commodity in Colonial and Postcolonial Worlds*. Berkeley: University of California Press.

Pratt, Mary Louise. 1992. *Imperial Eyes: Travel Writing and Transculturation*. New York: Routledge.

Price, Sally. 1989. *Primitive Art in Civilized Places*. Chicago: University of Chicago Press.

Robins, Steven, Elias Madzudzo, and Matthias Brenzinger. 2002. *An Assessment of the Status of the San in South Africa, Angola, Zambia and Zimbabwe, Regional Assessment of the Status of the San in Southern Africa*, Report No. 2. Windhoek: Legal Assistance Centre.

Rubin, William, ed. 1984. *"Primitivism" in Twentieth-Century Art: Affinity of the Tribal and the Modern*. New York: Museum of Modern Art.

Ryan, Judith. 1993. "Kunst der Aborigines Australiens: Andersartigkeit oder Ähnlichkeit?" In *Aratjara Kunst der ersten Australier*, Lüthi, 49–63.

Seagrave, Annalisa. 1998. "Regenerations: The Graphic Art of Three Young Artists." *Inuit Art* 18: 4–15.

Skotnes, Pippa, ed. 1996. *Miscast: Negotiating the Presence of the Bushmen*. Cape Town: University of Cape Town Press.

Smith, Andy, Candy Malherbe, Mathias Guenther, and Penny Berens. 2000. *The Bushmen of Southern Africa: A Foraging Society in Transition*. Cape Town: David Philip.

Smith, B., J. David Lewis-Williams, G. Blundell, and C. Chippindale. 2001. "Archaeology and Symbolism in the New South African Coat of Arms." *Antiquity* 74: 467–68.

Steiner, Christopher. 1994. *African Art in Transit*. Cambridge: Cambridge University Press.

Tomaselli, Keyan. 1993. "The Post-Apartheid Era: The San as Bridge between Past and Future." In *Eyes across the Water*, ed. R.M. Boonzaier Flaes and D. Harper. Amsterdam: Het Spinhuis.

———, ed. 1995. "Recuperating the San." Special issue of *Critical Arts* 9 (2).

Torgovnick, Marianne. 1990. *Gone Primitive: Savage Intellects, Modern Lives*, Chicago: University of Chicago Press.

Vinnicombe, Patricia. 1976. *People of the Eland: Rock Paintings of the Drakensberg Bushmen as a Reflection of their Life and Thought*. Pietermaritzburg: Natal University Press.

Volkman, Toby A. 1988. "Out of Africa: The Gods Must be Crazy." In *Image Ethics*, ed. L. Gross and J. Ruby. New York: Oxford University Press.

Whyte, Hilton. 1995. *In the Tradition of the Forefathers: Bushman Traditionality at Kagga Kamma*. Cape Town: University of Cape Town Press.

Williams, Nancy. 1976. "Australian Aboriginal Art at Yirrkala: Introduction and Development of Marketing." In *Ethnic and Tourist Art*, ed. Nelson Graburn. Berkeley: University of California Press, 266–84.

Wilmsen, Edwin. 1989. *Land Filled with Flies: A Political Economy of the Kalahari*. Chicago: University of Chicago Press.

———. 1992. Comment on *People of the Great Sandface*. *Visual Anthropology* 5: 175–80.

———. 1995. "First People? Images and Imaginations in South African Iconography, Recuperating the San." *Critical Arts* 9(2): 1–27.

Winberg, Marlene Sullivan. 2001. *My Eland's Heart*. Cape Town: David Philip.

Chapter 11

CLASS, CULTURE, AND RECOGNITION
SAN FARM WORKERS AND INDIGENOUS IDENTITIES[1]

Renée Sylvain

Introduction

Over thirty years ago, ethnographic research on the San challenged deeply held beliefs about "human nature." The work of Richard Lee, and other Kalahari researchers influenced by Lee, was especially important because it debunked Hobbesian stereotypes about "primitive people" that served to justify race, class, and gender inequalities, both within Western societies and in colonial contexts. Today, the challenges presented by the San to Western philosophical and political presuppositions go beyond exploding myths and stereotypes. Their current activism as indigenous peoples and their current engagement in identity politics requires activists and academics to rethink received definitions of "culture," "class," "autonomy," and "authenticity."

Meanwhile, the field of anthropology, and Kalahari hunter-gatherer studies in particular, has undergone a philosophical shift away from trying to uncover a universal human nature to examining what goes into the local production of distinct identities. The Canadian philosopher Charles Taylor highlights the distinction between "human nature" and "identity" in the following way:

Notes for this section can be found on page 200.

Herder put forward the idea that each of us has an original way of being human... This idea has burrowed very deep into modern consciousness... There is a certain way of being human that is *my* way ... this notion gives a new importance to being true to myself. If I am not, I miss the point of my life; I miss what being human is for *me*. (1994: 30)

Two key presuppositions provide the basis for contemporary identity politics. First, identity is predicated on what Taylor calls "the ideal of authenticity"—that is, an "authentic" identity cannot be imposed, but is something that only autonomous agents can articulate and define for themselves (Taylor, 1994: 31; see also Hall, 1997a; 1997b). This ideal sets the standard for cultural authenticity, as well: "Just like individuals, a *Volk* should be true to itself, that is, its own culture" (Taylor, ibid). The second presupposition is that identity requires recognition. As Taylor notes: "[O]ur identity is partly shaped by recognition or by its absence... Nonrecognition or misrecognition can inflict harm, can be a form of oppression, imprisoning someone in a false, distorted, and reduced mode of being" (1994: 25).

In this paper I address these two theses—that identities rest on an "ideal of authenticity," and that identities require recognition—in light of the situation of the farm San in the Omaheke Region of Namibia. I first examine some of the ideological causes and material consequences of misrecognition. I then outline how current San struggles for political recognition reveal important assumptions surrounding the terms "authenticity" and "the invention of tradition." Finally, I examine expressions of identity among the San in the Omaheke, a context in which the idea of San culture (as an autonomous creation) is in tension with their highly dependent underclass status. This is a tension that expressed itself in the field of hunter-gatherer studies as the central question of the Great Kalahari Debate: namely, should the San be seen as creations or as casualties of colonization and global capitalism? (See Gordon and Spiegel, 1993: 89).

Invisible and Indigenous Identities

Disappearing Bushmen

When I first arrived in Namibia, a researcher with the Namibian Broadcasting Corporation (NBC) who had grown up in the Omaheke informed me that there were no Bushmen left in the region—they had disappeared years ago. It turned out that Bushmen were conspicuously present in the Omaheke and that what the NBC researcher had meant to say was that there were no real or authentic Bushmen left in the region. This was a widespread and historically deep attitude among non-San in Namibia.

The "real" Bushmen have disappeared, first, through intermarriage with other ethnic groups. A white resident of Gobabis told me: "There are no pure Bushmen left anymore. They've been intermarrying with other ethnic groups far too long." Boldly tying group authenticity directly to its male members, he explained: "Real Bushmen have semi-erections all the time." More importantly, however, the San have "disappeared" because they have been forced to abandon their traditional hunting and gathering lifestyle. Once they become incorporated into a modern political economy and state system, they cease to be "authentic" Bushmen. This view is not confined to Namibia. A missionary in Ghanzi, Botswana, told me: "Once they get an education, they are no longer Bushmen ... when they go to look for work they are Basarwa."[2]

I initially treated stories about disappearing Bushmen as ill-informed stereotypes that contributed to the general neglect of the San by the state. But the more often I heard such stories, the more I was forced to acknowledge a deeper problem, and one that bore on larger issues of identity politics. During the first year of my field work (1996), the Working Group of Indigenous Minorities in Southern Africa (WIMSA) was established to assist the San in their claims for rights as indigenous peoples in national and international forums. It suddenly began to matter a great deal whether the underclass of farm laborers I studied in the Omaheke were "real" Bushmen. The class status of the Omaheke San—as well as doubts about cultural authenticity engendered by that status—was becoming increasingly linked to their prospects for political empowerment and to the form such empowerment might eventually take.

Exclusion and Exploitation

To understand how the Omaheke San became invisible, we need to take a brief glance back. Two very different historical trajectories of colonial rule and identity formation were followed in the case of the Namibian San. For those San living in what is now the Otjozondjupa Region, colonial rule, and later apartheid, took the form of geographical, economic, and political segregation and containment on reserves, and an ethnic homeland (Bushmanland), where they were able to maintain a foraging lifestyle until fairly recently. But other groups— such as the Omaheke San—experienced colonial rule and apartheid as a process of complete land dispossession and eventual incorporation into the lowest stratum of a racialized and ethnically hierarchical class system. These two historical trajectories were reflected by the colonial distinction between the "wild" hunting and gathering Bushmen, and the "tame" farm laboring Bushmen.

The distinction between "wild" and "tame" Bushmen was never part of an internally coherent ideological scheme. But it did provide opportunistic justifications for exploitative labor relations—justifications that are echoed by the Omaheke farmers today. For example, many farmers still do not see their San employees as workers (which, since independence, would imply rights to certain standards of housing and remuneration). The Bushmen are still considered "wild" enough to have no need for a living wage or for decent housing (see also Suzman, 2000; Sylvain, 1997; 1999). But, while their inherent "wildness" excludes them from cash transactions and state politics, the loss of their foraging lifestyle prevents their recognition as "real" Bushmen. Too conspicuously Bushmen for participation in the "modern" world, but too obviously farm laborers to claim an "authentic" Bushman identity, the Omaheke San have fallen from sight between our categories of class and culture.

Three connected assumptions in popular discourse influence how Bushmen identity is recognized (or misrecognized): first, Bushman identity is pegged to a unique relationship with the land;[3] second, this relationship is crucial to a premodern lifestyle and identity; and third, class relationships—by alienating the San from their land and incorporating them into "modern" social relationships—dissolve their cultural identity. As the San struggle for recognition by participating in international forums, we should ask whether, and to what extent, the prospects for recognition of indigenous peoples in southern Africa is tied to these neocolonial assumptions about racial "Others."

Two main goals of the international indigenous peoples' movement are to secure land rights and to achieve local self-determination.[4] San struggles around these issues have so far been impressive. For example, the ≠Khomani San in South Africa won an important land claim victory in 1999, and in 1998, the Ju/'hoansi in the north of Namibia were granted rights to what is now the Nyae Nyae Conservancy (Working Group of Indigenous Minorities in Southern Africa, 1998). Even in cases where the San have not yet been successful in their struggles over land rights—such as in the Central Kalahari Game Reserve—connections with the global indigenous movement and broader nongovernmental organization (NGO) networks have helped lend international support to their cause. Nonetheless, some aspects of international discourse on indigenous identity resonate uncomfortably close to the three assumptions I outlined above.

First, much of the rhetoric surrounding land rights invokes the ontological premise that what *distinguishes* indigenous peoples from the masses of the world's impoverished marginalized minorities is a unique (often spiritual) relationship with the land. For example, in a speech celebrating the ≠Khomani victory, the South African Minister of Agriculture and Land Affairs, Hon. Derek Hanekom, stated that "We are here celebrating more than just the settlement of a land

Class, Culture, and Recognition 193

claim: we are here celebrating the rebirth of the ≠Khomani nation" (cited in Brörmann, 1999: 43). The ≠Khomani San's lawyer told the *Globe and Mail* that "a return to their land will give them back their identity" (20 March 1999). However, if the formerly landless ≠Khomani nation is being "reborn," if their cultural identity is being "given back," then to whom were land rights given, if not the cultural community of the ≠Khomani San? This conceptual inconsistency provides as much room for the denial of rights to land and political representation as it does for the recognition of these rights.

Second, as Will Kymlicka (1999) points out, legal distinctions between indigenous peoples and stateless nations (or "national minorities") rest on the notion that indigenous peoples are defined by radical "Otherness." New international norms regarding the status of indigenous peoples are based on the belief that "Indigenous peoples do not just constitute distinct cultures, but ... entirely different forms of culture ... rooted in a pre-modern way of life that needs protecting from the forces of modernization" (Kymlicka, 1999: 289). The third, related assumption is found in the exclusive nature of the distinction between culture and class. For example, Anti-Slavery International and the International Work Group for Indigenous Affairs describe a consequence of slavery and other forms of unfree labor as the "loss of cultural and political identity as Peoples" (1997: 19).

Each of these three assumptions magnifies the distinction between indigenous peoples and impoverished minorities. This is worrisome for two reasons: first, it effectively isolates indigenous peoples' issues from class issues, making the two mutually exclusive concerns; and secondly, by essentializing the identities of indigenous peoples, it risks "deculturating" those indigenous people who were dispossessed of their land by colonization. Much like the popular discourse on the "disappearing Bushmen," international discourse on indigenism risks defining those San who happen also to be an underclass as casualties of colonization and capitalism.

Rights and Recognition

The Invention of Tradition and Traditional Authorities

An alternative to defining the farm San as casualties of colonization and capitalism is to describe them as creations of these same processes, which is the approach that Kalahari "revisionists" adopted (see Wilmsen, 1989; Wilmsen and Denbow, 1990). The revisionists' "invention of tradition" approach appears, superficially at least, to recommend itself in cases where the San live in conditions of extreme dependency and are subject to the stereotypes that more powerful groups impose on them. But despite the commendable historicism of the revisionists' approach, they remain wedded to a deeply essentialist view of ethnic identity: their claim is that if we do not find the Bushmen of "traditionalist" ethnography, but instead find slaves, serfs, or rural proletarians, then, first, the category "Bushmen" is merely a creation of capitalism and colonization and, second, if the category is "created" or "invented," then it is a Western fiction. As Robert Gordon says, in *The Bushman Myth*: "The term Bushman is thus a 'lumpen' category into which all those who failed to conform or acquiesce were dumped. It is not an ethnic group but a sociopolitical category derived from a wider setting." (1992: 6). Here the implication is that, if an identity has been constructed, if it is a product of history, it must be fictitious (or in Gordon's words "a myth"). Either ethnicity and culture are primordial, ontological categories, or they are nothing at all. A second problem with the revisionists' use of the "invention of tradition" approach—one that has been emphasized in Richard Lee's work—is that it attributes too much power to "the system" (see Lee, 1992; Solway and Lee, 1990). This perspective obscures San agency in the dynamic relationships between the San and their significant "Others," whether those Others are the agents of colonialism, capitalism, or newly independent governments.

After the Namibian government passed the Traditional Authorities Act in 1995 (amended in 1997), San groups in Namibia began petitioning for government recognition for their community leaders (see Felton, 2000).[5] Government recognition of community leaders may mean a seat on the Council of Traditional Leaders, which would give the San a voice in discussions about land reform (Felton, 2000: 5). San struggles for recognition under this act are shaped by the three assumptions outlined above: that is, Bushmen identity is pegged to the land, it is premodern, and it is incompatible with class relations. At the same time, however, their struggles for political recognition are also shaped by assumptions surrounding the term "invented": that is, invented traditions are "made up" and "fictitious." I will address each assumption in turn.

First, the obstacles some San communities have confronted are associated with making landedness a precondition for recognition. The Traditional Authorities Act defines a "traditional community" as inter alia one "inhabiting a common communal area" (i.e., living in a former homeland). According to this definition, those San who live as a farm laboring underclass on land owned by others do not qualify as a "traditional community," and so have been unable to gain official recognition. However, the minority of San who retained at least de facto land rights (that is, those most clearly "tribalized" by colonial rule and put into a homeland) are also those who are most unproblematically entitled to political recognition.

Second, the recognition of San traditional leaders is also hindered by a static definition of "premodern" and "primitive" San culture. A common view holds that the San traditionally lived in foraging band societies and therefore did not own land, nor did they have formal leadership structures (Felton, 2000: 6).[6] Introducing leadership structures and modern property relations would compromise their cultural authenticity. Finally, San struggles for political recognition under the Traditional Authorities Act are shaped by tensions between class status and cultural identity. Silke Felton notes that the San are generally regarded as "different" by other ethnic groups, but they "are not usually credited with characteristics of distinct tribes"; instead, they are seen by others "as a socially inferior, mainly cattleless *class*" (2000: 6, emphasis mine). The implication of this attitude is that the San are more appropriately placed under the jurisdiction of the Bantu-speaking Traditional Authority for the area in which San "serfs" are found.

In light of static definitions of "authentic" Bushmen identity—as inherently premodern and uncontaminated by class—San struggles for recognition are troubled by the question of whether "traditional leadership [is being] copied or 'invented'?" (Felton, 2000: 4). Where continuity with the past is taken as the standard for measuring cultural authenticity, any form of activism that appears to involve "inventing" becomes questionable, because "invented" is taken to mean "fictitious," "made up," and therefore "inauthentic" (Lee, 1992: 36; Li, 2000: 150; Linnekin, 1991; Solway and Lee, 1990: 110). The assumptions underlying common conceptions of "authentic" and "invented" put pressure on indigenous peoples, in particular the San who are still struggling for recognition, to conform to what are often stereotypical definitions of their cultural identity.

The Ideal of Authenticity and the Problem of Autonomy

Since the "invention of tradition" approach to ethnic identity is often seen to undermine the claims to cultural authenticity of indigenous peoples, some have suggested that promoting an essentialized identity is a politically effective strategy for indigenous peoples to adopt (see, for example, Lattas, 1993). However, strategic essentialism can also leave the San open to accusations that their own expressions of identity are merely opportunistic and therefore "inauthentic" (Li, 2000: 151). Furthermore, strategic essentialism may not help us avoid the problem of misrecognition. The case of the ≠Khomani San at the Kagga Kamma Bushman ecotourism scheme provides an important lesson here.

Public reaction to Kagga Kamma invoked rhetoric that contrasts "authentic primitives" with a "detribalized" underclass. One letter to the South African newspaper, the *Argus*, expressed the hope that "the local authorities in Ceres will not allow [...] these happy child-like people [...] to be used for 'exhibition' purposes" (cited in White, 1995: 16). Another letter claimed that "There are in fact no Bushmen today who still live in the traditional way as hunter-gatherers... Dressed in rags and on the edge of starvation, [the little people at Kagga Kamma] were happy to accept the chance *to act like Bushmen.*" (Cited in White, 1995: 16, emphasis mine.)

The distinction between "authentic," happy, "child-like" Bushmen and impoverished people who merely *act like* Bushmen is important for the following reasons: first, the stereotype of "happy child-like Bushmen" provides a common justification for denying the San the status of modern citizens and for their continued economic exploitation as an underclass; second, if cultural rights are meant to redress historical injustices and inequalities, and not merely create a space for the preservation of fossilized cultures, then it is counterproductive to deny cultural identity to those people most in need of economic and social justice.[7]

As public response to the Kagga Kamma ecotourism project and the case of the Traditional Authorities Act in Namibia both indicate, the San are struggling for rights on a very narrow and contradictory field of recognition: they may be denied rights as an ethnic group on the grounds that their underclass status dissolves their cultural authenticity; and they may be denied rights as modern citizens on the grounds that their "authentic" cultural identity is defined by premodern, prepolitical primitivism (Comaroff and Comaroff, 1999; Garland, 1999).

The assumptions about "cultural authenticity" and "invented traditions" make an invented but authentic culture a contradiction in terms, equivalent to a fictional, but real culture. They leave no room to acknowledge San agency in the creation ("invention") of their own identity. Solway and Lee have argued convincingly that "foragers can be autonomous without being isolated and engaged without being incorporated" (1990: 110). We can take this important point about autonomy further and apply it to the case of the farm San to challenge the view that underclass status (as a condition of dependency) is incompatible with a cultural identity (as an autonomous creation). Autonomy is never perfect and absolute—it is always partial and is usually negotiated and compromised, without being altogether lost. My own research found that the Omaheke farm San, despite their conditions of dependency, still exercise considerable autonomy in the creation of their own cultural identity—they have a hand in the invention of their own traditions. If we want to find the "authentic" San, we must look to the world the San made for themselves and not let our search be hobbled by an overdrawn contrast between class and culture.

Class versus Culture

Colonization and Class Formation

In the Omaheke Region, class relations both shape and are shaped by local cultural systems. Afrikaner settlers did not introduce an acultural global economy into the Omaheke when they established their cattle ranches, but brought with them their own culturally unique method of organizing the Omaheke political economy. Since the system of farm government in the Omaheke enjoyed (and still enjoys) considerable autonomy from state interference, the settlers were able to give expression to their culturally distinctive views of race, class, and gender. A central feature of this cultural political economy is the principle of farm government known as baasskap, which organizes race, gender, and class relations according to the model of an extended patriarchal family (see Sylvain, 2001). In the Omaheke, the settlers' complex and contradictory racial mythology of the "Bushman" relegates the San to the bottom rung in an ethnic labor hierarchy in which, under the baasskap system of family and farm government, the San are placed in the position of perpetual childhood. ("I am the Papa," an Afrikaner farmer will say of "his Bushmen," even if "his" Bushmen laborers literally helped to raise him from childhood on his father's farm.)

In the Omaheke, the San are subject to powerful stereotypes that shape their material conditions and their cultural context. Given the farmers' economic dominance and the hegemonic status their world view enjoys, we might expect to find that the cultural identity of the San has been imposed—that is, that they have come to understand themselves according to the farmers' terms (see, for example, Suzman, 2000). But this view of San cultural identity is far too simplistic.

Cultural Identity and Class Consciousness

The Omaheke San do have a cultural identity, and it is one that they have forged for themselves in relation to and in opposition to the definitions the farmers try to impose upon them. Their culturally unique ways of coping with and resisting class exploitation are an essential part of what it means for them to be San today. I will offer a few examples to illustrate the nature of the dynamic culture the Omaheke San have created for themselves.

The most significant challenge to the Afrikaners' paternalistic ideology and patriarchal "family-based" farm government is the vitality and adaptability of the San's own kinship ties. The San kinship system I encountered on the farms was remarkably similar to those described by Lee (1986; 1993) and Marshall (1976) among the foraging San in Dobe and Nyae Nyae, but with a few features that reflect their class situation.[8] In the past, farmers gave San servants European names.[9]

Over the years, the San appropriated these Afrikaner names and assimilated them into their own naming system so that specific "Afrikaans names" are now linked with specific San names. Thus, if a child is named after a grandmother who has the San name "N≠isa" and the Afrikaans name "Anna," then that child will also be called N≠isa-Anna. The San take their naming system very much to heart and get quite upset when, as sometimes happens, a farmer presumes to give a San child an "Afrikaans" name. They get upset for good reason: a name also marks a location in a kinship system. Their kinship system is crucial to their existence as a community and to their sense of who they are as a "people" (*nasie*). Kinship provides the basis for ordering a whole world of social interaction that is not directly under the farmer's control.

Beyond providing the basis for ordering social relationships, kinship ties, together with their very strong sharing ethos, also form the infrastructure connecting the widely scattered farm San community and enabling elaborate systems of mutual support and assistance. The San confront their conditions of dependency and exploitation by mobilizing their kinship system to provide a social safety net that helps them to cope with scarce resources, unemployment, and "homelessness" (Sylvain, 1999; 1997). This social infrastructure is especially important as men travel great distances from farm to farm seeking work, and for San living in conditions of extreme marginalization far from genealogical kin. In such cases, non-kin who have the same name will assume the kin relations of their namesakes, "making family," and thus form bonds of mutual assistance and support.

Despite the fact that the Omaheke San live in conditions of extreme poverty, their cultural resources provide for more than just bare survival; they also provide a sense of identity and unity. San expressive culture in the Omaheke reflects both a cultural identity and a class consciousness. For example, San healers ritualistically incorporate money into their healing ceremonies (trance dances), which are now often conducted in order to combat the psychological distress of poverty, exploitation, and alcoholism. The healers, who are also known for their ability to transform themselves into "dangerous" animals (e.g., lions and leopards) now purport to use this power to gain advantages in stock theft as well as hunting. Their menstrual (Besu) ceremony includes some recently invented symbols, such as dressing the initiate in the garb of a Herero woman—a symbol of higher class status—to signal her "upward" transition to "womanhood." Today the menstrual ceremony marking the transition to "womanhood" means not only that the young initiate is marriageable and ready for domestic duties, but also that she is ready for domestic service in white households.[10]

I can here only hint at the dynamic culture that the San have made for themselves in the Omaheke. But I suggest that what a closer exam-

Class, Culture, and Recognition 199

ination will show is that, in the Omaheke, class and culture are mutually constituting: the unique culture of the Omaheke San would not exist as it does today if it were not for their class experiences; and the class system in the Omaheke would not exist as it does today if not for the culturally unique responses and modes of resistance on the part of the San people themselves.[11]

Conclusion

The linguistically and culturally diverse San groups throughout southern Africa are only now building the institutional infrastructure necessary for gaining rights and recognition. The question of whether or not the San are merely creating a "distinct identity" or "traditions" will nag us only so long as we assume that whatever is forged by historical processes and political economy cannot be a real cultural identity. Current San activism self-consciously reflects their colonial and postcolonial experiences of dispossession, marginalization, exploitation, and stigmatization (see, for example /Useb, 2000; Gaeses,1998; Thoma and ≠Oma, 1999). The recognition of this historical, contextual, and emergent identity is critical to the empowerment of the San and to the improvement of their material conditions.

Andrew Spiegel (1994) notes that the invention and manipulation of tradition have the potential either to legitimate or, alternatively, to challenge dominant power asymmetries. However, the emancipatory potential of manipulating traditions or asserting cultural identity is linked to the form that the rhetoric of cultural rights takes. The challenge facing rights activists is that of minimizing the extent to which claims for cultural rights sustain unequal power relations in other areas of social and economic life (see Bond and Gilliam, 1994: 4; Stammers, 1999: 1005). Critics of identity politics have rightly noted that an overemphasis on representation and "discourse" distract us from pressing problems of poverty and economic inequalities (Craig and Tiessen, 1993; Nystrom and Puckett, 1998; Rorty, 1998). Lee suggests that "focusing [...] on the social construction of current indigenous realities" has led anthropologists to neglect "indigenous peoples' still precarious position in the political economy and class politics of their respective nation states" (2000: 20). Lee's point highlights the need to recognize that indigenous issues are inseparable from class issues.

San activism also represents a deeper challenge to postcolonial, neoliberal political categories since "rights are not just instruments of law, they are expressions of [a] moral identity as a people" (Ignatieff, 2000: 12; see also Stammers, 1999). San struggles are therefore also efforts to articulate and legitimate an alternative identity, one that challenges us to rethink conventional categories (such as class and culture), as well as the philosophical and anthropological concepts (such as "authentic" and "invented") that sustain postcolonial inequalities.

Notes

1. This research was generously supported by the Social Sciences and Humanities Research Council of Canada and the Izaak Walton Killam Foundation. I would like to thank the members of the Department of Sociology and Social Anthropology at Dalhousie University who provided useful comments on earlier versions of these ideas, the editors of this journal, and the anonymous reviewers for their helpful comments and suggestions. I am deeply grateful to the people in Namibia who provided invaluable assistance with my research, especially the many San who shared their experiences with me. Special thanks goes, of course, to Richard Lee for inspiring me to work with the San, and for guiding me through a challenging field. Deepest gratitude goes to Rocky Jacobsen, for all his support and encouragement.
2. In this context, the missionary meant that the San are "serfs" when they become "Basarwa."
3. The relevant relationship is more profound than mere territoriality. The implicit claim is that they have a unique *way of being* in the natural environment.
4. For a discussion of the debates surrounding "self-determination" in indigenous peoples' politics, see Kymlicka (1999).
5. This act defines a "traditional community" as: "an indigenous, homogeneous, endogamous social grouping of persons comprising families deriving from exogamous clans which share a common ancestry, language, cultural heritage, customs and traditions, recognizes a common traditional authority and inhabits a common communal area; and includes the members of that community residing outside the common area" (cited in Working Group of Indigenous Minorities in Southern Africa, 2000: 13, footnote 7). The use of the term "indigenous" here is problematic because it defines all Africans as "indigenous," and so has the potential to diminish the significance of San peoples' claims to indigenous status, and/or the application of international legal instruments on indigenous peoples' rights to the situation of the San people in Namibia (ibid).
6. Joram /Useb, a Hai//om community facilitator and researcher, reports: "Nowadays my San colleagues and I have to listen to government officials and others making statements to this effect: 'You people never had leaders. Why do you need leaders today?'" (2000: 1).
7. The importance of genuine recognition was expressed by /Useb in the following way: "[San community leaders] are convinced that if they all acquire the status of an officially recognized leader, they will be able to invalidate the prevailing stereotypical notion that all San live in former Bushmanland, speak one language, are unable to farm cattle and crops, live a nomadic lifestyle, have no roots in their ancestral lands and thus have never had leaders" (2000: 7).
8. Widlok (2000) offers a similar analysis of Hai//om kinship and naming systems.
9. Many of these European names carry the diminutive suffix "tjie"—for example, Vaetjie, and especially "Mannetjie" (boy or small man)—which serves to perpetu-

Class, Culture, and Recognition 201

ate the San's "childlike" status and reinforce the farmer's paternalistic role (see also van Onselen, 1992: 141–42). Other "European" names given by farmers are actually nicknames, such as "Grootmeid" (Big Maid) and "Boesjman" (Bushman).

10. Two important points Guenther has raised are useful to recall here. First, Guenther notes that Nharo identity must be understood in terms of their experiences of class exploitation, racial discrimination, and ethnic marginalization. In this context, a highly politicized San identity was expressed through cultural revitalization movements (1979, 1986). Second, Guenther argues that the Nharo can be described as "cultural foragers" who are capable of creatively incorporating new items and influences into their own cultural practices, without losing their cultural identity (1997 and 1996).

11. For more ethnographic detail on the mutual construction of class and culture in the Omaheke, see Sylvain (1999, 2001, 2002).

References

/Useb, Joram. 2000. "'One Chief is Enough!': Understanding San Traditional Authorities in the Namibian Context." Paper presented at the conference "Africa's Indigenous Peoples: 'First Peoples' or 'Marginalized Minorities?'", 24–25 May, at the Centre for African Studies, University of Edinburgh, Scotland.

Anti-Slavery International and International Work Group for Indigenous Affairs. 1997. *Enslaved Peoples in the 1990s: Indigenous Peoples, Debt Bondage, and Human Rights.* London: Anti-Slavery International; Copenhagen: International Work Group for Indigenous Affairs.

Bond, George Clement, and Angela Gilliam. 1994. "Introduction." In *The Social Construction of the Past: Representation as Power*, ed. George Clement Bond and Angela Gilliam. London and New York: Routledge, 1–22.

Brörmann, M. 1999. *Working Group of Indigenous Minorities in Southern Africa, Report on Activities, April 1998 to March 1999.* Windhoek: WIMSA.

Comaroff, John L., and Jean Comaroff. 1999. "Introduction." In *Civil Society and the Political Imagination in Africa: Critical Perspectives*, ed. John L. Comaroff and Jean Comaroff. Chicago and London: University of Chicago Press, 1–43.

Craig, Benjamin, and Rebecca Tiessen. 1993. "Indigenous Peoples in and against the Global Economy." *Labour, Capital and Society* 26: 252–61.

Felton, Silke. 2000. "'We Want our own Chief': San Communities Battle against Their Image." Paper presented at the Annual Conference of the Association for Anthropology in Southern Africa, 8–13 May, at the University of Namibia, Windhoek, Namibia.

Gaeses, Elfrieda. 1998. "Violence against San Women." Paper presented at the First African Indigenous Women's Conference, Morocco, 24 April 1998.

Garland, Elizabeth. 1999. "Developing the Bushmen: Building Civil(ized) Society in the Kalahari and Beyond." In *Civil Society and the Political Imagination in Africa: Critical Perspectives*, ed. John L. Comaroff, and Jean Comaroff. Chicago and London: University of Chicago Press, 72–103.

Gordon, Robert. 1992. *The Bushman Myth: The Making of a Namibian Underclass*. Conflict and Social Change Series. Boulder: Westview Press.

Gordon, R.J., and A.D. Spiegel. 1993. "Southern Africa Revisited." *Annual Review of Anthropology* 22: 83–105.

Guenther, Mathias. 1979. *The Farm Bushmen of the Ghanzi District, Botswana*. Stuttgart: Hochschul Verlag.

———. 1986. *The Nharo Bushmen of Botswana: Tradition and Change*. Hamburg: Heltmut Buske Verlag.

———. 1996. "Diversity and Flexibility: The Case of the Bushmen of Southern Africa." In *Cultural Diversity among Twentieth Century Hunter-Gatherers: An African Perspective*, ed. Susan Kent. Cambridge: Cambridge University Press, 65–86.

———. 1997. "'Lords of the Desert Land': Politics and Resistance of the Ghanzi Basarwa of the Nineteenth Century." *Botswana Notes and Records* 29: 121–41.

Hall, Stuart. 1997a. "The Local and the Global: Globalization and Ethnicity." In *Culture, Globalization and the World-System: Contemporary Conditions for the Representation of Identity*, ed. Anthony D. King. Minneapolis: University of Minnesota Press, 19–39.

———. 1997b. "Old and New Identities, Old and New Ethnicities." In *Culture, Globalization and the World-System*, ed. Anthony D. King. Minneapolis: University of Minnesota Press, 41–68.

Ignatieff, Michael. 2000. *The Rights Revolution*. Massey Lecture Series. Toronto: Anansi.

Kymlicka, Will. 1999. "Theorizing Indigenous Rights." *University of Toronto Law Journal* 49: 281–93.

Lattas, Andrew. 1993. "Essentialism, Memory and Resistance: Aboriginality and the Politics of Authenticity." *Oceania* 63(3): 240–68.

Lee, Richard B. 1986. "!Kung Kin Terms, the Name Relationship and the Process of Discovery." In *The Past and Future of !Kung Ethnography: critical essays in honour of Lorna Marshall*, ed. Megan Biesele, with Richard Lee and Robert Gordon. Hamburg: Helmut Buske Verlag, 77–102.

———. 1992. "Art, Science, or Politics? The Crisis in Hunter-Gatherer Studies." *American Anthropologist* 94: 31–45.

———. 1993. *The Dobe Ju/'hoansi*. 2d ed. Forth Worth: Harcourt Brace.

———. 2000. "Indigenism and its Discontents: Anthropology and the Small Peoples at the Millennium." Paper presented at the 2000 Keynote Address, American Ethnological Society, Annual Meetings, Tampa, Florida, 25 March 2000.

Li, Tania Murray. 2000. "Articulating Indigenous Identity in Indonesia: Resource Politics and the Tribal Slot." *Comparative Studies in Society and History* 42(1): 149–79.

Linnekin, Jocelyn. 1991. "Cultural Invention and the Dilemma of Authenticity." *American Anthropologist* 93(2): 446–49.

Marshall, Lorna. 1976. *The !Kung of Nyae Nyae*. Cambridge, Mass.: Harvard University Press.

Nystrom, Derek, and Kent Puckett. 1998. *Against Bosses, Against Oligarchies: A Conversation with Richard Rorty*. No. 11. Charlottesville, Va.: Prickly Pear Pamphlets.

Rorty, Richard. 1998. *Achieving Our Country: Leftist Thought in Twentieth-Century America.* Cambridge, Mass.: Harvard University Press.

Solway, Jacqueline S., and Richard B. Lee. 1990. "Foragers: Genuine or Spurious? Situating the Kalahari San in History." *Current Anthropology* 31(2): 109–22.

Spiegel, Andrew D. 1994. "Struggles with Tradition in South Africa: The Multivocality of Images of the Past." In *The Social Construction of the Past: Representation as Power,* ed. George Clement Bond and Angela Gilliam. London and New York: Routledge, 185–202.

Stammers, Neil. 1999. "Social Movements and the Social Construction of Human Rights." *Human Rights Quarterly* 21(4): 908–1008.

Suzman, James. 2000. *Things from the Bush: A Contemporary History of the Omaheke Bushmen.* Basel Namibian Studies Series 5. Switzerland: P. Schlettwein.

Sylvain, Renée. 1997. "Survival Strategies and San Women on the Commercial Farms in the Omaheke Region, Namibia." In *The Proceedings of the Khoisan Identities and Cultural Heritage Conference,* ed. Andrew Bank. Cape Town: Institute for Historical Research, University of the Western Cape, published in conjunction with Info Source, 336–43.

———. 1999. "'We Work to Have Life': Ju/'hoan Women, Work and Survival in the Omaheke Region, Namibia." PhD Dissertation, University of Toronto.

———. 2001. "Bushmen, Boers and Baasskap: Patriarchy and Paternalism on Afrikaner Farms in the Omaheke Region, Namibia." *Journal of Southern African Studies* 27(4): 717–37.

———. 2002. "'Land, Water, and Truth': San Identity and Global Indigenism." *American Anthropologist* 104(4): 1074–84.

Taylor, Charles. 1994. "The Politics of Recognition." In *Multiculturalism: Examining the Politics of Recognition,* ed. Amy Gutmann. Princeton, N.J.: Princeton University Press, 25–73.

Thoma, Axel, and Kxao Moses ≠Oma. 1999. "The Working Group of Indigenous Minorities in Southern Africa (WIMSA)." In *Indigenous Peoples' Consultation: Report on an Indigenous Peoples' Consultation on Empowerment, Culture and Spirituality in Community Development,* 6–9 September. Shakwe, Botswana: Kuru Development Trust and the Working Group of Indigenous Minorities in Southern Africa, 39–42.

van Onselen, Charles. 1992. "The Social and Economic Underpinning of Paternalism and Violence on the Maize Farms of the South-Western Transvaal, 1900–1950." *Journal of Historical Sociology* 5(2): 128–60.

White, Hylton. 1995. *In the Tradition of the Forefathers: Bushman Traditionality at Kagga Kamma.* Cape Town: University of Cape Town Press.

Widlok, Thomas. 2000. "Names That Escape the State: Hai//om Naming Practices versus Domination and Isolation." In *Hunters and Gatherers in the Modern World: Conflict, Resistance, and Self-Determination,* ed. Peter P. Schweitzer, Megan Biesele, and Robert K. Hitchcock. New York and Oxford: Berghahn Books, 361–79.

Wilmsen, Edwin. 1989. *Land Filled with Flies: A Political Economy of the Kalahari.* Chicago: University of Chicago Press.

Wilmsen, Edwin, and James R. Denbow. 1990. "Paradigmatic History of San-speaking Peoples and Current Attempts at Revision." *Current Anthropology* 31: 489–524.

Working Group of Indigenous Minorities in Southern Africa. 1998. *Working Group of Indigenous Minorities in Southern Africa, Report on Activities, April 1998 to March 1999*. Windhoek: WIMSA.

———. 2000. *Working Group of Indigenous Minorities in Southern Africa, Report on Activities, April 1999 to March 2000*. Windhoek: WIMSA.

Chapter 12

THE OTHER SIDE
OF DEVELOPMENT
HIV/AIDS AMONG MEN AND WOMEN
IN JU/'HOANSI VILLAGES[1]

Ida Susser

Since 1996, Richard Lee and I have been working in Namibia and Botswana to attempt to contribute to the struggle against HIV/AIDS: arguably, the most serious contemporary threat to the newly independent southern African nations. During this period, the prevalence of HIV/AIDS in Namibia and Botswana ranked among the highest in the world. Clearly, a crucial immediate intervention is necessary to provide treatment to save the lives of those already infected. Nevertheless, since currently no cure exists, treatment has to be accompanied by prevention, and, in order to be successful, both forms of intervention have to take into account the social relations of particular groups.

From the perspective of our research on HIV over the past decade (1996–2003), I would like to address two historic debates that have arisen with respect to the Ju/'hoansi: the question of poverty and the issue of women's autonomy. Although we did not have the opportunity to conduct extensive research, I hope that outlining these preliminary and suggestive findings may assist in further research and also help anthropologists and others consider useful expedients to protect local people from the AIDS epidemic.

Notes for this section can be found on page 219.

The Question of Poverty

As the question of poverty is crucial to the spread of HIV infection (Farmer et al., 1996; Schoepf, 2001; Parker, 2002), we need to examine when people are poor. Although poverty is self-evident within capitalism, it is less easy to define among groups with a long history of autonomous subsistence or at least, subsistence outside capitalism. In fact, in order to understand the dire costs of poverty within capitalism, it has always been salutary to examine different kinds of societies. As is well-known, Lee's fieldwork in the 1960s among the still-nomadic Ju/'hoansi provided confirming evidence for, or possibly even inspired, Marshall Sahlins's theoretical argument that hunters and gatherers did not have to work as hard as wage earners in industrial societies. According to Sahlins (1972), in their ability to feed themselves well, house themselves adequately, and still find many hours of leisure, the Ju/'hoansi constituted an early affluent society.

Others have pointed out that the Ju/'hoansi have long interacted with the surrounding settlers and colonial administrations and that nowadays they cannot be understood separately from their negotiations with the neighboring pastoral groups. They might more accurately be viewed as a perennial underclass within the world system (Gordon, 1992; for a review of these issues, see Solway and Lee, 1990).

The association of HIV/AIDS today with patterns of inequality led us to reexamine these contrasting perspectives. The Ju/'hoansi have managed to create unique patterns of subsistence, sharing, and ritual that partially protect them from being destroyed by the encroachment of surrounding groups and allow them to survive as a people (Lee, 2002). We needed to understand the particular ways in which the Ju/'hoansi might be protected from the exigencies of "poverty" and possibly HIV/AIDS infection by an ongoing degree of autonomy. In addition, it seemed imperative to understand the ways they currently might be categorized as the underclass in the encompassing regional political economy and as a result might be at particularly high risk for HIV/AIDS.

Poverty has always been understood as a relative phenomenon. Studies in international health have convincingly demonstrated that it is not the lack of material wealth but inequality and the widening gap between rich and poor that contributes to higher rates of disease among the poor in contemporary societies (Susser et al., 1985). The underclass in capitalist societies has little access to formal employment and is frequently deprived of nutrition, education, health benefits, and decent housing. This, in turn, undermines the efforts of the poor to provide for their families and support the next generation. Societies with less material wealth, such as the Ju/'hoansi, may have their own sources of subsistence and sharing of resources that allow them to maintain kin connections and reproduce supportive social relations from generation to generation. In the examination of a continuum of independence from capitalism towards marginalized dependence on capital, our work suggested that the degree of Ju/'hoansi autonomy as opposed to material poverty within a wider society might have a direct effect on the spread of HIV infection.

The Question of Women's Autonomy

The question of women's power, status, independence, and economic autonomy is also basic to the prevention of the spread of the HIV epidemic in southern Africa and, indeed, in many other regions of the world (Cook, 1999; Freedman, 2000; Piot, 2001; Preston-Whyte et al., 2000; Schoepf, 1997, 2001; Farmer et al., 1996; Susser, 2001, 2002). In southern Africa today, young women from the ages of fourteen to twenty-five are three times as likely to be infected with the HIV virus as young men of the same age. In Botswana, the prevalence of sero-positivity for young girls is 34 percent, in Namibia, 20 percent (UNDP, 2000). Gendered inequality is fueling the epidemic, as women, marginalized in the informal economy and responsible for supporting themselves and their children, are often forced to depend on men with more resources in the struggle to survive.

In light of HIV/AIDS, the arguments initiated by Eleanor Leacock (1972) and Kathleen Gough (1971) and further developed by feminist anthropologists since the 1970s (Gailey, 1987) become newly and tragically significant. From her archival work with respect to the Algonquin of North America, Leacock (1972) argued that, while women maintained autonomy in hunting and gathering societies, such autonomy was undermined as people in these societies came in contact with missionaries, traders, and other mercantile influences. As the relations of production shifted towards capitalism, women lost their previous independence. Based on fieldwork among the Ju/'hoansi in the 1960s, Lee's (1979) path-breaking ethnography, *The !Kung Ju/'hoansi*, stands as a classic benchmark in providing systematic contemporary evidence for women's autonomy in a foraging society. His later cooperation with Leacock (1982) in research on the relations between men and women in hunting and gathering societies takes on new meaning in the face of the current threat. The ensuing work by Marjorie Shostak (1981), Patricia Draper (1975), and others documenting the life experiences of sex, work, and family among the Ju/'hoansi provide us with a rich history on which to base our current efforts with respect to HIV.

Much has changed among the Ju/'hoansi over the past forty years (Lee, 2002; Lee and Hurlich, 1982; Becker 2003). As a result of colonialism, wars, agricultural incursions by both settlers and African farmers, much of their way of life has disappeared, and some aspects have been retained or recreated. In addressing the HIV/AIDS epidemic, we need to understand the extent to which Ju/'hoansi women may still be autonomous or in what ways they are able to control their sexuality and their life choices. Our ethnographic research sheds some light on contemporary Ju/'hoansi women's autonomy and sexual authority and the particular ways in which their history may protect them from HIV as well as their current vulnerabilities.

Ethnographic Work in the Kalahari

Funded by a Fogarty Award for Training and Research with respect to HIV/AIDS in Namibia and Botswana (the only Fogarty Award yet targeted for training in ethnographic research), we trained local researchers in the ethnographic method and, simultaneously, with the help of our trainees, conducted research among many groups, urban and rural. As part of this project, we made trips to the Namibian Ju/'hoansi villages, including Tsumkwe and Baraka in 1996, 1997, and 2003. In 1999 and 2001, we conducted exploratory fieldwork with respect to AIDS at Kangwa, Dobe, and /Xai/Xai villages on the Botswana side of the border. Up until 2003, the border between Namibia and Botswana was virtually closed to motor traffic. As a result, we had to select only one side of the border each year, although the Ju/'hoansi crossed the border frequently by foot. On each occasion we interviewed local women, men and Ju/'hoansi political representatives, as well as administrative, health, and religious personnel (including folk healers) and shebeen owners and migrant laborers when they appeared in the villages.[2]

The Ju/'hoansi village populations have been interacting with the surrounding populations for at least 150 years, and they have not been living by hunting and gathering for decades. Nevertheless, people do still gather berries and nuts. Men still set snares for small animals—we saw the snares, the mongongo nuts, and the berries as we walked through the villages of Dobe in July 2001. However, we also observed men and women stringing beads, making twine, and carving wooden spoons, drums, and other objects for sale to ecotourism traders as well as missions.

In Botswana, both men and women also participate in work groups to clear brush and complete other tasks and are paid through government supplements. Despite the fact that men are paid almost twice as much as women, reflecting the institutionalized discrimination of the state, men and women labor equally side by side. Although households congregate in proximity to the boreholes constructed and maintained by the government and external funding agencies, the Ju/'hoansi still move their families from place to place. Significantly, in terms of the maintenance of ongoing social supports, they rebuild their grass and clay shelters to reflect kin relations and are able to move to live near other kin apparently at will. I would suggest that these strong manifestations of earlier patterns allow couples to maintain some stability in their households.

In another manifestation of the strong continuity of family relations in the face of adversity, in Dobe, Lee and I noted an older daughter, in a family where her mother had died of an unknown cause, who was breastfeeding her own newborn baby as well as her infant sister. Since HIV can be transmitted through breast milk, such customary practices might offer a potential opportunity. If a woman had been tested in pregnancy and knew she was HIV positive, she could ask another pregnant woman, who had tested HIV negative, to take over the nursing of her newborn. Such practices could be implemented in villages with extensive supportive kin relations.

Although still remote and inaccessible in comparison to other rural settlements in southern Africa, Tsumkwe, Namibia and Kangwa, Botswana, initially small Ju/'hoansi villages, now each houses a clinic, a few stores, and a boarding school. Brick houses have been constructed and many people from other groups live there. Although even more remote, /Xai/Xai has a school, clinic, store, and Baraka, constructed as a cooperative center, has some rustically built rondavels. The other Ju/'hoansi villages in both Namibia and Botswana are now largely clusters of clay rondavels and brush shelters surrounded by bush and sand.

HIV/AIDS in the Kalahari

In Dobe and /Xai/Xai, in 1999 and 2001, we conducted house-by-house censuses. Lee, speaking the Ju/'hoansi language, asked in each village about births, deaths, and marriages. Using his intricate knowledge of past kin relations, he was able to trace children to grandparents and identify relationships among the various households. At each hut we asked whether there was anyone not well or lying inside the rondavel and whether people knew about HIV/AIDS. Most people mentioned that they had heard about AIDS on the radio.

On only one occasion, at Dobe, were we told that a woman was lying sick in her hut. Also at Dobe, there were two occasions when people came to us for help with medical problems. Once a family messenger came to ask us to help a young man who had broken his leg, and on another occasion a mother asked us about her sick child. Such events suggested that people were not hiding illness from us. More likely, they regarded us and our van as a resource to help them seek medical care. In addition to visiting households and talking with men, women, and children outside their rondavels, we also informally interviewed some of the young unmarried women of the village, in small groups of two or three, about their relationships. The girls seemed more willing to talk in little groups than one at a time, as they teased each other and giggled and helped the conversations along.

In 2001, at /Xai/Xai, we interviewed folk healers and sat and talked with them, among much else, about their knowledge and experience of HIV/AIDS. We also noted the formation of the Tlhabololo Development Trust which was set up as a wildlife management area controlled by the Ju/'hoansi. It allowed the village to sell hunting rights to safari tours and to contribute the proceeds to the development of local institutions (Lee 2003:184). In 1999 and 2001, we also assembled several larger groups of young men and young women. Lee, accompanied by his son, David, and my teenage son, Phil, talked to the young men who congregated after the informal nightly soccer game about their views of women, sex, condoms, and HIV/AIDS. The group included local Ju/'hoansi boys and young Herero men who also lived in the village and some visiting Ju/'hoansi. The local Herero youth seemed much more knowledgeable about condoms than the local Ju/'hoansi, although one of the Ju/'hoansi from Tsumkwe (Namibia) seemed familiar with them. David and Phil, who also played soccer every night and generally spent time with the young men, distributed boxes of condoms, which the soccer players all took eagerly.

A young unmarried woman, who was the Dobe preschool teacher, helped me to gather and talk several evenings with a group of young married women about male condoms, female condoms, and HIV/AIDS. She had been born in the village with a Herero father and Ju/'hoansi mother, had previously attended boarding school, and spoke both English and Ju/'hoansi. We sat on the sandy ground, outside the huts and away from view of the men who were meeting with Lee at the soccer game. I brought female condoms, which always interest people and have been a conversation starter all over the world. We talked about their usefulness. I also gave out boxes of condoms to the women.

Although we spent more time at Dobe, a main site of Lee's long-term work, we also met with groups of men and women at /Xai/Xai and Kangwa in Botswana and Baraka, Tsumkwe and other villages in Namibia. While staying at Baraka in 1996, we met with a mixed

The Other Side of Development 211

group of men and women to discuss condoms, female condoms, and HIV/AIDS.

We were able to make some comparisons among the experiences of women in different groups, since as part of our ethnographic training workshop at the University of Namibia we took Ovambo-speaking students with us to conduct fieldwork among other populations in Namibia (Susser and Stein, 2000; Susser, 2001; Lee and Susser, 2002). Findings that emerged from this fieldwork serve to highlight certain issues with respect to gender and poverty.

Tsumkwe: A Village in Poverty

In 1996, we initiated our discussions of HIV/AIDS at Baraka, Namibia, among the elected representatives of the Nyae Nyae Conservancy (then the Nyae Nyae Farmers Cooperative), a local group set up for self-government among the Ju/'hoansi (for more detail on the history of this organization, see Lee 2003:184). In the meeting, which the representatives called at Baraka, all the participants were men. When we asked about their knowledge of HIV/AIDS, the representatives told us that they knew about AIDS. A visiting linguist had, in fact, translated a handbook on AIDS into Ju/'hoansi a few years earlier, before he, himself, died of the disease. The men at the meeting implied that they expected AIDS was brought among the Ju/'hoansi by Ju/'hoansi women who had sexual relations with men from other groups. They spoke disapprovingly of the women. We were told that at Tsumkwe there were many men who were not Ju/'hoansi who came to buy beer from the numerous temporary grass shelters set up as bars and then met with the Ju/'hoansi women. Drinking was widely discussed and seemed a major problem both to the local people and the anthropologists.

Throughout our research, Tsumkwe emerged as a main center for the spread of HIV for a variety of overlapping reasons. First, the South African army was based there in the 1980s and the local soldiers, from many populations, may have introduced new diseases among the Ju/'hoansi. Second, the border guards and other administrative personnel spend many lonely nights in the region and some frequent the local nightlife. Third, nowadays there are passable gravel roads from Namibian towns into Tsumkwe (although the nearest non-Ju/'hoansi village is about 200 kilometers away), as well as a nearby air strip. Although there had been very little alcohol and none locally brewed among the Ju/'hoansi when Lee began his fieldwork in the 1960s, nowadays the Ju/'hoansi who live in Tsumkwe, and those who live elsewhere but have visited the area, talk about the incidence of drinking and sexual exchange as different from the surrounding villages.

However, it was not until 2003 that we finally pursued the implications of the comments made by the council members in our first visit to Baraka.

On the Namibian side, Tsumkwe was once a Ju/'hoansi village centered around an ancient baobab tree; since 1960, it has been the site of a government resettlement station with many social problems. It is now the administrative center for the Tsumkwe District, a Ju/'hoansi region. Before Namibia won its independence in 1990, the South African government built a clinic, a store, and rows of cement houses similar to those that were constructed under the disreputable Bantustan policy in South Africa (Lee, 2002). There is also a coeducational boarding school at Tsumkwe. Although some Ju/'hoansi children attend this school, most children are not Ju/'hoansi but are sent to it from several hundred kilometers away. At least two well-known films, the commercially successful film by Jamie Uys, *The Gods Must Be Crazy*, and the documentary by John Marshall *!Nai*, focus on Tsumkwe. The star of *The Gods* used to live there before he died in 2003, diagnosed with tuberculosis. In the early 1990s, his wife had also died of a long illness. The main protagonists of the documentary still live there intermittently. By 1997, a Safari Lodge was operating in Tsumkwe to provide a base from which tourists could visit the Ju/'hoansi villages and witness Ju/'hoansi dancing and healing rituals staged for their consumption.

In 1996, in Tsumkwe, we interviewed two health workers employed by Health Unlimited, an internationally funded nongovernmental organization (NGO). They visited the Ju/'hoansi villages monthly to provide some medical assistance and health education. The two health workers were aware of HIV and had begun to discuss it on their monthly rounds to the villages. This was the extent of AIDS prevention in the Namibian Ju/'hoansi area at that time. Testing and diagnosis were not yet readily available, and treatment at that time was not even considered. Although, tuberculosis had long been epidemic in the Kalahari, the fact that it was sometimes resistant to treatment suggested that AIDS might have been present, if not recognized.

By 2001, AIDS had been diagnosed by doctors who served the Ju/'hoansi region. A preschool program, initiated by Megan Biesele, had begun to incorporate training for their Ju/'hoansi teachers about AIDS prevention. In 2001, we met one of the teacher trainees, who spoke excellent English, visiting his relatives in Dobe (on the Botswana side). He was extremely well-informed and helpful in discussing AIDS with his kin in the community. This suggests that such minimal investment has an important multiplying effect for knowledge and prevention far beyond the confines of the original preschool setting.

In 1999, at Dobe, a young teenage girl who had spent several weeks staying with kin at Tsumkwe said: "There is no AIDS here, but I know

The Other Side of Development 213

they have it at Tsumkwe. The girls over there told me not to sleep with the boys because they have that disease there. I am afraid of AIDS at Tsumkwe."

In 2001, a discussion with an older couple and two younger men in a village at Dobe led to their naming three women who they believed had died of AIDS. All the women named lived at Tsumkwe, although they were near kin to the people at Dobe. We were told that one young woman died, unmarried, at age twenty. The ages of the other two were estimated at thirty-five and forty. The two older women had young children, but there was no knowledge of children's deaths. No sense of shame or stigma seemed to be expressed in this conversation.

As a result of the conservations in Baraka, Dobe, and elsewhere, we spent the summer of 2003 interviewing Ju'/hoansi men and women, administrative personnel, health workers, tour guides, and shebeen owners in Tsumkwe (Lee and Susser, 2003). We found that, since the late 1990s, to meet the demands of currently unemployed men who had fought in the battles for Namibian Independence from South Africa, the government had begun to create jobs for veterans in many regions, including Tsumkwe. Large numbers of laborers looking for work had migrated to Tsumkwe. Alongside this growing population, shebeens flourished, run by both men and women (Lee and Susser, 2003.)

Although the Ju'/hoansi were neither government employees nor shebeen owners, they were clearly shebeen customers. Much of the money Ju'/hoansi received from selling trinkets to tourists or even from the machines providing pension money in Tsumkwe appeared to land in the pockets of the alcohol sellers. We observed couples we knew drinking at the shebeens when we went to interview the shebeen owners at midday. We were told frequently by Ju'/hoansi men and women that drunkenness and sexual violence were associated with shebeen drinking in this area. This was certainly not confined to the Ju'/hoansi, but the Ju'/hoansi women seemed to be at risk for violence both from their own Ju'/hoansi husbands and from interactions with long-term partners or brief encounters with the migrant laborers (Lee and Susser, 2003).

At a village meeting, Ju'/hoansi men and women talked of the violence of Ju'/hoansi men against their own wives when drunk on the powerful liquor now being distilled at the shebeens. One woman told a story about her friend whose husband beat her on a night when she refused to give him any more money to buy drink. Other men and women at the meeting nodded in agreement. We met two children whose father had killed their mother in an argument at a shebeen (Lee and Susser, 2003).

In 2003, in contrast to the all-male group of leaders we met in Baraka in 1996, an articulate and well-informed woman had become one of the leading members of the Ju/'hoansi village council. She spoke eloquently in English as well as in Ju/'hoansi of the problems she saw posed by the wide availability of concentrated alcohol to Ju/'hoansi households. The woman council leader was also knowledgeable about the implications of the situation for HIV. The Ju/'hoansi Council had joined with the local church to try to address the issue. However, they had been unable even to enforce any of the existing government liquor regulations.

In 2003, we were told of at least seventeen Ju/'hoansi from Tsumkwe who were known to have died of AIDS over the last seven years. Many of them were women whose partners were among the new population of migrant workers. In fact, a local doctor told us that, in 2003 alone, she knew of seven AIDS deaths in the area. One was a Ju/'hoansi man, while the other deaths were among the itinerant workers who lived in the encampments surrounding the Ju'/hoansi villages and who may have been carrying the virus for some time (Lee and Susser, 2003.)

In contrast to Tsumkwe, among the Ju/'hoansi villages at Dobe in Botswana and also the Ju/'hoansi villages in Namibia outside Tsumkwe, there was no center of liquor shops and fewer outside visitors. Possibly due to a lack of diagnosis, but more likely because couples appear more stable, there were not yet any clear cases of HIV/AIDS known to the local people outside Tsumkwe.

Although the known HIV/AIDS cases are concentrated in Tsumkwe, the case of this village is an indication of future threats. Tswana and Herero cattle farmers, border guards, and construction workers pass through most of the Ju/'hoansi villages. Indeed, an improved gravel road into the heart of the Dobe area is fast nearing completion, heralding new forms of tourism, economic development, and increased possibilities of infection. Among the mothers living in the remote Ju/'hoansi villages, most were married. However, we interviewed an unmarried Ju/'hoansi woman who lived along the paved road to a Botswana rural town. She told us that her daughters, too, had children but no husbands, and she was afraid they were at risk for HIV.

It would appear that the patterns of inequality so evident at Tsumkwe—the Ju/'hoansi with few possessions and the people from other groups, soldiers, border guards, construction workers with money to attract or pay for sexual partners—was fuelling the transmission of HIV/AIDS.

The Ju/'hoansi have a long history of both economic and sexual negotiations with outside men and women. However, new forms of capital penetration—such as the cash payments for trinkets, cash for sex, and the extensive sale of concentrated liquor—have accompanied the new development projects in both tourism and agriculture. The resulting increasing relative inequality and the privatization of resources

The Other Side of Development

has precipitated the disintegration of household reciprocities and couples' relations and contributed to individual competition for scarce resources. This might be one useful way to understand the manifestation of poverty in capitalism in comparison to a subsistence economy coping with scarce resources. We are seeing the destructive penetration of capitalism and the creation of poverty in Tsumkwe, and also possibly in many similar settlements, such as Kangwa and Sehitwe in Botswana. Perhaps, although they travel frequently to Tsumkwe and Kangwa the people living in the more stable Ju/'hoansi villages should not be seen as poor in the same way. They maintain social organization and conjugal relations based partially on a subsistence economy. They are, also, perhaps, partially shielded from the market by cooperative organizations such as the Nyae Nyae Conservancy, centered at Baraka, and the /Xai/Xai Trust which attempt to mediate collectively between the market and the villages. Villagers who are somewhat protected from the individual risk and insecurity involved in marginal work and the lowest rung of the tourist economy, appear to be less vulnerable to the ravages of HIV/AIDS.

Next, I would like to highlight our observations with respect to gender and HIV transmission.

Women's Autonomy and HIV/AIDS

Preliminary findings suggest that Ju/'hoansi women differ in their sense of autonomy from other women whom we interviewed in Namibia. Our conversations with women and young girls among the Ju/'hoansi revealed a different kind of confidence in sexual negotiation with men than Ovambo women in the rural homesteads of northern Namibia. In 1996, we asked young Ju/'hoansi women at Baraka whether they would ask their husbands or boyfriends to use a condom. They insisted, without apparent doubt, that if the men did not do as the women and young girls asked, the women would not hesitate to refuse sex.

This finding might be usefully compared to our interviews in the same year with a group of Ovambo women in a rural homestead, who said they would not dare to ask their partners to use a condom. In fact, although the Ovambo women were obviously outspoken and confident in many situations, they told us that they would not discuss anything with their husbands or boyfriends during a sexual interaction (Susser and Stein, 2000.)

In 1996, Ju/'hoansi women whom we interviewed saw no particular advantage to the female condom, as they said if they wanted a man to use a male condom they would ask him to. In contrast, Ovambo women claimed that they could not ask a man to use a male condom. They were extremely enthusiastic about the possibilities of the female condom, as they saw it as an alternative strategy that would be under the woman's control and acceptable to men (Susser and Stein, 2000)

In Dobe in 2001, I asked a group of young married Ju/'hoansi women if they would be able to use a box of male condoms. "Give us some and we will teach our husbands how to use them," they said. Ovambo and Kavango women only expressed such a sense of empowerment through the woman's control of the female condom (Susser and Stein, 2000; Susser, 2001). The remarks of Ju/'hoansi women expressed a sense of entitlement and straightforwardness with respect to sexual decisions, which was not evidenced in the same way among the Ovambo women with whom we spoke.

When Lee interviewed the young men in Dobe in 1999, their responses seemed to corroborate the women's views. They talked as if women had the power to turn down sexual advances, and they said that if a young woman were to accept such advances, they would regard her behavior as representing the opportunity to marry her. Ethnographic findings by one of our research associates, Pombili Iipinge, suggested that Ovambo men in contrast expected to have sexual relations with more than one woman and did not say they expected to marry a woman if she agreed to a sexual relationship.

This picture is complicated by the many relationships between Ju/'hoansi women and Ovambo, Herero, and Tswana men. The availability of relationships with men from surrounding populations who have more money and resources in general than the Ju/'hoansi may allow women more negotiating power with men from their own village. Nevertheless, the terms in which Ju/'hoansi women speak, for example seeing the opportunity to "teach" their husbands about condoms, suggests a different kind of autonomy.

Unfortunately, Ju/'hoansi women seem to have less leeway in their relationships with men from the surrounding populations. Women we spoke with mentioned that their Tswana or Herero boyfriends might give them presents but were, in fact, married to other women. As noted above, a woman visiting Dobe said she lived far from the Ju/'hoansi villages near the road to Sehitwe, where men worked in highway construction. She was afraid her daughter might be at risk for HIV.

As the men at the first meeting at the Nyae Nyae Conservancy pointed out, it may be the women who have broader outside contacts. In fact, women may be the first Ju/'hoansi to come in contact with HIV/AIDS. Mirroring the situation throughout southern Africa, young women are also more likely to be the first to die from the disease. As we were told in 2001, three women were known to have died from HIV/AIDS at Tsumkwe. Another woman, whose family had just returned to

The Other Side of Development   217

Dobe, had died from an unknown cause. Her husband, who had been taken from Dobe as a young boy and spent decades in farm labor, had stayed on in Dobe with the rest of his family. No deaths among Ju/'hoansi men in Dobe were reported to us. In Tsumkwe, in 2003,we learned that the majority of the seventeen Ju'/hoansi who were thought to have died of HIV/AIDS were young women.

Conclusion

Both the debate around poverty and the discussions of gender autonomy are significant for identifying possibilities for prevention of HIV/AIDS among contemporary Ju/'hoansi. When the Ju/'hoansi leave their villages, around the newly dug boreholes, and work along the roads and on the cattle ranches, they are clearly transformed into the underclass or the poor of the new African states. As a result, they become vulnerable to HIV/AIDS. Men work far from home and seek sexual partners elsewhere. Poor Ju/'hoansi, women no longer protected from the sexual discrimination of the surrounding capitalist society, are seldom hired for construction or farming. They are forced to earn money through casual sex work or simply seek sexual relations with men who will provide gifts for themselves and their children.

In villages such as Dobe, where foraging was still a possibility, women and men expressed much more stable views of their relationships. Women seemed to maintain a degree of power and independence in marriage. Certainly, to supplement their subsistence, people earned small sums of money in government work groups, and both men and women worked at a variety of crafts, such as beading and carving. However, such partial incorporation into wage labor combined with market exchange did not lead to the destruction of sturdy, longstanding strategies of survival. If people were poor, in terms of their clothes and their shelter, they did not seem to suffer the poverty of an underclass in which family and household relations are undermined. The historical autonomy of women seemed to offer the opportunity for forthright sexual negotiations and mobilization to prevent the spread of HIV/AIDS.

Clearly, none of the villages are isolated from tourism and development efforts today. Our research suggests that every small outpost of development, whether it be sending men from a nearby town to dig the foundation for a new store, or developing a trust to allow tourist hunting from safaris, also introduces the threat of HIV. However, the incursions on social organization will be different for a collectively operated trust than for a store that sells individual crafts. Development must obviously be immediately associated with HIV education and strategies, such as male and female condoms, testing and access to treatment. In addition, however, broader social issues need to be considered.

Mobilization for HIV prevention among the Ju/'hoansi will have to take different approaches in different villages, but might well be able to build upon the autonomy of the women and the respect of the Ju/'hoansi men. However, every new development effort will have to be understood not only in individual economic terms but also in terms of its impact on collective social organization. As Solway and Lee (1990) argued, the resilience of the foraging societies in the Kalahari Desert has protected people, so far, from many of the exploitative incursions of capitalism. However, this too is a historical phenomenon, and as other populations are forced to impinge on the lands of the Ju/'hoansi, and as global capital brings tourism, safaris, and development plans further and further into the centers of their territory, their survival strategies are drastically threatened. In Tsumkwe, Kangwa, and other villages that have been torn apart by the invasion of capitalist relations, and where the Ju/'hoansi clearly constitute a poverty stricken, demoralized underclass, the women too have become more dependent on cash from men and especially susceptible to HIV. In villages such as Dobe and /Xai/Xai, which continue to center around a foraging way of life and where the various efforts at community development trusts and supplemental work payments allow families to sustain their households and women to maintain aspects of their historic autonomy, the spread of HIV infections appears so far to have been limited, if not prevented.

Acknowledgements

I want to thank Jackie Solway and Christine Gailey for their comments and support and Richard Lee for his generous and inspiring collaboration in all aspects of this research. David and Louise Lee, Rebecca Rosenberg, and Philip and Jonah Kreniske contributed extensively to the fieldwork. This research was partially supported by the Columbia University HIV Center for Behavioral and Clinical Research, the University of Toronto, and the City University of New York. I also wish to acknowledge the support of a MacArthur Foundation Research and Writing Fellowship, and a National Endowment for the Humanities/ National Institutes of Health Fellowship Award.

Notes

1. An earlier version of this paper, "Ju/'hoansi survival in the face of HIV: Questions of Poverty and Gender," appeared in *Anthropologica* 45 (2003): 121–28.
2. A shebeen is frequently a makeshift shelter where home brew is sold and which often serves as a local gathering place.

References

Cook, Rebecca. 1999. "Gender, Health and Human Rights." In *Health and Human Rights,* ed. Jonathan Mann, Sofia Gruskin, Michael Grodin, and George Annas. New York: Routledge, 253–65.

Becker, Heike. 2003 "The least sexist society? Perspectives on gender change and violence among southern African San." *Journal of Southern African Studies* 29 (1):5–23

Draper, Patricia. 1975. "!Kung Women; Contrasts in Sexual Egalitarianism in the Foraging and Sedentary Contexts." In *Toward an Anthropology of Women,* ed. Rayna Rapp Reiter. New York: Monthly Review Press, 77–109.

Farmer, Paul, Margaret Connors, and Janie Simmons, ed. 1996. *Women, Poverty and AIDS: Sex, Drugs and Structural Violence.* Monroe, Minn.: Common Courage Press.

Freedman, Lynn. 2000. "Human Rights and Women's Health." In *Women and Health,* ed. Marlene Goldman and Carolyn Sargent. New York: Academic Press, 428–41.

Gailey, Christine. 1987. "Evolutionary Perspectives on Gender Hierarchy." In *Analyzing Gender,* ed. B. Hess, Ferree. Beverly Hills: Sage, 32–67.

Gordon, Robert. 1992. *The Bushman Myth.* Boulder, Col: Westview.

Gough, Kathleen. 1971. "Nuer Kinship: A Re-Examination." In *The Translation of Culture: Essays to E.E. Evans-Pritchard,* ed. T.O. Beidelman. London: Tavistock, 79–121.

Leacock, Eleanor Burke. 1972. "Introduction." In *The Origin of the Family, Private Property and the State,* ed. Eleanor Burke Leacock. New York: International, 7–69.

Leacock, Eleanor Burke, and Richard B. Lee, ed. 1982. *Politics and History in Band Societies.* Cambridge, UK: Cambridge University Press.

Lee, Richard B. 1979. *The !Kung San: Men, Women and Work in a Foraging Society.* Cambridge, UK: Cambridge University Press.

———. 2003. *The Dobe Ju/'Hoansi.* U.S.: Wadsworth, Thomson Learning, Toronto, Ontario.

Lee, Richard B., and Susan Hurlich. 1982. "From Foragers to Fighters: South Africa's Militarization of the Namibian San." In *Politics and History in Band Societies,* ed. Eleanor Burke Leacock and Richard B. Lee. Cambridge, UK: Cambridge University Press, 327–46.

Lee, Richard, and Ida Susser. 2002. "Confounding Conventional Wisdom: Women's Power and Low HIV/AIDS Rates among the Ju/'Hoansi of

Namibia and Botswana." Paper presented at the XIV International AIDS Conference, Barcelona, Spain, July.

———. 2003. "Confounding Conventional Wisdom: The Ju/'Hoansi and HIV/AIDS." Paper presented at the annual meeting of the American Anthropological Association, Chicago.

Parker, Richard. 2001. "Sexuality, Culture and Power in HIV/AIDS Research." *Annual Reviews in Anthropology* 30: 163–79.

Piot, Peter. 2001. "A Gendered Epidemic: Women and the Risks and Burdens of HIV." *Journal of the American Medical Women's Association* 56: 90–91.

Preston-Whyte, Eleanor, Oosthuizen Varga, Rachel Roberts, and Frederick Blose. 2000. "Survival Sex and HIV/AIDS in an African City." In *Framing the Sexual Self,* Richard Parker, Regina Barbosa and Peter Aggleton (eds.), Berkeley: University of California Press, 165–90.

Sahlins, Marshall. 1972. *Stone Age Economics.* Chicago: Aldine-Atherton.

Schoepf, Brooke. 1997. "AIDS, Gender and Sexuality during Africa's Economic Crisis." In *African Feminism: The Politics of Survival in Sub-Saharan Africa,* ed. Gwendolyn Mikell. Philadelphia, Penn.: University of Pennsylvania Press, 310–33.

———. 2001. "International AIDS Research in Anthropology: Taking a Critical Perspective on the Crisis." *Annual Reviews in Anthropology* 30: 335–61.

Shostak, Marjorie. 1983. *Nisa: The Life and Words of a !Kung Woman.* New York: Vintage Books.

Solway, Jacqueline, and Richard Lee. 1990. "Foragers, Genuine or Spurious: Situating the Kalahari Ju/'hoansi in History." *Current Anthropology* 109: 109–46.

Susser, Ida. 1996. "The Construction of Poverty and Homelessness in U.S. Cities." *Annual Reviews in Anthropology* 25: 411–35.

———. 2001. "Sexual Negotiations in Relation to Political Mobilization: The Prevention of HIV in a Comparative Context." *AIDS and Behavior* 5(2): 163–72.

———. 2002. "Health Rights for Women in the Age of AIDS." *International Journal of Epidemiology* 31: 45–48.

Susser, Ida, and Zena Stein. 2000. "Culture, Sexuality, and Women's Agency in the Prevention of HIV/AIDS in Southern Africa." *American Journal of Public Health* 90: 1042–48.

Susser, M., Watson, W., and K. Hopper. 1985. *Sociology in Medicine.* Oxford: Oxford University Press.

UNDP. 2000. *Botswana Human Development Report: Towards an AIDS-Free Generation.* Botswana: Government of Botswana.

PART III

Richard Borshay Lee: An Appreciation

Chapter 13

RICHARD B. LEE AND COMPANY
A KALAHARI CHRONICLE, 1963–2000

Compiled by Jacqueline Solway

1963

1963

1964

1964

1973

226   The Politics of Egalitarianism

1983

1983

Richard B. Lee and Company

1983

1987

1987

2000

Chapter 14

RICHARD B. LEE:
THE POLITICS, ART, AND SCIENCE
OF ANTHROPOLOGY

Christine Ward Gailey

In its original sense, a *Festschrift* is a celebration in writing by people who have drawn on and grown to appreciate the work of a major figure, at a time when he or she can respond and contribute further to the discussions for which the honoree is so pivotal. For Richard Lee, this demands that writers address a range of controversies that are far from concluded, areas of debate that point to the vitality of a four-fields approach in anthropology and long-term, socially engaged field research, with both agendas committed to redressing oppression. Only in such a way can we ensure that later generations will have an alternative view than seeing human nature as either a biological reflex or a narrow range of attributes serving a global imperium.

No *Festschrift* is complete without providing readers with a sense of the person and the emergence and development of the themes that occupy the scholar's intellectual life and social and political engagement. With the objective of portraying the person behind the work, politics, and scholarship, I arranged a meeting with Richard to record some biographical details. The following is based on our taped exchanges, which took place in Riverside, California, 14–15 March 2002.

Notes for this section can be found on page 240.

230   *The Politics of Egalitarianism*

Early Cultural Milieu

Richard Borshay Lee was born in Brooklyn, New York, on 20 September 1937. His sister Rhea was 16 years older, born to his mother in her first marriage. Although Rhea married when Richard was only five years old, they have remained close throughout their lives and share a love of *Yiddishkeit*[1] and Major League Baseball.

Richard's parents were in their thirties at the time he was born. They had met in New York in the 1930s when both were active in left-wing circles. Anne Borshay worked for AMTORG, the Soviet-American trading company; Charles Liberman (later Lee) worked for the Longshoreman's Union as a bookkeeper. In early 1942 they decided to move to Toronto, "where my mother's family had settled after emigrating from Minsk, Russia at the turn of the century."[2] One of his earliest memories was crossing the U.S.-Canadian border in a vintage automobile, driving "to our new life in Canada."

Politics and Culture: Toronto in the 1940s and 1950s

For Lee, being the child of progressives became "the core of my consciousness." In Canada they moved to the edge of a well-to-do Toronto suburb, Forest Hill Village, which later became part of Toronto proper. Richard's father became a certified public accountant and built up a modest practice. Lee went to the local public school, "South Prep," where he became aware that most of his schoolmates' families were far better off than his was:

> I had vivid memories of my mother and father saying, "Well, always remember, Richard, the poor, the working people are the salt of the earth, and so you have nothing to be ashamed of or apologize about," and that's the way I grew up ... our family culture was classical music and literature while [some of my richer classmates' families] were going on gambling junkets to Havana.

Still, in the late 1940s the institutions of Jewish community life in Toronto were relatively progressive. For several summers Lee went to Camp Northland through the YMHA, where the counselors taught the campers Woody Guthrie and labor songs. The era was, for these twelve and thirteen year olds, exciting and full of hope for the future:

> The world of fascism had been defeated, the New World was being created, the quarrels of the Cold War hadn't really taken hold, and so there was a lot

of optimism and progressive politics among the youth. This contributed to my basically optimistic view that revolution is possible, change is possible, and the condition of oppression under capitalism is not the natural state, not the inevitable state of humankind.

But alongside this enthusiasm, he realized that geopolitical struggles were real and could scar the lives of individuals. He recalls that one wealthy woman who lived in the exclusive Rosedale neighborhood invited him and his parents to her home to meet Paul Robeson, who made a lasting impression on them. He followed Robeson's

> epic battles with the Immigration and Naturalization Department ... we weren't in Vancouver, but we heard about when he came to Blaine, Washington and they wouldn't let him travel out of the U.S. into Canada, and so he stood on the U.S. side at the Peace Arch and gave a concert across the border for several thousand people who had gathered on the Canadian side.

Because of their involvement in progressive causes, the dynamic in his natal family was less transnational than internationalist. His mother held Canadian citizenship (in those days, a British passport), while his father retained landed immigrant status until some forty years later, when he became a dual citizen. As an adolescent in the 1950s, Lee considered New York the place to go, but gradually the strengths of the Canadian way of life began to grow on him. Inspired by the political message of Tommy Douglas, a pioneering Canadian socialist, and given that all American eighteen year olds had to register for the draft, he applied for and was granted Canadian citizenship in 1956.[3]

Although he had no call to become an anthropologist in those days, the politics of culture and race as they permeated Lee's community and family prefigured an abiding opposition to racism and the denial of agency and cultural creativity to those deemed socially inferior. As he puts it,

> In this progressive Jewish milieu, there was always a strong presumption that, for example, people of color were an oppressed minority, ... that out of their suffering has come some of the most important cultural productions of history.

His love of folk music, blues, and jazz was fostered by his ten-year career through high school and university playing drums in various bands around Toronto, selling his drum set only when it came time to go off to graduate school.

One of his favorite authors at the time was Howard Fast, whose book *Freedom Road,* on post-Civil War Reconstruction in the South, helped to shape his ethics and sense of human agency:

> [T]he world was a mess, but the people were strong and were going to rise ... oppression couldn't go on indefinitely because ... the righteous anger of the people would rise up—this was my childhood view of the world.

His simple sense of right and wrong would be challenged by what was for his family—and his father especially—a cataclysmic event: the Twentieth Congress of the Communist Party of the Soviet Union in 1956, when Nikita Khruschev denounced Joseph Stalin's crimes. The "fairly uncritical" discussions of the USSR that had been part of his childhood ceased abruptly. While his mother's politics had always appeared to be more "pragmatic, less ideologically driven" than his father's, as a young man of nineteen Lee saw his father become deeply disillusioned:

> One of the things I took from that time period ... was that one must never allow oneself to become so ideologically trustful and ideologically driven that one could find oneself in a situation where your world could collapse ... because everything, everything you had believed in was a sham. Science, with its reliance on empirical evidence and verifiability, offered a more intellectually satisfying alternative.

The unmasking of Stalin's repression, he recalls, did not embitter his mother:

> She would say, "Well, I still believe in the basic goodness of humanity, and I still believe in the basic truth of the underlying principles, but we have to see how they could go so horribly wrong with Stalin."

He remembers repeatedly arguing at the supper table with his disillusioned father, who would say, "I've had it, I'm going to join the synagogue!"—the ultimate right wing for a committed atheist. Lee recalls defending the Soviet Union to his father, since despite Stalin's monstrous actions, he recognized the USSR had played the pivotal role in defeating Hitler in World War II.

Lee's maturing sense of cultural politics drew from his upbringing in a leftist milieu sensitive to the influence of race, class, and state oppression on culture creation. His awareness of the dangers of uncritical acceptance of any ideology—even as he remained critical of capitalist society—grew from the critique by leftists throughout the world of the Soviet state that was spurred by revelations about the 1956 Party Congress and that ultimately led to the more vigorous and grounded progressive commitments of the 1960s and 1970s.

Becoming an Anthropologist:
The University of Toronto in the 1950s

Richard's family aspired for him to become a lawyer, and Lee concurred, until it came time to choose courses for his first year at the University of Toronto. Richard had written a paper on Indian-White relations in Canada before Confederation in the thirteenth grade, and opted for an honors anthropology course. The instructor for this pivotal first-year course was Robert C. Dailey, who inspired Richard to go into anthropology. As it turns out, Dailey had the same influence some eight years later on Harriet Rosenberg, who some sixteen years in the future would become Richard's life companion and many years after that, his wife. Dailey's approach was Boasian, weaving the physical, the social, and the archaeological into the course. Dailey's discussion of his fieldwork among the Inuit of Rankin Inlet (west coast of Hudson's Bay) sparked Richard's abiding concern with foraging societies. Halfway through the term, Lee told his parents he was going to go into anthropology. He recalls his father saying, "Can you make a living at that? Can you really make a living at that?" but soon "coming around"; his mother was supportive from the outset.

Lee's subsequent training in kinship and social organization brought him under the tutelage of one of Meyer Fortes's former students, Canadian anthropologist R.W. Dunning, who at the time was writing and sharing with his students the 1959 volume that would become a classic in Canadian anthropology, *Social and Economic Change among the Northern Ojibwa*. Dunning was not reluctant to reveal to his classes his deep mistrust and dislike for the bureaucracy. To him, the Department of Indian Affairs was bent on destroying Indian culture, whom the local peoples had to resist in order to survive. Largely due to Dunning's influence, Lee's first field research was with Northern Ojibwa on the north shore of Lake Superior. Still in his second year, Richard grew closer to Professor Ronald Cohen, whom he knew slightly through interlaced family networks; Cohen's field research was in Bornu, an emirate in northern Nigeria. Unlike Dunning, whose training under Fortes would have eschewed such theorizing, Cohen was a social evolutionist. He introduced Lee to the works of Leslie White and Julian Steward, and urged Richard and other students in the cohort to do field research in Africa.

At the University of Toronto in the 1950s, Lee recalls reading Wittfogel's work and being more influenced by Steward than White. Although his immersion in the Marxian tradition shaped his political consciousness, Lee also embraced the "scientism" of Julian Steward's "cultural ecology"; he would not include Karl Marx's work explicitly in the construction of his theoretical apparatus until the 1970s. Among the British anthropologists taught at the university, Fortes and E.E. Evans-Pritchard figured larger than others. Among US anthropologists, Richard found the early work of Marshall Sahlins intriguing, but was most influenced by Eric Wolf's 1959 *Sons of the Shaking Earth* and the work of Steward's more historically grounded former students such as Morton Fried and Sidney Mintz.

Thus, Lee's early theoretical framework was social evolutionist, but with a concern for understanding kinship and social organization as dynamic rather than fixed, due largely to colonial histories and confrontational processes that involved community attempts to sustain ways of life in the face of state incursions. These aspects would make Lee's social evolution distinct from that of Steward and others, since his concern for history as process and local resistance subverted the view of the forces of production as the motor of history favored by Wittfogel and White.

After doctoral studies at the University of California at Berkeley with Sherwood L. Washburn, Robert Murphy, and J. Desmond Clark, Lee first conducted field research in the Kalahari in 1963. He was part of a loose international coterie of academics studying hunters and gatherers in the last decade of British rule in southern Africa.

Contributions to Ethnological Theory

Lee's earliest writings, from the late 1960s to the latter half of the 1970s, fit comfortably into a framework that emphasized the cultural framing of environmental use, a four-fields approach to cultural ecology, the cultural dimensions of production and reproduction, and historically attentive social evolution. Lee noted that the foragers spent considerably less time in "subsistence" than was typical of workers in industrial capitalist societies. He stressed the ways that their far-flung kinship networks, flexible group membership, and patterns of sharing and exchange buffered local groups against the vicissitudes of seasonality and drought. Implicitly, he argued that in the long sweep of history, want was less a result of environmental scarcity than of evolving human relations that limited access to necessary resources and led eventually to the permanent inequalities of state societies. Hence the appellation "Original Affluent Society" (see Sahlins, Solway and Susser, this volume) emerged for groups such as the San.

In contrast to some of the other articles in *Man the Hunter* (Lee and DeVore, 1968), Lee's contribution did not focus exclusively on men's hunting contributions to the food supply, but emphasized subsistence activities of both women and men as contributing to the adequacy of the diet and availability of greater leisure time even amid "scarce resources" in a desert environment (1968).

While Lee's evolutionism at that time had more in common with Julian Steward than Marvin Harris, he was critical of Steward's "composite band" versus "family band" typology for hunter-gatherers, suggesting, based on the !Kung case, that these are better seen as seasonal variations (1972a). Even so, one senses a tension in his article on group composition and in those on fertility and reproduction (1972b) and subsistence strategies among foragers (1972c). Lee's work in this early period emphasizes how successful the strategies are: we do not find here the techno-environmental motor force of history that we see in other social evolutionist writings of the era (1968).

His changing choice of terms for the people with whom he worked reflects a growing sense of how apartheid and colonialism influenced the very naming of a people: the uncritical adoption of the common usage of "Bushmen" in the 1960s is followed by the transition to the more respectful term "San" in the early 1970s, and in the late 1980s, to the self-appellation "Ju/'hoansi." Each refinement reflects the development of a stronger indigenous rights movement worldwide, and the reassertion by local peoples of their persistent identities. In this way, and even in the early work, he brings changing interactions with surrounding peoples into the arguments. Lee never ignored historical dynamics, pointing out the relations of the !Kung with the incoming Herero and Tswana in different regions, while emphasizing the historical depth of San occupation in the Kalahari relative to other peoples (1972c).

Tracing his trajectory as a scholar from the early to the late 1970s demands that we see Lee's growing attention to gender, on the one hand, and mode of production debates, on the other. He never loses his concern with the ways people construct their usable environments, and with what is now called political ecology. In short, while Lee's theoretical armature becomes more subtle and more explicitly linked with indigenous rights, feminism, and a critique of capitalism, his appreciation of the holistic nature of anthropology remains important: his work iterates the centrality of a four-fields approach, with culture at the core.

Gender and Egalitarianism in Foraging Societies

In our conversations, Lee stated that his development as a scholar owes more to the influence of Marxist-feminist work than any other corpus of scholarship; he is one of the few senior male ethnologists who acknowledge such influence. Because his ethnographies on the San are so widely read in US and Canadian universities (see Lee, 2003a), generations of women and men have become attentive to gender dynamics and structures that challenge patriarchal paradigms.

The early 1970s saw the emergence of Marxist-feminist anthropologists who interrogated the theorizing of sex roles and reproductive institutions among peoples in precolonial and marginalized capitalist settings (Gough, 1968; Leacock, 1954; 1972; [Brodkin] Sacks, 1971, 1976; Siskind, 1973, 1978). Together with the British feminist Marxist critique of *Precapitalist Modes of Production* (Edholm, Harris, and Young, 1977; Hindess and Hirst, 1975), these writings presented ways to integrate cultural dynamics and human agency with a concern for the structures that shape production and social reproduction, without sacrificing history or gender politics. Lee brought a range of such Marxist-feminist influences to his writings beginning in the late 1970s, notably in his 1979 *The !Kung San: Men, Women, and Work in a Foraging Society.*

Unlike many ethnographers in the 1960s and early 1970s, Lee's early writings discussed the division of labor by sex and the role women played in production and reproduction among the San. Through the descriptions one can see the enactment in everyday life of what constitutes comparable worth of women and men in the San foraging context. Especially since the early 1970s, he has highlighted the voices of actors shaping local communities, through a language of rough joking and banter that helps to reproduce non-hierarchical relations (1992b). This central ethos was later given the label "complaint discourse" by Harriet Rosenberg in her studies of Ju/'hoan aging and caregiving (1997).

He and Irven DeVore drew Marjorie Shostak into their volume on Kalahari foragers. This 1976 volume premiered Shostak's exploration of one woman's perspective on girlhood among the San, later emerging in 1982 as the classic life history, *Nisa: The Life and Words of a !Kung Woman.* Through his cooperation with and encouragement of other researchers on the San, Lee avoided stereotyping gender relations among the various groups in the Kalahari.

Lee's concern with gender was anticipatory of what became the study of the cultural construction of masculinity. "Eating Christmas in the Kalahari" begins as a "cultural misunderstanding" piece, but soon delves into the gendering of hunting and how !Kung concepts of masculinity eschew the machismo associated with hunting in Euro-American contexts. Contrary to images fostered by "man the hunter" mythologies, Lee shows how the !Kung practice of "insulting the meat" subverts what they perceive as a potential for arrogance that, in turn, might shift into domination and violence within the group

(1969). In later pieces, Lee explores women's attitudes toward meat and the ways sexual joking plays with hunting metaphors (see, e.g., Lee, 1979).[4]

The Mode of Production Debates

In the late 1970s and 1980s a range of Marxist anthropologists in North America and Europe debated how production and reproduction were articulated in precapitalist social formations—both state and nonstate—and in colonial and capitalist industrial contexts. Beginning with the publication of Eric Hobsbawm's reexamination of arguments on modes of production in Marx's *Grundrisse* (1965), orthodox, structural, and dialectical Marxist scholars in the Soviet Union, Europe, and the Americas developed a critical discourse on the role of culture and agency in the transformation of political economies and the social formations associated with them. Among the debates that emerged was whether or not egalitarian societies existed and persisted in the face of state encapsulation and colonization. Many of these debates took place in the pages of *Critique of Anthropology, Culture, Dialectical Anthropology, Economy and Society* and in the first Conference on Hunting and Gathering Societies (CHAGS) organized by Maurice Godelier in Paris in 1978, which Lee and Leacock attended.

Lee's "Is There a Foraging Mode of Production?" appeared in *Anthropologie et société* in 1980 and signaled his first explicit engagement with the precapitalist mode of production debates. *Politics and History in Band Societies*, the collection of CHAGS essays he edited with Leacock, appeared in 1982. Their position in the latter volume emphasizes a historical appreciation of shifting political terrains among foraging societies, the centrality of gender in the analysis of social formations (and not only in terms of social reproduction), and the complex and simultaneous significance of both structure and concerted human agency in social transformation. They also made a larger claim: that egalitarian societies exist, albeit today under genocidal or ethnocidal threat from the expanding world system. The positions taken by Leacock and Lee in their introduction and respective essays for the volume center on the importance of appreciating local histories. The argument stresses that politics are intrinsic to the reproduction of social relations in foraging societies, that existing "primitive communist" social formations do not conform to liberal notions of equality in their egalitarian relations, and that the reproduction of foraging and other band societies is due to the active engagement of their constituents in changing social and ecological contexts.

Foragers versus the Scholars without History:
The Kalahari Revisionist Debate

Lee's long-term field research provides his work with a depth of time and a sense of transformation with processes of colonization, sedentarization, militarization, and other issues confronting indigenous peoples that virtually no other ethnographer has framed. In light of his efforts to portray the contemporary issues faced by the San peoples in the region in which he worked, it is astonishing that he was attacked in the late 1980s and early 1990s for romanticizing them and ignoring history (see Wilmsen, 1989; Wilmsen and Denbow, 1990; see Lee 1992a for his far-ranging response to the controversy and his broadest theoretical statement on contemporary issues across the discipline of anthropology).

With Jacqueline Solway, Lee based his defense of the historical validity of egalitarianism and autonomy among Kalahari foragers on archaeological, ethnohistorical, and ethnographic evidence that contradicts the claims of Wilmsen and Denbow of early San subordination under a regional power grid (Solway and Lee, 1990; see also Lee and Guenther, 1991). The Solway-Lee argument is not that San had no history, but rather that their insertion into relations of domination by neighboring polities is rather late and highly uneven, so long as foraging has remained an option. Far from denying dynamism to the society, Lee emphasizes the social engagement of particular San peoples—or human agency if you will—in reproducing egalitarian relations. Daily practices, evasions, and acts of resistance emerge time and again in San efforts to remain autonomous under pressure from surrounding pastoral and sedentarized peoples, as well as recent South African and other state domination (e.g., Lee and Hurlich, 1982). Solway and Lee urged scholars to document the region's varied histories and the responses of the peoples, instead of imposing a Procrustean bed of an early "world system" for which there is no evidence (Solway and Lee, 1990). For them, and for those who sided with them in the face of this virulent attack, the major theoretical point was that exchange was a universal of human experience and did not automatically translate into political dependency or economic subordination (see also Lee and Guenther, 1993).

Indeed, in moving beyond the Kalahari debate, Lee provides new intellectual life to the notion of primitive communism (1992b). The term, he points out, had its origins not so much in the writings of Marx and Engels as it was found in the work of Lewis Henry Morgan, who called it "communism in living" (Lee, 1990b). Lee's appreciation of what a real social safety net entails, as a feature of preclass societies, as distinct from the imagery associated with the current fast-disappearing

Richard B. Lee: The Politics, Art, and Science of Anthropology

welfare state apparatus, provides contemporary peoples with a measure of how societies need not replicate the Hobbesian "Warre of all against all" that underlies neoliberal policies and practices.

Parallel to Leacock and Gailey's essay in the same 1992 volume, Lee presents relations in primitive communism as more or less equal rather than the hypothetical ideal of equality in the classic liberal sense. Inequities exist, but they are not structural: they are artifacts of personal achievement, skills or talents, or moments in the life course, and are contained and prevented from crystallizing into permanent hierarchies through the normal operation of systems of kinship, production, and reproduction. What results from this fundamental security—the right to exist in one's multifaceted social personhood—is not utopian similarity of being but an individuation that can be explored actively through the life course. In keeping with the work of Stanley Diamond (1974), there is in Lee's continuing appreciation of primitive communism an abiding commitment to indigenous rights. Lee's unromantic view of indigenous rights rejects preservation strategies (see 2002). His view is that people will continue to make their own histories whether or not they control the conditions in which they must live. Gaining greater control over those conditions is the struggle facing indigenous peoples and their advocates throughout the world (see, e.g., Lee and Biesele, 2002; Lee, Hitchcock, and Biesele, 2002).

The Work Today

In 1996, the HIV/AIDS crisis in southern Africa drew Lee to undertake work on the social and cultural aspects of HIV/AIDS. In a region ravaged by the epidemic, Lee expects that the Ju/'hoansi may be less affected by the disease. With Ida Susser, he has studied San men's and women's responses to AIDS prevention (2002, 2003). They see a clear link between what may be the Ju/'hoansi's success at keeping the epidemic at bay and the high status of women, contrasting so markedly with women in less gender-equitable settings. In contrast to Namibian and South African township women, who said that they could not ask their male partners to use condoms, Ju/'hoan women and men spoke freely. Ju/'hoan women said that they were willing to ask or teach their husbands about condom use. Otherwise, they said "women could get sick!" Lee and Susser acknowledge, however, that San people elsewhere in the region working in underpaid or unpaid jobs on farms and ranches and exposed to the gender dynamics of the wider society are at much greater risk of succumbing to AIDS. This brings home the point that fighting AIDS and the struggle for indigenous rights in post-Apartheid southern Africa must go hand in hand (Lee, 2003b). Lee continues active research projects in both areas. Richard Lee's lines of ongoing research, combining medical anthropology, indigenous rights, political ecology, and social activism, augurs well for the coming decades.

Richard Lee has learned the lesson of !Kung masculinity well: while he is clearly a pivotal figure in anthropology today, he remains an affable sort, an optimistic intellectual: deeply engaged and deeply influenced as a person by the people with whom he has worked for decades. Lee's intellectual generosity has helped colleagues around the world, from politically marginalized scholars laboring under repressive regimes to marginalized academics at home, and, always, the countless students, both graduate and undergraduate. Despite his outspoken stands on issues of the day including US adventures in the Middle East and Israel's continuing occupation of Palestine, he has been honored with two honorary degrees. As an advocate for indigenous rights, his deft weaving of political ecology, social, cultural, historical, and medical anthropology gives his argumentation a singular and lasting persuasive force.

Acknowledgments

I thank Jackie Solway for her patience through a difficult period and editorial suggestions, Tom Patterson for reviewing the manuscript and listening critically to drafts, and Winnie Lem for bearing with me. I thank the audience and panel participants in the CASCA/AES meetings in Toronto for their contributions to shaping this *Festschrift*. I thank Louise Rosenberg Lee and Sarah Gailey for helping Richard and me find time to do the interviews and keeping us grounded in the process. Most of all, I thank Richard Lee for his characteristic honesty, good humor, insight, and spirit of intellectual exploration during the interviews and the drafting of the chapter. I thank Maggie Ham at UC Riverside for her cheerfully undertaken research assistance.

Notes

1. *Yiddishkeit*, literally "Yiddishness," roughly translates as "Jewish lore." The concept is weighted heavily toward the more humorous and the more political aspects of Eastern European shtetl (ghetto) and New World immigrant experiences.

2. All quotes and information in the biographical section are taken from a series of interviews I conducted with Richard Lee in Riverside, California, 14–15 March 2002.
3. Later, when he was offered a job at Harvard University, Lee had to go through the usually bureaucratic entanglement of applying for a "green card," although he had been born in the United States.
4. The only other anthropologist at the time who explored this kind of everyday construction of gender in subsistence practice was Janet Siskind in her pioneering study of marginalized indigenous communities in the Peruvian Amazon (1973).

References

Diamond, Stanley. 1974. *In Search of the Primitive: A Critique of Civilization.* New Brunswick, N.J.: Transaction Books.

Edholm, Felicity, Olivia Harris, and Kate Young. 1977. "Conceptualising Women." *Critique of Anthropology* 3(9–10): 101–30.

Gough, Kathleen. 1968. "The Nayars and the Definition of Marriage." In *Marriage, Family, and Residence,* ed. Paul Bohannan and John Middleton. Garden City, N.Y.: Natural History Press.

Hindess, Barry, and Paul Hirst. 1975. *Precapitalist Modes of Production.* London: Routledge and Kegan Paul.

Hobsbawm, Eric. 1965. "Introduction." In *Karl Marx, Pre-capitalist Economic Formations,* trans. Jack Cohen, ed. Eric Hobsbawm. New York: International.

Leacock, Eleanor B. 1954. "The Montagnais 'Hunting Territory' and the Fur Trade." *American Anthropological Association, Memoir No. 78.*

———. 1972. "Introduction." In *The Origin of the Family, Private Property, and the State,* by Frederick Engels. New York: International.

Leacock, Eleanor B., and Christine W. Gailey. 1992. "Primitive Communism and Its Transformations." In *Civilization in Crisis: Anthropological Perspectives,* Vol. 1, *Dialectical Anthropology: Essays in Honor of Stanley Diamond,* ed. Christine Gailey. Gainesville, Fl.: University Press of Florida, 95–110.

Rosenberg, Harriet. 1997. "Complaint Discourse, Aging, and Care Giving among the Ju/'hoansi of Botswana." In *The Cultural Context of Aging: Worldwide Perspectives,* ed. Jay Sokolovsky. Westport, Conn.: Bergin and Garvey, 33–55.

Sacks, Karen Brodkin. 1971. *Economic Bases of Sexual Equality: A Comparative Study of Four African Societies.* Ann Arbor: University of Michigan.

———. 1976. "State Bias and Women's Status." *American Anthropologist* 78: 565–69.

Sahlins, Marshall. 1972. *Stone Age Economics.* Chicago, Ill.: Aldine.

Shostak, Marjorie. 1976. "A !Kung Woman's Memories of Childhood." In *Kalahari Hunter-Gatherers: Studies of the !Kung San and Their Neighbors,* ed. Richard B. Lee and Irven DeVore. Cambridge, Mass.: Harvard University Press, 246–77.

———. 1981. *Nisa: The Life and Words of a !Kung Woman.* Cambridge, Mass.: Harvard University Press.

Siskind, Janet. 1973. *To Hunt in the Morning.* New York: Oxford University Press.

————. 1978. "Kinship and Mode of Production." *American Anthropologist* 89(4): 860–72.

Slocum, Sally. [1971] 1975. "Woman the Gatherer: Male Bias in Anthropology." In *Toward an Anthropology of Women*, ed. Rayna Rapp Reiter. New York: Monthly Review Press, 36–50.

Wilmsen, Edwin. 1989. *Land Filled with Flies: A Political Economy of the Kalahari*. Chicago, Ill.: University of Chicago Press.

Wilmsen, Edwin, and James Denbow. 1990. "Paradigmatic History of San-Speaking Peoples and Current Attempts at Revision." *Current Anthropology* 31(5): 489–524.

Wolf, Eric. 1959. *Sons of the Shaking Earth*. Chicago, Ill.: University of Chicago Press.

See "Selected Bibliography" for all Lee references.

SELECTED BIBLIOGRAPHY

Richard Borshay Lee
Fellow, The Royal Society of Canada
University Professor, University of Toronto.
Winner, 1980 Herskovits Award of the African Studies Association, for the best book of the year in English on Africa, for *The !Kung San: Men, Women and Work in a Foraging Society.*

Books and Monographs

Jorgenson, Joseph B., and Richard Borshay Lee, ed.
    1974 *The New Native Resistance: Indigenous People's Struggles and the Responsibility of Scholars.* Module No. 6. New York: MSS Modular Publications.
Leacock, Eleanor, and Richard Borshay Lee, ed.
    1982 *Politics and History in Band Societies.* Cambridge and Paris: Cambridge University Press and La Maison des Sciences de l'Homme.
Lee, Richard Borshay
    1965 *Subsistence Ecology of !Kung Bushmen,* PhD Dissertation, University of California, Berkeley. Available from University Microfilms, Ann Arbor, MI, #66-3636: 1–209.
    1979 *The !Kung San: Men, Women and Work in a Foraging Society.* Cambridge and New York: Cambridge University Press.
    2003 *The Dobe Ju/'hoansi.* 4th ed. Toronto: Thomson Learning/Wadsworth.
Lee, Richard Borshay, and Richard Daly, ed.
    1999 *The Cambridge Encyclopedia of Hunters and Gatherers.* Cambridge and New York: Cambridge University Press.
Lee, Richard Borshay, and Irven DeVore, ed.
    1968 *Man the Hunter,* Chicago: Aldine.
    1976 *Kalahari Hunter-Gatherers: Studies of the !Kung San and Their Neighbors,* Cambridge, Mass.: Harvard University Press.
Lee, Richard Borshay, Robert Hitchcock, and Megan Biesele, ed.
    2002 The Kalahari San: Self-Determination in the Desert. *Cultural Survival Quarterly,* Special Issue, 26(1).

Articles

Lee, Richard Borshay

1963 "The Population Ecology of Man in the Early Upper Pleistocene of Southern Africa." *Proceedings of the Prehistoric Society* 29:235–57.

1968a "Sociology of !Kung Bushman Trance Performances." In *Trance and Possession States*, ed. R. H. Prince. Montreal: R.M. Bucke Memorial Society.

1968b "What Hunters Do for a Living, or, How to Make Out on Scarce Resources." In *Man the Hunter*, ed. Richard B. Lee and Irven DeVore. Chicago, Ill.: Aldine.

1969a "!Kung Bushmen." *South African Medical Journal*, January 11: 48.

1969b "!Kung Bushman Subsistence: An Input-Output Analysis." *Ecological Essays: Proceedings of the Conferences on Cultural Ecology*, ed. D. Mamas, Bulletin 230. Ottawa: National Museum of Canada, 73–94.

1969c "Eating Christmas in the Kalahari." *Natural History*, 14–22 December 1969: 60–63 (reprinted over 40 times).

Lee, Richard B., and Irven DeVore

1970 "Ngamiland !Kung Bushmen: Research in Progress." *Botswana Notes and Records* 2: 122–25.

1971 "The Bushmen of the Kalahari Desert, Record and Filmstrip." In *Studying Societies: Patterns in Human History*, developed for the Anthropology Curriculum Study Project, American Anthropological Association. New York: Macmillan.

1972a "Work Effort, Group Structure, and Land Use in Hunter-Gatherers." In *Man, Settlement, and Urbanism*, ed. Peter Ucko, Ruth Tringham, and G.W. Dimbleby. London: Duckworth.

1972b *The !Kung Bushmen of Botswana, Hunters and Gatherers Today*, ed. M. Bicchiere. New York: Holt Rinehart and Winston.

1972c "Population Growth and the Beginnings of Sedentary Life among the !Kung Bushmen." In *Population Growth: Anthropological Implications*, ed. Brian Spooner. Cambridge, Mass.: MIT Press.

1972d "The Intensification of Social Life among the !Kung Bushmen." In *Population Growth: Anthropological Implications*, ed. Brian Spooner. Cambridge, Mass.: MIT Press.

1972e "!Kung Spatial Organisation: An Ecological and Historical Perspective." *Human Ecology* 1(2): 125–47.

1973a "The Evolution of Technical Civilization." In *Communication with Extra-Terrestrial Intelligence (CETI)*, ed. Carl Sagan. Cambridge, Mass.: MIT Press.

1973b "Mongongo: The Ethnography of a Major Wild Food Resource." *Ecology of Food and Nutrition* 2: 307–21.

1974 "Male-Female Residence Arrangements and Political Power in Contemporary Hunter-Gatherers." *Archives of Sexual Behavior* 4: 163–67.

1975a "The !Kung's New Culture, Science Year: 1976." In *World Book Encyclopedia*, Chicago.

1975b "The !Kung San: Life in a Hunting and Gathering Community." In *The Study of Anthropology*, ed. David Hunter and Philip Whitten. New York: Harper and Row.

Bibliography

Lee, Richard B., H. Harpending, and N. Howell
  1977 "!Kung Bushmen." *Science* 197: 1232.
  1978a "Hunter-Gatherers in Process: The Kalahari Research Project, 1963–76." In *Long-Term Field Research in Social Anthropology*, ed. G. Foster et al. New York: Academic Press.
  1978b "The Ecology of a Contemporary San People." In *The Bushmen*, ed. P. Tobias. Capetown: Human and Rousseau.
  1978c "Politics, Sexual and Non-Sexual in an Egalitarian Society." *Social Science Information* 17(6): 871–95.
Hurlich, Susan, and Richard B. Lee
  1979 "Colonialism, Apartheid and Liberation: A Namibian Example." In *Challenging Anthropology*, ed. D. Turner and G. Smith. Toronto: McGraw-Hill Ryerson.
  1980a "Lactation, Ovulation, Infanticide and Women's Work." In *Biosocial Mechanisms in Population Regulation*, ed. M. Cohen et al. New Haven: Yale University Press.
  1980b "Is There a Foraging Mode of Production?" *Anthropologie et société*. Reprinted in 1981 in *Canadian Journal of Anthropology* 2(1): 13–19.
  1982a "Politics, Sexual and Non-Sexual, in an Egalitarian Society." In *Politics and History in Band Societies*, ed. Eleanor Leacock and Richard Lee. New York: Cambridge University Press.
Lee, Richard B., and Susan Hurlich
  1982b "From Foragers to fighters: the militarization of the !Kung San." In *Politics and History in Band Societies*, ed. Eleanor Leacock and Richard Lee. New York: Cambridge University Press.
  1982c "Forward." In *Boiling Energy: Community Healing Among the Kalahari !Kung*, by R. Katz. Cambridge, Mass.: Harvard Univ. Press.
  1982d "SWAPO: Best Hope for the San." *Anthropology Resource Centre (ARC Inc.) Newsletter* 6(1): 10.
Lee, Richard B., and Carolyn Filteau
  1983 "Notes on the Politics of Teaching Anthropology in Canada." In *Consciousness and Inquiry*, ed. Frank Manning. Ottawa: National Museum of Canada, Mercury Series.
  1984 "Ethnicity, Militarism and Human Rights in South Africa and Israel." *Dialectical Anthropology* 10: 121–28.
  1985a "Work, Sexuality and Aging among !Kung Women." In *In Her Prime: A New View of Middle-Aged Women*, ed. Judith Brown and Virginia Kerns (reprinted in 1992 by University of Illinois Press). New York: Bergin and Garvey.
  1985b "Models of Human Colonization: San, Greeks and Vikings." *Interstellar Migrations*, ed. E. Jones and B. Finney. Berkeley and Los Angeles: University of California Press.
  1985c "Greeks and Victorians: a re-examination of Engels' theory of the Athenian Polis." *Culture* 5(1): 63–73.
  1985d "Foragers and the State: Government policies towards the San in Namibia and Botswana." *Cultural Survival: Occasional Papers*, No. 18: 37–46.
  1986a "!Kung Kinship, the Name Relationship and the Process of Discovery." In *Critical Reflections on !Kung Ethnography: Essays in Honour of Lorna Marshall*, ed. Megan Biesele. Hamburg: Helmut Buske Verlag.

1986b "The Gods Must Be Crazy but the State Has a Plan: Government Policy Towards the San in Namibia." *Canadian Journal of African Studies* 20(1): 181–90.

Lee, Richard, B, and Richard Daly

1987a "Man's Domination and Women's Oppression: The question of origins, Beyond Patriarchy." In *Essays by Men on Pleasure, Power, and Change*, ed. Michael Kaufman. Toronto and New York: Oxford University Press.

1987b "The impact of development on foraging peoples: a world survey." *Tribal Peoples and Development Issues*, ed. John Bodley. Mountain View, Calif.: Mayfield.

1988 "Reflections on Primitive Communism." In *Hunters and Gatherers*, Vol. 1, *Ecology, Evolution, and Social Change*, ed. Tim Ingold, David Riches, and James Woodburn. London: Berg.

Lee, Richard B., et al.

1989 "Hunters, Clients, and Squatters: the Contemporary Socio-Economic Status of Botswana Basarwa." *African Studies Monographs*, Kyoto 9(3):109–51.

Solway, J., and Richard Borshay Lee

1990a "Foragers, Genuine or Spurious? Situating the Kalahari San in History." *Current Anthropology* 32: 106–46.

1990b "Comment to Wilmsen and Denbow. Paradigmatic History of San-Speaking Peoples and Current Attempts at Revision." *Current Anthropology* 31: 510–12.

1990c "Primitive Communism and the Origin of Social Inequity." In *The Evolution of Political Systems: Sociopolitics in Small-Scale Sedentary Societies*, ed. Steadman Upham. Cambridge, UK: Cambridge University Press.

Lee, Richard B., and Mathias Guenther

1991a "Oxen or Onions: The Search for Trade (and Truth) in the Kalahari." *Current Anthropology* 32(5): 592–601.

1991b "The !Kung in Question: Evidence and Context in the Kalahari San Debate." *Michigan Discussions in Anthropology* 11: 73–91.

1992a "Art, Science, or Politics? The Crisis in Hunter-Gatherer Studies." *American Anthropologist* 90(1): 18–45.

1992b "Demystifying Primitive Communism." In *Civilization in Crisis: Anthropological Perspectives*, Vol. 1: *Dialectical Anthropology: Essays in Honor of Stanley Diamond*, ed. Christine Gailey. Gainesville: University Press of Florida.

1992c "Making Sense of the Tasaday." In *The Tasaday Controversy*, ed. Thomas Headland. Washington: American Anthropology Association Special Publication.

Lee, Richard B., and Mathias Guenther

1992d "Problems in Kalahari Historical Ethnography and the Tolerance of Error." *History in Africa* 20: 185–235.

1993a "The Primitive as Problematic." Guest Editorial. *Anthropology Today*, December: 3–5.

Lee, Richard B., and Karen Sacks

1993b "Anthropology, Imperialism and Resistance: The Work of Kathleen Gough." Special Issue of *Anthropologica* 35(2): 175–301.

Lee, Richard B., and Harriet Rosenberg

1994 "Fragments of the Future: Aspects of Social Reproduction among the Ju/'hoansi." In *Papers of the Seventh Conference on Hunting and Gathering Societies*, ed. Moscow. L. Elleana. Fairbanks: University of Alaska Press.

Lee, Richard B., and Mathias Guenther

1995 "Errors corrected or compounded? A Reply to Wilmsen." *Current Anthropology* 36: 299–305.

1996 "AIDS in Southern Africa: The Struggle Continues." *Southern Africa Report* 16: 21–25.

Biesele, Megan, Robert K. Hitchcock, and Richard B. Lee

1996 "Thirty Years of Ethnographic Research among the Ju/'hoansi of Northwestern Botswana: 1963–1993." *Botswana Notes and Records*, 28, Gaborone, Botswana.

Lee, Richard, B., and Robert Hitchcock

1998a "African Hunter-Gatherers: History and the Politics of Ethnicity." In *Transformations in Africa: Essays on Africa's Later Past*, ed. Graham Connah. London: Cassels.

1998b "Forward." In *Limited Wants, Unlimited Means*, ed. John Gowdy. Washington: Island Press.

1998c "Anthropology at the Crossroads: From the Age of Ethnography to the Age of World-Systems." *Social Dynamics* 24: 34–65.

1998d "Precapitalist Work: Baseline for and Anthropology of Work or a Romantic Delusion." *Anthropology of Work Review* 20: 9–15.

1999 "Science and Constructivism: Notes Towards a Reconciliation." In *The New Physical Anthropology*, ed. Shirley Strum, David Hamburg, and Don Lindburg. Englewood Cliffs, N.J.: Prentice-Hall.

Lee, Richard B., and Megan Biesele

2002a "Local Cultures and Global Systems: The Ju/'hoansi-!Kung Forty Years On." In *Chronicling Cultures: Long-term Fieldwork in Anthropology*, ed. Robert Kemper and Anya Royce. 2d ed. Walnut Creek, Calif.: Altamira Press.

2002b "Solitude or Servitude? Ju/'hoan Images of the Colonial Encounter." In *Ethnicity and Hunter-Gatherers: Association or Assimilation*, ed. Susan Kent. Washington, D.C.: Smithsonian Institution Press.

2002c "Foragers to First Peoples: The Kalahari San Today." Special issue, *The Kalahari San: Self-Determination in the Desert*, ed. R.B. Lee, R. Hitchcock, and M. Biesele. *Cultural Survival Quarterly* 26(1): 3–10.

Lee, Richard B., and Ida Susser

2002d "The San and the Challenge of AIDS." Special issue, *The Kalahari San: Self-Determination in the Desert*, ed. R.B. Lee, R. Hitchcock, and M. Biesele. *Cultural Survival Quarterly* 26(1): 18–20.

2002e "Foragers to First Peoples: The Dobe Ju/'hoansi Today." (In Japanese.) *Humanities and Sciences, Journal of the Kobe/Gaikuin University, Humanities and Sciences* 17: 1–16.

Lee, Richard B., and Ida Susser

2003a "AIDS, women's power, and the Ju/'hoansi of Southern Africa." *Culture Matters* 1(1), Available at, http://www.nyu.edu/fas/ihpk/CultureMatters/index2.htm

2003b "Human Rights and Indigenous People in Post-Apartheid South Africa." In *At the Risk of Being Heard: Identity, Indigenous Rights and Post-Colonial States,* ed. Bart Dean and Jerome Levi. Ann Arbor: University of Michigan Press.

2005 "Power and Property in Twenty-first Century Foragers: A Critical Re-examination." In *Property and Equality: Encapsulation, Commercialization, Discrimination,* ed. Thomas Widlok and Tadasse Wolde. London: Berghahn.

NOTES ON CONTRIBUTORS

Megan Biesele helped found one of the first US anthropological advocacy organizations, the Kalahari Peoples Fund, in 1973 and currently serves as its coordinator. For the past four decades, Biesele worked with Ju/'hoan San communities in Botswana and Namibia as an advocate and documentarian, and served as director of a nongovernmental organization, the Nyae Nyae Development Foundation of Namibia. Currently, she is preparing her collected folklore and other texts in the Ju/'hoan language for use by linguists and other scholars, and for return to Ju/'hoan community educational projects and archives. Her many books include *Women Like Meat: The Folklore and Foraging Ideology of the Kalahari Ju/'Hoan*.

Karen Brodkin is a professor of Anthropology and Women's Studies at the University of California at Los Angeles. She is the author of *How Jews Became White Folks and What that Says about Race in America*. She is currently working on social activism in Los Angeles.

Christine Ward Gailey is Professor of Anthropology and Chair of the Women's Studies Department at the University of California, Riverside. Gailey has written extensively on contemporary kinship formation, on gender, race, and class dynamics in adoption and more generally on cultural resistance to state formation. She has written intellectual biographies of Stanley Diamond and Eleanor Leacock and her books include, *Kinship to Kingship: Gender Hierarchy and State Formation in the Tongan Islands*.

Mathias Guenther is a professor of Anthropology at Wilfrid Laurier University. He has conducted field research among the farm San (Bushmen) of western Botswana, on such topics as social change, ethnohistory, social organization, religion, folklore, and art. His publications include *The Nharo Bushmen of Botswana: Tradition and Change,*

Bushman Folktales: Oral Traditions of the Nharo of Botswana and the /Xam of the Cape and *Tricksters and Trancers: Bushman Religion and Society.*

Robert K. Hitchcock is professor of Anthropology in the Department of Anthropology and Geography and coordinator of African Studies at the University of Nebraska, Lincoln. He is also a member of the board of the Kalahari Peoples Fund. He has worked among San in southern Africa since the mid-1970s. Currently he is serving as a member of the Panel of Environmental Experts of the Lesotho Highlands Water Project and is working with Sudanese refugees on the Great Plains of the United States. He recently coedited *Indigenous Peoples' Rights in Southern Africa* with D. Vinding.

Tom Patterson is distinguished professor and chair of Anthropology at the University of California, Riverside. He recently published *Marx's Ghost: Conversations with Archaeologists* and *A Social History of Anthropology in the United States.*

Marshall Sahlins is the Charles F. Grey Distinguished Service Professor Emeritus of Anthropology and Social Sciences in the College, University of Chicago. He is presently doing research focused on the intersection of culture and history, especially as those play out in early-modern Pacific societies. His many books include *Culture and Practical Reason, Islands of History, How "Natives" Think: About Captain Cook, For Example* and most recently, *Apologies to Thucydides: Understanding History as Culture and Vice Versa.*

Jacqueline Solway is associate professor of International Development Studies and Anthropology at Trent University. She has conducted research in North and East Africa but has worked primarily in Botswana, southern Africa, studying rural socioeconomic change, culture, and development, and multiculturalism in the context of liberal democracy. Her articles appear in numerous books and journals, including *Current Anthropology, Ethnos, Interventions, Anthropological Quarterly, Journal of Anthropological Research, Development and Change,* and *Journal of Southern African Studies.*

Ida Susser, professor of Anthropology at Hunter College and the Graduate Center of the City University of New York, has been working in southern Africa on questions of gender, HIV/AIDS, and collective action since 1992 with support from the National Endowment for the Humanities, the National Institute of Health and a MacArthur Fellowship in Research and Writing. She has also conducted research in Puerto Rico on social movements and the exportation of health hazards and in New York City on poverty, homelessness, and working-class resistance. Her selected publications include *Wounded Cities*, coedited with Jane Schneider; *Medical Anthropology in the World System*, coauthored with Hans Baer and Merrill Singer; *AIDS in Africa and the Caribbean*, coedited by George C. Bond, John Kreniske, and Joan Vincent; and *Norman Street: Poverty and Politics in an Urban Neighborhood*. She was awarded the SANA prize for Distinguished Achievement in the Critical Study of North America and is president-elect of the American Ethnological Society

Renée Sylvain is an associate professor in the department of Sociology and Anthropology at the University of Guelph. She has conducted research on San farm laborers and domestic servants in the Omaheke Region of Namibia since 1996. She has published articles in journals including *Anthropos, American Anthropologist, Journal of Southern African Studies*, as well as a forthcoming piece in *American Ethnologist*.

Elizabeth Marshall Thomas is a professional writer living in New Hampshire. She has conducted extensive fieldwork among the Bushmen of the Kalahari, and also among animal populations in Africa and the Arctic. She has published nonfiction as well as fiction books: her titles include *The Harmless People, The Hidden Life of Dogs, Tribe of the Tiger, Reindeer Moon*, and *The Animal Wife*. Her work has also appeared in *The New Yorker, The Atlantic Monthly, National Geographic, Behavioral Ecology and Sociobiology*, and others.

Bruce G. Trigger is James McGill Professor in the Department of Anthropology at McGill University. A graduate of the University of Toronto and Yale University, his numerous books include *The Huron: Farmers of the North, The Children of Aataentsic, A History of Archaeological Thought, Sociocultural Evolution*, and *Understanding Early Civilizations*.

INDEX

A

advocacy, 153
  essentialism and, 99, 195–196
  Kalahari Peoples Fund and, 145,
    133–144, 152–156
  identity and, 99, 100, 194,
    199–200
agropastoralists
  Herero, 151, 153, 154, 198, 210,
    216, 235
  Tawana, 151, 157n
AIDS
  See HIV
American Anthropological
    Association, 11, 134
Anthropology
  feminist, 4, 5, 16n4, 207, 236
  four-field approach, 11, 229, 235
Art
  appropriation and, 178–179
  "ethnic art," 177, 180, 183n11
  Kuru Art Project, 162, 179, 180
  politics and, 163, 172–174
  primitivism discourse and San art,
    13, 160, 176–180
  rock art, 160, 175
  Schmidtsdrift, 160–161, 163,
    182n4
Australian Aborigines, 69, 70, 80,
    87–88, 95
  Australian Fish Creek Study, 73
"authenticity"
  See indigenous peoples
autonomy, 195–196

women and, 207–208, 215–216,
  217

B

baasskap, 197
Barnard, Alan, 69–71
Basarwa, 134, 191, 200n2
  See also San, Ju/'hoansi, !Kung,
    Zhu
Basarwa Development Office (BDO),
    140, 142
Biesele, Megan, 6–7, 8, 10, 13, 15,
    211
Bird-David, Nurit, 67, 71–72
Botswana, 132, 134
  Department of Wildlife and
    National Parks, 153
  Dobe, 154, 208, 209–210
  Kalahari People's Fund in (Dobe),
    140–141, 142, 144
  North West District (Ngamiland),
    150, 154
  Northwest District Council, 153,
    155
  Shaikarawe, 141, 155
  XaiXai, 153–154, 208, 209, 210
  See also Ditshwanelo, the
    Botswana Centre for Human
    Rights
Brodkin, Karen, 6–7, 15
Buntman, Barbara, 177, 178, 179
Bushmen 122, 235
  identity politics and, 190–192,
    194, 195

relationship with lions, 119–128
subsistence, 88–89
See also Basarwa, San, Ju/
'hoansi, !Kung, Zhu

C

Capitalism, 22, 27, 32–33, 40–43,
45–46, 48, 58, 60, 190,
193–194, 206–207, 215, 218,
231, 235
Chagnon, Napoleon, 56–58
China, 21, 37, 47
Class, 36–39, 46–47, 99–100
cultural identity and, 13, 192,
193, 197–199, 201n11
the "traditional community" and,
194, 195
Clastres, Pierre, 6, 23
"coercive conservation," 134
Cohen, Ronald, 232
Communism
See social formations
Community-Based Natural Resource
Management Program
(CBNRM), 139, 153–155
community-based organizations
(CBOs)
Ju/Wa Farmers Union (JFU), 135,
136
Nyae Nyae Conservancy, 137,
140, 142, 191, 211, 215
Nyae Nyae Farmers Cooperative,
131, 133, 135, 137, 140
Tlhabololo Development Trust,
139, 140, 153, 156, 210
/Xai/Xai Trust, 215
See also non-governmental
organizations (NGOs)
community-controlled hunting area
(CCHA), 154
cultural ecology, 11–12, 233, 234

D

Dada (San painter), 163, 167–168,
182n5
Dailey, Robert C., 232
dependency theory, 61
DeVore, Irven, 3, 11, 12, 236

Ditshwanelo, the Botswana Centre
for Human Rights, 133, 155
Dobe
See Botswana
Draper, Pat, 4–5, 16n1, 207
Dunning, R.W., 232

E

early civilizations
See social formations
Eastern Bushmanland, 135
egalitarianism, 2, 4–6, 10, 31, 25,
27, 58–59, 60, 238
egalitarian societies
gender relations in, 59, 235–237
Engels, Friedrich, 31, 38, 42, 44
Enlightenment, 22, 25
ethnotourism, 179, 183n13
The *Ethnological Notebooks*
critical anthropology and, 42–43
marginalization of, 44, 45
See also Marx, Karl
ethnological theory, 234–235
evolution,
Social, 4, 12, 21, 24, 94–95, 234
See also Marx, Karl

F

First Peoples of the Kalahari
See non-governmental
organizations
foraging societies, 2–5, 12, 237
history and, 234, 235, 238
See also hunter-gatherer societies
formalism and substantivism, 3, 66

G

Gailey, Christine Ward, 2, 5, 14, 15,
239
Geographic Positioning Systems
(GPS), 154
gender relations, 55–57, 58, 59,
234–235, 236–237
HIV transmission and, 207,
215–217
postwar American Jews and,
106–107, 108–110
Gowdy, John, 67, 69

Index 255

Graburn, Nelson, 177, 159
Guenther, Mathias, 7, 9, 10, 13, 15,
  201n10

H

Harris, Marvin, 235
Harvard Kalahari Research Group
  (HKRG), 2, 7, 11–12,
  132–133, 150
Hadza, 69, 89
Health Unlimited
  See non-governmental
    organizations
Herero
  See agropastoralists
Hitchcock, Robert, 7, 9, 10, 15,
  134, 141, 145n
HIV
  female autonomy and, 14, 15,
    207, 215–217, 239
  poverty and, 206–207, 211–215,
    217, 218
  prevention, 211, 218
human nature, 5, 6, 14, 21–23, 27,
  62, 189–190
human rights, 2, 143, 145, 149
hunter-gatherer societies, 2–3, 22,
  75n1
  affluence and, 65–66, 69–74,
    75n5, 80, 84–86, 90
  anthropological understandings
    of, 69–74, 80–83, 235
  as theoretical category, 4, 12
  "diminishing returns" and, 91–92
  leisure and, 68, 71, 93
  mobility and property, 85–86, 91
  present-orientation, 70, 75n5
  sharing and, 58–59, 60, 80, 84,
    90, 234
  social hierarchy and, 23, 25
  social control and, 27
  subsistence and, 84, 86–91,
    92–93, 234
  the "anti-state" and, 23, 26
  witchcraft and, 23
  See also foraging societies,
    "Original Affluent Society," the
Huron, 23

I

identity
  activism and, 99–100, 199
  class consciousness and,
    197–199, 201n10
  collective memory and, 103, 112
  descent and, 7–8
  gender and, 106–107, 108–110,
    111
  identity formation, 99–100
  politics and, 13–14, 99–100,
    103, 110, 190, 194, 195,
    199
  recognition and, 190, 194–195,
    200n7
immediate and delayed return
  systems, 69–70, 72, 75n5
indigenous peoples
  "authenticity" and, 13–14,
    190–191, 195–196
  "indigenousness," 7–9, 150–151,
    193, 200n5
  impoverished minorities and, 192,
    193, 196
  political struggles of, 192,
    194–195, 196
  recognition and, 190, 193–195,
    200n7
  relationship to land and,
    192–193
  See also identity, indigenous rights
    movement
indigenous rights movement, 1,
  156, 192, 200n4, 235, 239
inequality, 23, 24, 46–47,
  199–200, 206–207
  HIV and, 214–215
Integrated Rural Development and
  Nature Conservation
  See non-governmental
    organizations
"invention of tradition," 193–196,
  199

J

Jewish identity (North America)
  activism and, 6, 100–103,
    104–105, 110–111, 231

256 Index

collective memory and, 102, 103, 112

feminism and, 109–112

masculinity and, 108–109

postwar gender relations and, 106–107, 108–110

Ju/'hoansi, 135, 150–151, 208–209, 235

as Remote Area Dwellers, 156

coalition-building and, 150, 153, 155

collective identity and, 154, 155

community-based organizations and, 135, 153–154, 156

HIV and, 211, 212, 214, 216–217, 239

Kalahari People's Fund and, 133, 135, 141–144

land rights and resource management, 134, 136–139, 151–155

language preservation, 134, 139, 143, 144

non-governmental organizations and, 139, 152, 153

political participation and self-determination of, 134, 136–138, 140, 153, 155–156

poverty and, 206–207, 214–215, 217

water rights and, 152, 154

Ju/Wa Farmers Union
See community-based organizations

K

Kalahari

Kalahari Debate, 10, 14, 61–62, 90, 238

Kalahari Peoples Fund, 7, 9, 131, 135, 139–140, 150, 152

activism and, 141–143

funding and, 143–144

history of, 132–133

collaborations with other organizations, 133–134

Kaplan, David, 73–74, 76n7

!Kung, 23, 60–61, 65, 135

Dobe !Kung, 58–59, 88–89

division of labour among, 59

poverty, 206–207

subsistence and, 58–59, 76n7, 84

See also Basarwa, Bushmen, Ju/'hoansi, San

Kuper, Adam, 7–8

Kuru Development Trust
See non-governmental organizations

Kymlicka, Will, 193, 200n4

L

land

activism and, 134, 135–136, 139–141, 142, 153–155, 192, 194

"back to the land" movements, 134

Bushman identity and, 192–193, 194, 200n3

community mapping of, 154–155

de facto rights, 141, 152, 194

de jure rights, 138, 150, 155

settlements, 135, 151

territory (n!ore), 122, 136, 141, 154

territory "owner" (n!ore kxausi), 75, 138, 152

"traditional communities" and, 194–195

water infrastructure and San land tenure, 140–141, 152–153, 154

liberalism, 26

liberal social theory, 54, 55–56, 58, 60, 61–62

livestock, 151, 155

Bushman-lion relationship and, 121–122, 127

Contagious Bovine Pleuropneumonia (CBPP), 151

Leacock, Eleanor, 5, 42, 58–59, 206, 207, 238, 239

Lee, Richard, 1–3, 6, 15, 42, 73, 74, 206, 207, 234, 240

activism and, 100–101, 102, 239

on agency and autonomy of indigenous peoples, 194, 196, 199, 218, 238, 239

AIDS research and, 205, 209, 210, 216, 239
childhood, 230–231, 232
cultural ecology and, 11–12, 233, 234
on Dobe !Kung, 58–59, 60, 65, 88–89, 235
education, 233, 234
ethnography and, 9–10
feminist anthropology and, 4, 5, 16n4, 235–236
Harvard Kalahari Research Group and, 2, 132, 133, 150
on human nature, 25–26, 56, 189
Marxist social theory and, 5, 54, 59–60, 61, 233
on "primitive communism," 5, 31, 58, 60, 238, 239
on social evolution, 234, 235
lions
//gauasi (spirits of the dead) and, 120
Bushman-lion truce, 121, 124–127, 128n5
Bushman precautions against, 119–120, 125–127
in Etosha National Park, 121
influence of domestic animals on, 121–122, 127
territory of, 123
Locke, John, 56–57
long-term research, 10, 43, 238
Kalahari People's Fund and, 131–132, 145

M
"Man the Hunter" conference, 3, 12, 65, 75n1
market economy
scarcity and, 67, 80–82, 90, 214–215
market principle, 3, 67, 68
Marshall, Lorna, 128n6, 128n7, 132–133, 135, 144, 197
Marshall, John, 121, 128n5, 135, 141
Marx, Karl, 5, 14–15, 80
Engels and, 31, 38, 42, 44

on communal relations, 32, 40–41, 45, 47–48
critical anthropology and, 42–43
critique of social evolution, 34–36, 40–41, 42, 46
on human nature, 22, 25
on hunter-gatherer societies, 22
on racial classification, 36
on state and customary law, 36, 37, 45–46
on superstition, 38
Marxist social theory, 25
historical and dialectical, 59–60
non-dialectical and structural, 61
Ministry of Agriculture (Botswana), 156
mode of production, 40–41, 45–47, 48, 58, 60, 61, 70, 71, 74, 237
Morgan, Lewis Henry, 35, 238

N
n!ore (territory)
See land
Namibia
Baraka, 208, 209, 210–211
Etosha National Park, 121, 125, 127, 150
Namibian Conference on Land Reform and the Land Question, 136, 140
Omaheke, 190, 197
Otjozundjupa, 132, 135, 136, 137, 144, 191
Tjum!kui (Tsumkwe), 131–132, 135, 144, 208, 211–215
See also Nyae Nyae
National Council of Jewish Women, 101
neo-classical economics, 65–66
neoconservatism, 26–27
neoliberalism, 3, 32–33, 34, 43, 49, 238–239
Netherlands Development Organization (SNV), 153
Ngamiland
See Botswana
non-governmental organizations (NGOs), 8–9, 13

First Peoples of the Kalahari, 133, 161, 172
Health Unlimited, 211
Integrated Rural Development and Nature Conservation, 138
Kuru Development Trust, 9, 134, 139–141, 161, 172, 182n3
Nyae Nyae Development Foundation, 134, 135, 136, 138, 141
South African San Institute (SASI), 134
Survival International, 8–9
Trust for Okavango Cultural and Development Initiatives (TOCADI), 134, 139, 140, 141, 142, 152, 154
Working Group of Indigenous Minorities in Southern Africa (WIMSA), 9, 134, 137, 161, 162, 153, 191, 192
See also community-based organizations (CBOs), Ditshwanelo, the Botswana Centre for Human rights
Northwest Coast Aboriginals (Canada), 83
Novick, Peter, 102, 110
Nyae Nyae (Namibia)
Bushman-lion relations in, *See* lions, Bushmen
Kalahari People's Fund in, 142–143
re-organized San communities in, 140
San literacy programs in, 143, 144
water infrastructure and San land-use, 141
Nyae Nyae Conservancy
See community-based organizations
Nyae Nyae Development Foundation
See non-governmental organizations
Nyae Nyae Farmers Cooperative
See community-baased organizations

O
Omaheke,
See Namibia, San
optimal foraging strategy, 67–68
"Original Affluent Society" the, 3, 14, 65–66, 74–75, 206, 234
critiques of, 67–68, 71–74
popular readings of, 66–67, 75n4
Otjozondjupa
See Namibia

P
participatory rural appraisal, 154
Patterson, Thomas, 5, 14, 42
Polanyi, Karl, 90
"political economy of sex," 57
poverty, 81, 84, 91, 95, 206–207, 214–215
Paleolithic, 80
praxis, 6–7
"primitive communism"
See social formations

Q
Qwaa (San painter), 163–165, 168–171, 182n5

R
race, 100, 101–102, 107–108, 109, 110, 112n1, 231
revisionists, 5–6, 10, 193–194
Ritchie, Claire, 121, 128n5
Rosenberg, Harriet, 74, 232, 236

S
Sahlins, Marshall, 3, 65–66, 68, 73, 206, 234
on "economic man," 66, 70
on formalism and substantivism, 67
practical reason, 71
on Zen road to affluence, 66, 71, 80
See also "Original Affluent Society," the
San, 2, 4, 6, 16n2, 235
academics and, 141
language initiatives, 143

healers, 198
Khomani San, 192–193, 195–196
kinship and naming, 198
struggle for political recognition, 7, 134, 140, 144–145, 149–150, 155, 192–195, 199
Omaheke San, 13–14, 191–192, 196–199
small stature of, 73
primitivism discourse and, *See* Art
See also Bushmen, Basarwa, Ju/'oansi.!Kung. Zhu
seasonal weight loss, 73
self-interest, 26–27
Setshogo, Thamae (San painter), 159, 165, 168, 182n5
sharing, 69–70, 71–72, 74, 80, 234
development of human society and, 54–56
Siskind, Janet, 58
Snow, C.P., 11
Socialism
See social formations
social formations
Communism, 39–41, 42, 45, 48, 58
early civilizations and precapitalist societies, 24, 25, 36–37, 47
"primitive communism," 5, 31, 43, 46, 47, 60–61, 237
Socialism, 22, 26, 39–40, 44, 45–48
See Captialism
Solway, Jacqueline, 3, 12, 196, 218, 238
South African San Institute (SASI)
See non-governmental organizations
South West African Peoples Organization (SWAPO), 140
Soviet Union, 26, 48–49, 232
special game license (subsistence hunter's license), 153
Steward, Julian, 233, 235
"strategic essentialism," 8, 195–196
Survival International

See non-governmental organizations
Susser, Ida, 2, 5, 6, 10, 11, 12, 14, 15, 239
Sylvain, Renee, 5, 7, 9, 10, 12, 13, 14, 15, 201n11

T
Tawana Land Board (Botswana), 152–153, 154, 155
Taylor, Charles, 189–190
Thomas, Elizabeth Marshall, 12
Thompson, E.P., 65, 75n2
Thompson, John Eric, 24
Tjum!kui (Tsumkwe)
See Namibia
Tlhabololo Development Trust
See community-based organizations
Traditional Authorities Act (Namibia), 194, 195
Triangle Factory Fire (New York), 100
collective memory and, 102
activism and, 103, 105–106
literature on, 104
women and, 104, 105, 106, 111
Trigger, Bruce, 5, 6, 14
Trust for Okavango Cultural and Development Initiatives (TOCADI)
See non-governmental organizations
Tupinamba (Brazil), 23

U
Union of American Hebrew Congregations, 101

W
Washburn, Sherwood, 54–56, 234
well-digging, 152, 154, 155
White, Leslie, 233–234
Wiessner, Polly, 140
Wilmsen, Edwin, 54, 61–62, 72–73, 74, 238
Wolf, Eric, 11, 234
Woodburn, James, 5, 69–71, 89

Working Group of Indigenous
    Minorities in Southern Africa
    (WIMSA)
  See non-governmental
    organizations
world systems theory, 61

X
/Xai/Xai
  See Botswana

/Xai/Xai Trust
  See community-based
    organizations

Y
Yanomami, 56–58

Z
Zhu, 72–73